Writing Device Drivers
for SCO UNIX

Writing Device Drivers for SCO UNIX

A Practical Approach

Peter Kettle
The Santa Cruz Operation Ltd

Steve Statler
Sequent Computer Systems Ltd

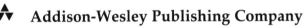 **Addison-Wesley Publishing Company**

Wokingham, England · Reading, Massachusetts · Menlo Park, California
New York · Don Mills, Ontario · Amsterdam · Bonn · Sydney · Singapore
Tokyo · Madrid · San Juan · Milan · Paris · Mexico City · Seoul · Taipei

Cover designed by Designers & Partners of Oxford and printed by The Riverside Printing Co. (Reading) Ltd.
Typeset by CRB (Drayton) Typesetting Services, Norwich, Norfolk.
Printed in Great Britain at the University Press, Cambridge.

First printed 1992.

British Library Cataloguing in Publication Data
A catalogue record for this book is available from the British Library.

Library of Congress Cataloging in Publication Data
Kettle, Peter.
    Writing device drivers for SCO UNIX : a practical approach / Peter Kettle, Steve Statler.
        p.   cm.
    Includes index.
    ISBN 0-201-54425-3
    1. UNIX device drivers (computer programs)   I. Statler, Steve.
II. Title.
QA76.76.D49K48   1992
005.4'3--dc20   92-36521
                                                          CIP

*This book is dedicated
to our parents.*

Foreword

UNIX started life as an operating system for technical or scientific users, and following its adoption as the basis for the Open System operating environment, it has now progressed to become a general purpose operating environment for business applications. By combining UNIX and computer systems based on industry standard Personal Computer hardware, solutions based on Open Systems are now becoming increasingly popular in an ever-expanding range of applications. This move into new territories has been largely as a result of the desire by large scale users of computers to build complex systems out of standard low-cost components and to break free from the restrictions created when they have a single source provider for their computer hardware.

The Open Systems standards established by organizations such as X/Open and the commitment to these standards from software providers such as SCO, have meant that highly powerful systems that are capable of running the most sophisticated applications can be put together at previously undreamed of costs to match the users' needs exactly.

This flexibility to produce powerful and sophisticated systems has created a need for special software device drivers to be produced to run the ever-increasing range of special hardware products available for standard PC hardware. There are already many hundreds of device drivers available for SCO UNIX and yet every week many new requirements appear. These might be for a new point-of-sale terminal, a new type of tape back-up drive, a new graphical display card, or maybe for an intelligent telephone exchange!

We at SCO are totally committed to the Open System process, and through this process, to providing our customers with the freedom to put together the very best systems that precisely meet their needs. The development of special device drivers for incorporating the optimum components into a system is a key element in our approach to Open Systems. I believe that this excellent book based on training courses delivered by the Santa Cruz Operation provides you with an insight into the requirements for producing a device driver for SCO UNIX and I hope that it will encourage you to take on the challenge of developing many new device drivers.

Lars Turndal
Senior Vice President and Managing Director
The Santa Cruz Operation Ltd

Preface

Welcome!

This book is written for students of computer science and systems programming professionals. Our objective is to offer information about writing UNIX device drivers and the operation of the UNIX kernel that is practical and accessible.

On successful completion of this book you will be able to write a variety of device drivers. If you have completed the exercises set at the end of each chapter, you will have built a UNIX kernel, written a device driver for a mouse, experimented with interrupts, written a simple line discipline, written a Stream driver and modified a disk driver. You are likely to have a better grasp of operating system functions and the inside of UNIX than most of your colleagues in the computer industry.

Although it is rare for most systems programmers to have to write device drivers, the investigation of this topic can pay many dividends. It yields an understanding of the following areas:

(1) The structure and mechanisms of an Operating System.

(2) Device drivers and the concept of device independence.

(3) Computer and peripheral hardware architecture.

To provide an accessible environment, the exercises are designed for SCO UNIX. At the time of writing the current release is SCO UNIX Release 3.2 Version 4.0. The exercises are set at the end of each chapter with hints and model answers to aid the reader. They can be readily adapted to operate on other vendors' versions of UNIX after consultation with the appropriate implementation-specific documentation. Although we use UNIX as the basis for this book, many of the principles that we discuss extend to other operating systems.

The information that we have distilled into this book has traditionally been fragmented in many different places: computer science text books, hardware manuals, software guides and the minds of a few developers who may be difficult to contact or to understand.

Conventions

Throughout the text of the book, when UNIX system calls or commands are mentioned, they will be followed by an abbreviation in parentheses to indicate where they are documented in the SCO UNIX manual set. For example nm(CP) indicates that the nm command is documented under Commands: Programming (CP) in the Programmer's Reference Manual.

UNIX commands, system calls and function names will be in constant width type, as will code extracts, structures and variables.

Where UNIX commands are listed they will be preceded by a prompt that will indicate whether the command needs to be typed as root (#) or any user ($).

A convention that we have not adhered to is the use of troff(CT) in the preparation of this book. We used Microsoft Word!

Prerequisites

In order to gain the most from this book it is necessary to have experience of using the C programming language, including an understanding of the use of libraries, system calls, pointers and bitwise operations. In order to attempt the exercises it will be necessary to have experience of developing programs using UNIX and access to a machine running SCO UNIX. Some knowledge of the issues relating to UNIX system administration would also be useful but is not essential.

Choice of operating system

UNIX is supported by nearly every major mainframe, mini and microcomputer manufacturer in the world. Since its appearance in the early 1970s it has been adopted by Altos, Amdahl, AT&T, Bull, Cray, Data General, DEC, Fujitsu, HP, IBM, ICL, Intel, MIPS, Motorola, NCR, Olivetti, Prime, Sequent, Siemens/Nixdorf, Sun, Tandem, Tandy, Unisys, Wang and many others.

SCO XENIX and latterly SCO UNIX have proliferated throughout industry and academia, running on many different manufacturers' computers and in greater quantities than any other variant of UNIX.

The latest estimates run at 500 000 SCO licences sold, most of which are multi-user licences. SCO UNIX will run on some of the least expensive Intel i386 and i486 microprocessor-based computers. It is likely that if you have a Personal Computer in your office that is running UNIX, it will be running SCO UNIX.

Device drivers for SCO XENIX and SCO UNIX differ in some areas. We have chosen SCO UNIX as a basis for the examples in this book, as most developers are working with SCO UNIX rather than XENIX.

How to use this book

At the end of each chapter there is a short quiz. We recommend that you use these to test your understanding of the chapter. There is also a practical exercise at the end of each chapter. Answers to quizzes and exercises are provided in separate chapters at the end of the text.

If you attempt the quizzes and the exercises, you are more likely to retain more of what you have read, gain a deeper understanding of the topics that we have discussed, derive more satisfaction and have an opportunity to learn about related issues through the process of exploration.

We also suggest that you discard the conventional reverence for books and annotate the text wherever needed.

Materials required to perform the exercises

If you are going to attempt the exercises, the following materials will be useful:

(1) A copy of SCO UNIX and the SCO UNIX Development System.
(2) A computer based on either the Intel i386 or i486 microprocessor, with the above software installed.
(3) A copy of the *SCO UNIX Device Driver Writer's Guide*, which contains more information about SCO-specific details.
(4) For a number of the exercises, you will need a mouse. The model answers assume that you have a Microsoft InPort Bus Mouse®.

Acknowledgements

We are very grateful to the following people for their technical assistance and constructive and courteous feedback during the preparation of this book: Rob Adams, Tony Booker, John Forrest, Steve Gzesh,

Craig Heath, Dave McLeman, Simon Plackett, Pete Shephard, Hendrik Jan Thomassen at AT Computing, Dave Tollow (who wrote the original mousey test program), Nadeem Wahid, John Warnants and many others.

Many thanks go to Jo and Miranda for their support, patience and coffee, and to Rattle and Hum for their miaows, purrs and assistance at the keyboard.

Parts of this book were prepared and tested on an Olivetti M380 computer.

A special thank-you to Nicky Jaeger at Addison-Wesley, for her infinite patience and continuous support and encouragement over the past two years.

And finally, thank-you to Doug Michels and SCO, who first suggested that the book should be written, and who granted free access to the necessary research materials.

Peter Kettle
Steve Statler
August 1992

Contents

Trademark notice
SCO™ is a trademark of The Santa Cruz Operation, Inc.
UNIX™ and 3b2™ are trademarks of AT&T
Microsoft InPort Bus Mouse^R and XENIX^R are registered trademarks and
Word™ is a trademark of Microsoft Corporation
Motorola 68000™ is a trademark of Motorola Corporation
IBM PS/2™ and AIX™ are trademarks of International Business Machines
Corporation
8088™, 80286™, 80386™, 80486™ and Multibus™ are trademarks of Intel
Corporation

1

Fundamentals

1.1 Overview

Before we launch ourselves into the midst of writing device drivers it is advisable to revisit some fundamental facts. We will review:

- The definition of a UNIX device driver
- Computer hardware architecture
- The role of an operating system
- The structure of the UNIX operating system
- The purpose of a device driver
- What device drivers do and what they don't do
- How device drivers communicate with peripherals
- An overview of character and block drivers.

The objective of this chapter is to ensure that the reader has an understanding of the foundation concepts necessary to progress with the later material. This chapter may be omitted if you feel you have an adequate understanding of all the above topics.

1.2 The definition of a UNIX device driver

A device driver is a collection of software routines that make up part of an operating system. It allows the UNIX kernel and user programs to communicate with peripheral devices.

A UNIX device driver hides hardware device-specific details from the user and the rest of the operating system. It provides an interface between the kernel and the device which allows the device to be

1

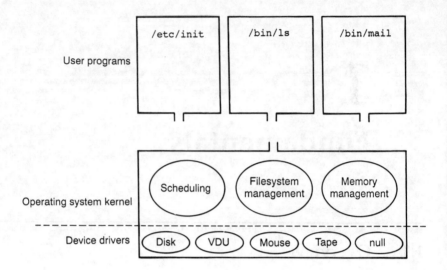

Figure 1.1   User programs, the kernel and device drivers.

accessed using the same system calls as those associated with accessing a regular file. Figure 1.1 shows device driver modules along with other parts of the operating system kernel offering services to user programs.

1.3   Computer hardware architecture

For the sake of our discussions computer hardware can be divided into the Central Processing Unit (CPU), memory, peripheral controllers and the peripherals themselves.

Device drivers typically are written by computer manufacturers, peripheral manufacturers, system integrators and sophisticated end users with specialized needs. The devices supported by these device drivers include hard disks, visual display units, keyboards, speakers, printers and sometimes even the flashing lights on the front of the computer. All of these need to be controlled by the computer using sets of software routines called device drivers.

The connection of the CPU to its peripherals is via a component known as the system bus. This normally takes the physical form of the system back-plane, a printed circuit board with a large number of address, data and control lines, joining together most of the cards in

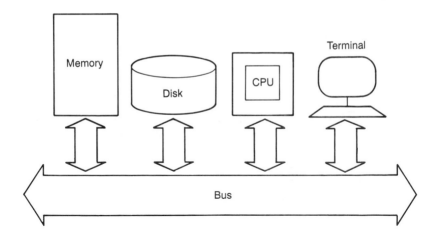

Figure 1.2 The logical structure of a computer.

the computer chassis. Examples of types of bus are the original IBM PC Bus (known as Industry Standard Architecture, ISA), the Extended Industry Standard Architecture Bus (EISA), Intel's Multibus and the IBM Micro Channel Architecture (MCA) bus. Other examples used on larger machines include the VME bus, the IEEE Future Bus and a multitude of proprietary designs from many manufacturers. The system bus acts as a data highway, linking the CPU, memory and peripherals. The relationship between these is shown in Figure 1.2. Although it is useful to be aware of its existence, the device driver writer rarely becomes involved in the details of the system bus operation.

Some machines employ a hierarchy of buses, with a peripheral bus attached to the system bus. This allows larger numbers of peripherals to be connected to the system and also makes possible the integration of peripherals that are not directly compatible with the interface used on the system bus. In these cases the driver writer needs some knowledge of the bus operation in order to achieve access to these peripherals.

An example of this is the Small Computer Systems Interface (SCSI) bus which can be attached to the ISA, EISA and MCA buses as well as many others. The SCSI bus attaches to the system bus using a host adaptor, which is addressed in the same way as any peripheral controller would be. This adaptor manages access to the SCSI bus, which usually takes the form of a cable, connecting up to seven SCSI controllers. Each controller may support up to eight devices. In this way a single slot in the system bus yields connections with up to 56 peripherals.

1.4   The role of an operating system

The operating system of a computer manages the hardware resources and provides an environment that allows users' application programs to run.

The kernel, as its name suggests, is at the centre of the operating system and performs the following low level functions.

- Input/Output (I/O) from and to peripherals
- Management of memory
- Process creation and scheduling
- File system management.

It also provides a set of entry points into the kernel code that allow programs to make use of facilities such as device access and process creation, through a system call interface. A system call is a request for action from the kernel, such as 'read some bytes from a file'.

In the same way that one might consciously decide to blink one's eyes without having to consider the speed, start and stop point of each eyelid, an application program such as a spreadsheet will make a system call to display a character on the terminal, without considering issues of what bit patterns are to be placed on the terminal's communications line and determining the state of the peripheral controller.

1.5   The structure of the UNIX operating system

The UNIX operating system is divided into two classes of software: the routines that make up the kernel and the programs that make up a broad set of utilities.

The utilities consist of hundreds of separate executable programs. One can subdivide the utilities into two separate groups. The first is quite remote from the workings of the low-level operating system, for example, the spelling checker, the sort program or the hangman game. The other group is closely linked to the operation of the kernel. It includes the programs /etc/init, /etc/login and /bin/sh. Despite the fact that these programs are fundamental to the use of the system (they allow users to log in, type commands and log out again), they are distinctly separate from the kernel code and operate through the same system call interface as the hangman program. Figure 1.3

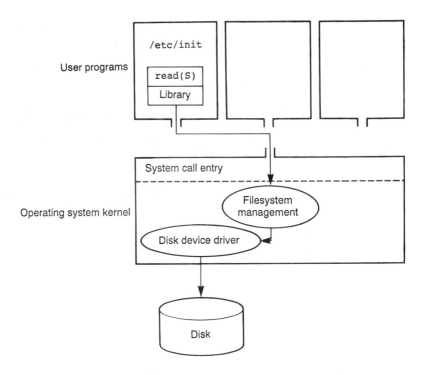

Figure 1.3　The /etc/init program making a system call in order to read the disk.

illustrates the request for kernel services from the read(S) system call in a user program.

During the period that the CPU is executing the code of a user program or utility it is said to be in user mode. When it executes code within the kernel (the /unix binary) it is in system mode.

When programmers make a system call in their code, they are setting up a request for services from the operating system. If we examine the assembly language instructions generated by compiling a program which makes a single system call, we see the following sequence.

A system call such as open(S) consists of a short library routine. This library routine switches the flow of execution from the instructions in the user's executable file, for example a.out, over to instructions in the operating system kernel, by performing the following operations:

(1)　Setting up parameters (a file name and a number which signifies the access mode (read or write) to be used). These are pushed onto the user program's stack.

(2) Executing a special machine code instruction to switch from user mode into the system call entry point in the UNIX kernel. SCO UNIX on the Intel i386/i486 CPU uses a call gate machine code instruction (see the *Intel i80386 Programmer's Reference Manual* for further details). On other CPUs the instruction is commonly referred to as a 'trap'. Once this has been executed, the kernel then takes control, checks the parameters on the user's stack, ascertains the system call operation that is required and then executes the relevant kernel functions. When this has been completed the kernel returns control to the user's code.

(3) In the user's code the call gate is immediately followed by instructions that test to see if the system call has been successful.

In between execution of the call gate (step 2) and the return to user mode (step 3), many thousands of kernel instructions will have been executed.

The instructions that implement the open(S) system call are contained within the kernel. The system call mechanism is quite different from a library call, although from the programmer's view point there is little noticeable difference.

System calls and library routines are linked into executable object files or binaries using the link editor ld(CP). Library routines, which are generally made up of many thousands of instructions, are copied from library archives such as /lib/libc.a and linked with the library function call in the program to create the object file. For a system call, the library consists of only a short piece of code that contains a call gate. As in the case of a library routine, it is copied and linked with the program; however, the bulk of the code that implements the system call is not in the library, it is contained in the kernel.

Device drivers are part of the UNIX kernel. Therefore they cannot make system calls and do not have the standard set of library functions available to them (such as those within the library /lib/libc.a). Use of a system call within a device driver would be like using the front door of a house as an entry point into the kitchen, when you are already in the living room. Functions such as printf(S), which are sometimes mistakenly considered to be part of the C language, are in fact library routines contained within libc.a and hence are not available for use within kernel code.

Familiar library routine names sometimes reappear within the kernel but this time with different functionality. For example, putc(S) changes from being a general function to pass characters to a file, to a mechanism for adding characters to a kernel buffer structure.

Routines that are provided for the device driver writer are known as 'kernel support routines'. These routines should always be used to ensure the portability of the device driver code. Potentially you can call any routine in the kernel, but if you choose to use undocumented ones, device drivers may stop working when the routines change their functionality or disappear in future releases of the operating system. If all operations are coded explicitly within the source of the driver, rather than using the documented support routines, the same problems can occur when kernel structures and mechanisms evolve. To avoid these problems, the kernel support routines which are documented in the *SCO UNIX Device Driver Writer's Guide* should always be used. These routines are identified in this book as follows: putc(K).

As UNIX has evolved, larger numbers of support routines are provided by operating system vendors in order to offer uniform and sophisticated implementations of functions such as disk partitioning and screen handling, across ranges of different devices.

The UNIX kernel is a stand-alone executable file. A copy of it resides in the filesystem and is usually called /unix. Just like any other program its source can be modified, compiled using the C compiler cc(CP) and linked using ld(CP). It is written in a mixture of C and a small amount of assembly language code. Less than 1% of the code is written in assembly language.

Users rarely have access to all the source code of the operating system. It is usually jealously guarded by the lawyers of its authors and only released at great expense, although traditionally, academic institutions receive UNIX source for a token sum. However, certain parts of the source code escape these restrictions and are 'freely' available to the UNIX user (albeit copyrighted). These parts include nearly all of the header files which define the data structures used within the kernel (the majority of these are contained in the /usr/include/sys directory on most UNIX systems) as well as source files containing definitions of configurable values such as process table size, file table size and user-defined device drivers.

The kernel can be investigated with standard UNIX development utilities such as the debugger adb(CP) and the name list display utility nm(CP). The command

```
# nm -p /unix
```

can be run on a system to list the address, type and name of all the routines and variables used within your kernel. adb(CP) can be used to disassemble your driver routines, as well as modify constants and variables. You will find this very useful when you come to do any practical work.

1.6   The purpose of a device driver

A device driver is a set of routines linked into the kernel which are used as part of the mechanism to translate the general file handling system calls open(S), read(S), write(S) and close(S) into commands that will operate the specific peripheral device being accessed.

The system call interface and most of the kernel routines below it are not hardware specific, but the device driver is. The device driver provides an interface between the low-level parts of the kernel and the hardware.

One of the great strengths of UNIX is the simplicity of being able to use the same file handling primitives (read(S) and write(S)) on any type of file. These files can be regular files, directory files, pipes, symbolic links or the special device files that control peripherals such as disks, terminals and tapes. A device is seen by the users as an extension of the filesystem, so that just as they open(S) and read(S) a text file, they may use the same system calls to access a peripheral. As a result of this a utility such as od(C), the octal dump program, can be used to examine text or binary files as well as the contents of a disk partition or the data arriving on a communications line. This gives great flexibility to the programmer and simplifies the building of what would otherwise be complex and unportable software.

When accessing regular files and directories, the following command might be used:

```
$ od /etc/passwd
```

A layer of software between the system call interface and the disk device driver provides the filesystem management functions. This is almost completely bypassed when special device files are accessed directly:

```
# od /dev/root
```

The modularity of the UNIX kernel combined with the increase in compatible computer hardware, based on common chip sets, means that once the initial CPU-specific implementation of UNIX has been completed (often by the chip vendor or an industry consortium), the bulk of the programming task involved in porting UNIX to a new machine is the writing or modification of device drivers.

Part of the device driver writer's task is to hide the complexities of the peripheral from the kernel and hence the user. If programmers had to write the code to operate a specific type of disk at the register level every time they developed a general ledger accounting application, then their task would be complicated many times over. It would also be very difficult to port any software that was finally produced to other machines that did not use the same hardware interface to control the disk. Some large computer manufacturers have done very well offering solutions similar to this despite these disadvantages.

There is a trade-off however between using a simple standard system call interface to a peripheral and accessing the device at a lower level. The trade is in the area of performance. This is best illustrated in the world of MS-DOS, first developed for the Intel 8088 processor. Some application writers have been tempted to access display devices at a low level, bypassing the machine's Basic Input Output System (BIOS) and writing directly to the registers of a device in order to gain maximum control and performance. Often this is in order to access display devices such as a VGA graphics card. Programs written in this way are less portable and may not run on another manufacturer's PC. These applications are also more difficult to transfer to other operating systems. Machines such as the IBM PC which were based on comparatively simple processors without memory management units permitted the accessing of a machine's hardware directly from application programs. This practice is becoming less common. With the advent of the Intel 80286 processor, the CPU has a protected mode which can be used selectively to control access to a machine's hardware.

In protected mode a mechanism is enforced which is built on four levels of privilege. Level 3 is the least privileged and under normal circumstances it is not possible to use the processor's I/O instructions. At level 0 it is possible to use all of the processor's instructions and have access to all of the machine's memory. These levels of privilege are like the layers of an onion, as shown in Figure 1.4. SCO UNIX uses only two levels of privilege. It disregards the middle levels and runs user processes at level 3 and the kernel at level 0. These two levels correspond to user mode and system mode. These modes have no relationship with the root and user account privileges or file permissions which are implemented in software by the kernel.

On an Intel 8088-based machine, running MS-DOS, a user can use an assembly language routine to read directly from a device. That same routine, if it were executed on an Intel 80286 machine running in protected mode, would fail to complete its execution. The CPU would detect that a protected instruction was about to be executed whilst the CPU was at privilege level 3 and would generate an exception. This would cause the CPU to switch to system mode to deal with the exception and the offending process would probably be terminated. These restrictions on the use of I/O instructions are

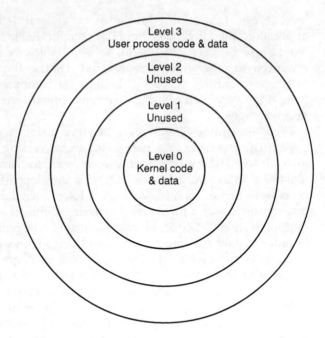

Figure 1.4 Privilege levels on SCO UNIX.

necessary when the hardware is being shared in a multi-user environment, where users need to be protected from the actions of themselves and others on the system.

1.7   Demarcation between drivers and the rest of the kernel

If we examine the events following a read(S) system call, we will be
able to appreciate the areas of demarcation between a device driver
and the rest of the kernel. When a program executes a read(S) system
call to retrieve data from a file, a hierarchy of kernel functions are
invoked. Eventually these result in device driver routines being
executed.

In response to a read(S) system call the kernel will look up the
current offset of the file pointer from the file table and map this offset
to the location of the disk block within the filesystem containing the
data.

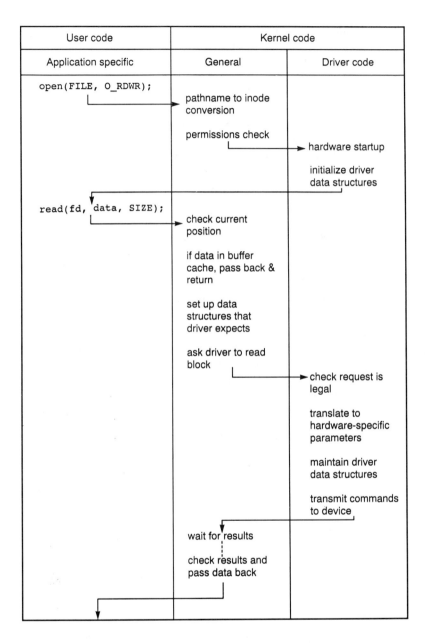

Figure 1.5   Functions performed by the kernel and a device driver.

The kernel keeps copies of recently accessed disk blocks in RAM. This memory area is known as the disk buffer cache. If there is a copy of the desired block in the disk buffer cache, the kernel copies the data from the cache back to the user and so completes the read without using the device driver or accessing the disk hardware. If there is not a cached version of the block, the kernel must call the driver.

Parameters will be set up by the kernel so that the driver will know how far from the beginning of the filesystem to start reading the disk, how much data to read and where in memory to put the data. The device driver code then takes over.

The driver validates the request, determining whether the block is actually contained on the disk and whether the size of the request is reasonable. This depends on whether the requested data extends past the end of the division, partition or disk that is being read. Divisions and partitions divide a disk into separate areas. This allows more than one operating system (each in its own partition) with a number of filesystems (each in their own division) to reside on the same disk. Partitions and divisions are implemented by the device driver. They are not physical attributes of a disk.

Before the request can be passed to the disk controller, the block number provided by the kernel must be translated from an offset within a filesystem to a physical location on the disk. The block number received from the kernel does not include offsets for the partitions and divisions, neither does it take into account any bad tracks. The disk driver must deal with all of these issues.

Having translated the block number, a request is formulated in terms that the disk controller understands. It will probably need to be told the cylinder, sector and track being accessed and how many sectors to read.

Once the driver has programmed the disk controller with the request, control returns from the driver back up to the kernel. The kernel waits for the transfer to be completed by the controller which will send an interrupt when the data has been transferred into the buffer cache. The kernel then copies the data from the buffer cache out to the user process and the read(S) system call returns.

The functions performed by the kernel and device driver are illustrated in Figure 1.5.

1.8 Communicating with devices

A device driver communicates with hardware devices in a similar way that PC programmers do when they bypass the BIOS. It outputs instructions directly to the controller's registers.

The procedure is similar to that which a customer might use to communicate with a waiter in a Chinese restaurant. Predefined numbers are used to signify what is required. At the restaurant, the numbers are defined in a menu and transmitted by the customer to the waiter, indicating for instance that number 96 (sweet and sour pork) is required. When dealing with the device, the numbers and their meanings are detailed in a hardware specification (often harder to obtain than a menu). The device driver outputs these numbers into the controller's registers, indicating that a disk read is required, for example. The command 'read the disk' might be specified by placing the value 96 into the disk controller's command register. There will also be numbers used to specify where on the disk the read is to be made and how much data is to be read and where to put the data in memory.

Passing these commands between the device driver and the peripheral is achieved by one of two methods, depending on whether the device has been designed to be I/O mapped or memory mapped.

1.8.1 I/O mapped transfers

Accessing I/O space and the devices that are mapped within it requires use of specific machine instructions. These instructions pass commands and data to and from the I/O space address locations. They do not work with ordinary memory address locations. In the case of the Intel-based machines, these instructions are called IN and OUT and can normally be executed only by the UNIX kernel running at privilege level 0. I/O space is a special address space which is limited to 64K on the Intel iX86 and is logically separate from physical memory. The SCO UNIX kernel only allows access to the first 4K of I/O space.

Having the two address spaces removes the possibility of peripheral addresses conflicting with those used for program storage. Processors such as the Motorola 68000 series do not offer the facility of a separate I/O address space and use memory mapped I/O instead.

1.8.2 Memory mapped transfers

Memory mapped I/O means that the CPU's general purpose instruction set can be used to pass commands and data to and from memory locations which are linked to the registers of a device. Memory mapped I/O can be used on Intel-based machines despite the fact that they have a separate I/O space. This is illustrated in Figure 1.6.

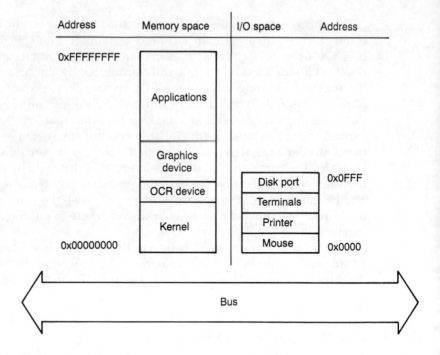

Figure 1.6   Diagram of I/O and memory mapped devices.

Memory mapped I/O allows the hardware integrator to tie specific physical memory addresses to the registers of a peripheral. This has the advantage that a full complement of assembly language instructions is available to the programmer to manipulate these registers. Typically, devices such as graphics displays are memory mapped so that programmers may easily modify bit patterns in memory, which are then transformed into related patterns on the display screen by the graphics device.

1.9   Controllers

It is important to distinguish between devices and controllers. Device drivers usually communicate with a controller rather than directly with the device itself. A controller interprets the commands sent to it by the device driver, often using an embedded processor that executes code stored in firmware. There are a number of standard controller command sets. A device driver written to use a particular command set (for example SCSI) can communicate with controllers produced by any manufacturer that conforms to that standard. This gives the user a choice of supplier for device controllers and minimizes the number of device drivers that need to be written for different peripherals.

The controller commands are translated into signals which are passed to the device by the controller over an electrical interface. Examples of different controller/device interfaces are Storage Module Device (SMD) and Seagate Technology 506 (ST506). This standardization allows different controllers to be used in combination with a variety of devices.

Successive generations of controllers are becoming more intelligent, which usually makes the task of writing device drivers for them more straightforward. Unfortunately, the intelligence of the controller is sometimes wasted when it does not fit the method of operation expected by the operating system.

Hence a device driver is a layer of software that is positioned between two other layers of code. The upper layer is the kernel's system call and filesystem management routines and the lower layer is the controller's firmware.

In order to communicate with a controller the device driver uses three types of data:

- Commands and parameters passed to the controller via command registers.

- Data moving to and from the controller via data registers.

- Status information received from the controller's status registers.

These registers are provided at predetermined I/O or memory addresses where this information can be read or written (see Figure 1.7). These addresses may be configurable via jumper connections on the controller board.

Some devices map many registers to the same address. The mapping can be done in a number of ways. One method (used by a disk controller found in the IBM PS/2 machine) is for the controller to map two different registers to a single address, depending upon whether the location is being read or written. The controller can sense this by examining the system bus to see if a read or write is being performed by the CPU. If the address is written to, the command register is mapped, if the address is read from, the status register is mapped (see Figure 1.8). Given that you will only write commands and only read the status of a device, this works well. The problem with this approach to hardware design is that it makes drivers more difficult to write and understand.

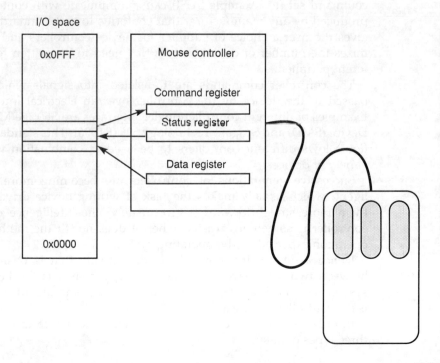

Figure 1.7   Each register has an address in order to allow the CPU to read and write its contents.

The main disadvantage with registers sharing addresses becomes apparent when a device is memory mapped and an instruction that the programmer assumed only writes to the location actually performs an implicit read as well. Unexpected results will occur in this situation when using C's bitwise operators such as |= and &=, which are frequently used to set and unset bits within variables, or any operator which performs an implicit read.

An example of this can be seen if you increment the value held in a command register which is also mapped to the same address as a status register. Common sense dictates that this would result in a write. However, after consideration it becomes apparent that the memory location will need to be read first in order to know what value is to be incremented. If the initial value in the command register is 2 and the status register is set to 41, the result of incrementing the command register would be to set it to 42, not 3 as one might have wanted. The solution to this problem is to use a static variable in the

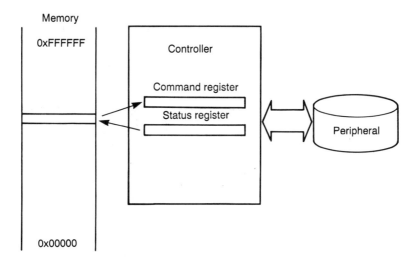

Figure 1.8 Registers can be mapped into place depending upon the operation being performed.

driver to record the last value written to the command register. It can be safely incremented and then copied to the command register.

Another complication which often exists is when registers are switched into place depending upon the value that has been written to another register. Effectively you have a register selection register, as well as the actual register that you want to access. The advantage of this scheme, from the hardware designer's point of view, is that it conserves physically mapped locations. This technique is often used for graphics cards, for example the IBM Video Graphics Adaptor (VGA), where one may want to have a palette of many colours, each one programmable to different shades but without having to use up hundreds of memory locations.

1.10 An overview of block and character drivers

There are two basic types of interface to devices offered to users on a UNIX system, block and character device files. You can verify this by typing ls -l /dev, which should produce output similar to that shown in Figure 1.9. The field on the left displays the access permissions of the device files and has either a b or a c to indicate whether

```
crw-r--r--    1 sysinfo  sysinfo    7,   0 Jun 26 00:27 cmos
crw-------    3 bin      terminal   3,   1 Aug 16 09:39 console
brw-rw-rw-    5 bin      bin        2,  52 Jun 25 04:52 fd0
brw-rw-rw-    1 bin      bin        2,  36 Jun 26 00:27 fd0135ds9
brw-------    2 sysinfo  sysinfo    1,  23 Jun 25 04:52 hd02
brw-rw-rw-    1 bin      bin        2,  64 Jun 25 04:52 install
c---r-----    1 bin      mem        4,   1 Jun 26 00:27 kmem
crw-------    2 bin      bin        6,   0 Jun 26 00:27 lp
crw-rw-rw-    1 root     other     43,   0 Aug 14 14:08 pts000
crw-------    2 sysinfo  sysinfo    1,  47 Jun 25 04:53 rhd0a
b---r-----    1 bin      backup     1,  40 Aug  9 13:42 root
crw-rw-rw-    1 bin      terminal   3,   0 Jun 25 04:52 tty
crw-------    1 root     terminal   0,   0 Aug 16 09:40 tty01
crw-rw-rw-    1 bin      bin       52,   5 Jun 26 00:27 vga
```

Figure 1.9   Part of the output from the command 'ls -l /dev'.

the device has a block or character interface. The implications of this categorization represent one of the many hurdles at which most people fall when trying to get to grips with UNIX device drivers.

1.10.1 Block drivers

Block devices are usually associated with peripherals used to support filesystems such as disks. They read and write fixed-size blocks of data. A large number of kernel support routines are provided to do buffering, sorting of requests and read-ahead functions that work with the device-specific driver code.

1.10.2 Character drivers

Character interfaces cover a wide range of drivers. A character interface usually exists for all peripherals supported on the system. A common misconception of character device drivers is that they only transfer data one character at a time. In fact transfers can be of a variable size depending upon the characteristics of the device. There are no fixed-size transfers of data that are inherent in the character interface and as a result character device drivers can be written for all peripherals.

Serial drivers

The most obvious category is that of serial drivers used to interface to asynchronous terminals. These use additional device-independent kernel support functions which provide a lot of the more complex but standard functionality associated with terminal modes such as character erase and keyboard signals.

STREAMS drivers

The STREAMS interface became available when UNIX System V Release 3.0 was introduced. It provides a framework for implementing and using software modules within a driver. STREAMS is most commonly used to implement layered protocol stacks to support use of communications devices. It allows the modularization of drivers that were previously very large, complex and hence difficult to maintain and port to other systems. The architecture offers the potential flexibility of easily combining various different communication protocols (such as TCP/IP running over X.25) that were not originally designed to work together.

Raw drivers

Another category of character device drivers are those which are associated directly with block device drivers. These provide an alternative mechanism for accessing the same physical device as the block driver. They bypass the buffering mechanism provided through the block driver and allow variable-sized transfers directly between a user process and a device such as a tape. Raw drivers also offer device-specific control of the peripheral to the user through the ioctl(S) system call. This invokes additional routines in the driver which implement functions such as formatting or retensioning a tape.

Pseudo-drivers

Pseudo-device drivers are unique in that they do not talk directly to a peripheral device but offer an entry point to the kernel in order to gain access to a kernel facility. An example of this is the /dev/null device driver which acts as a benevolent black hole in the operating system, absorbing any output that is sent to it. Another example is /dev/kmem which allows programs to access kernel virtual memory.

Other drivers

Most other drivers are also implemented as character devices. Devices such as mice and Ethernet cards which have a variable data-unit size and do not use the standard kernel support routines associated with filesystems or terminals fall into this category.

1.11   Summary

In this chapter we have reviewed some fundamental information about the architecture of a computer system and the UNIX operating system that runs on it. We have drawn the lines of demarcation between user processes and the kernel, kernel code and driver code, as well as character and block device drivers.

QUIZ

To test your understanding of this chapter, try to answer the following questions.

1.1   Can programmers bypass UNIX device drivers in order to control peripherals directly?

1.2   The /etc/init program is part of the operating system. Is it part of the kernel?

1.3   Which file conventionally contains the UNIX kernel object file?

1.4   Can character device drivers be used to access disks?

1.5   Can a UNIX device driver make system calls?

1.6   Does a disk device driver writer have to implement the code to perform buffer caching?

EXERCISES

(1) Using nm(CP), examine the names of the routines within the kernel and locate all of the routines associated with reading.
Hint: The routines will have *read* in their name.

(2) Using adb(CP), examine the read(S) library routine. How is the transition made from user mode to system mode?

Hint: Write a very short C program which has one statement, a
read(S) call, with no parameters. Use adb(CP) on the resultant
executable file. Print the instructions that follow the 'main' and
the 'read' symbol.

Users of systems other than SCO UNIX should use the sdb
debugger instead.

2

Getting started

2.1 Overview

Chapter 1 established some of the fundamentals necessary to understand the environment that device drivers work in. This chapter describes:

- An approach to follow when writing device drivers.
- How accessing a UNIX special device file results in device driver routines being called.
- An introduction to the routines that make up a UNIX device driver.
- Some initial rules to follow when writing device driver code.

The objective of this chapter is to offer readers a methodology and a foundation of information that will allow them to understand and write the various types of device drivers described in the following chapters.

2.2 A methodology for writing device drivers

During this chapter we will introduce a practical, exploratory method of learning. It is necessary to adopt this approach in order to be successful when working at the complex level of operating system internals. Much of the information that is needed is not documented. This is because of the small target audience for such documentation, the complexity of the subject matter and its dynamic nature. Therefore the device driver writer has to adopt a methodology which moves away from reliance on documentation or consulting local experts and relies instead on experimentation, use of source code and reference to first principles.

Use of operating system source code is an important part of the methodology that needs to be adopted in order to understand device drivers. The full source code of the operating system can be expensive to obtain, but other useful sources of information include:

(1)   The header files which contain the definitions of the data structures used within the operating system.

These are available on nearly every UNIX system which offers a C compiler. They can normally be found in the /usr/include and /usr/include/sys directories. Examination of the files in these directories will pay dividends. We will demonstrate the use of these files in this chapter.

(2)   The source code of other related device drivers.

If the source code supports a device similar to yours, it will contain useful information about the device, even if it is written for another operating system. This may include the locations of registers, how they can be used, comments about problem areas and idiosyncrasies of the device that might need to be dealt with.

(3)   Example device drivers that illustrate how specific types of devices are normally handled by UNIX.

Some examples are available in this book.

We will now use the discussion on 'how device drivers are invoked' to illustrate this practical, exploratory methodology.

2.3   How device drivers are invoked

The two objectives of this section are:

(1)   To give you an understanding of how and when device driver routines are invoked by the kernel. From this you will gain a perspective on where the device driver fits within the overall scheme of things.

(2)   To illustrate the process of using header files to understand kernel data structures and the examination of data held in these structures using UNIX utilities. This will be achieved through the use of a tutorial style for the rest of this section.

We will now describe the relationship between the special device file and the device driver. This will include the mechanism which is used to translate the reading and writing of a special device file to physical operations on the peripheral device which it references.

2.3.1   From the special device file to the inode

The Index Node or inode is the central data structure that holds the detailed information describing a file. For regular and directory files it stores the file type, access permissions, ownership, file size, location of the file's data blocks on the disk and records of access times. The kernel reads this structure from the disk when a file is open(S)ed and uses it to locate the necessary data blocks that the read(S) and write(S) system calls need to access.

Each UNIX file name has an inode number which is used to index into an inode list. This list is part of the filesystem structure held on the disk. Inodes that are currently in use are cached in the inode table, an array of inodes held in RAM.

A directory is a type of file. A directory entry for a file consists of an inode number and an array containing the file name. This is true for all types of file. Many different file names can use the same inode number. These file names are all linked to the same file. New links are established with the ln(C) command or the link(S) system call. The relationship between directory entries and inode table entries is illustrated in Figure 2.1 which shows multiple directory entries linked to single entries in the inode table.

All of the information necessary for the system to locate the correct set of device driver routines for a device is stored in the inode associated with the relevant special device file.

A special device file is distinguished from other types of file by the contents of the file type member of the inode structure. The special file type is displayed as either a b or a c in the first column of a directory listing.

A file's inode number can be listed using the ls(C) command with the -i flag, for example:

```
$ ls -i /dev/console
```

All this does is format the entry in the /dev directory file. Since all of the requested information is held in the directory file, the operating system does not need to access the inode table. If the command

```
$ ls -il /dev/console
```

had been entered, the system would need to use the inode number to index into the inode table where all the remaining information relating to the file resides (as a result of this, on heavily loaded systems you will find that ls and ls -i execute much faster than ls -l).

Special device files can exist anywhere in the UNIX filesystem, but conventionally they are grouped below /dev.

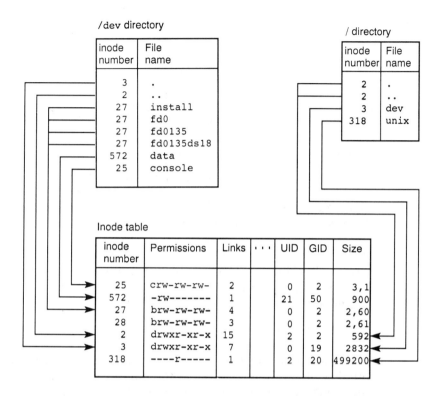

Figure 2.1 Diagram showing relationship between directory entries and an inode.

The ability to have multiple file names linked to the same inode is often used with special device files in order to designate a particular device as being the default. For example, in Figure 2.2 the output from the command

```
$ ls -i /dev/fd0* /dev/install | sort
```

shows that the default devices fd0 and install use the same inode as /dev/fd0135ds18 (on this particular system it is inode number 27). This allows us to infer that the default format for floppy disks on this system is 135 cylinders, double sided, 18 sectors and that the installation device relies on reading disks of this format. The fd0135ds18 notation is a device naming convention peculiar to SCO.

Another application of this facility is to maintain compatibility with previous names given to devices following name changes. A new name can be used to access the device whilst the old one remains. In this way versions of software that explicitly reference the old device

```
  27 /dev/fd0
  27 /dev/fd0135
  27 /dev/fd0135ds18
  27 /dev/install
1494 /dev/fd048ds8
1496 /dev/fd048
1496 /dev/fd048ds9
1516 /dev/fd096ds9
1517 /dev/fd096
1517 /dev/fd096ds15
1518 /dev/fd096ds18
1493 /dev/fd048ss8
1495 /dev/fd048ss9
1609 /dev/fd0135ds9
```

Figure 2.2 Example output from the command
ls -i /dev/fd0* /dev/install | sort.

name will still work. An example of this is the special device file for
the cartridge tape unit. These can be examined with the following
command:

```
$ ls -il /dev/rct0 /dev/rmt/0b
```

whose output is shown in Figure 2.3. The -il flag displays the inode
number (first column) as well as the number of file names linked to
the inode (third column). The first device name is used to preserve
compatibility with programs written for XENIX systems, whilst the
second is compatible with the UNIX System V convention.

The numbers 10, 0 taken from the example output in Figure 2.3 are
examples of major and minor device numbers. Each character/block
device driver has a unique major device number associated with it.
The major and minor device number are separated by a comma and
are seen in place of the size field which is displayed for regular files
and directories. The way these numbers are used will be explained
later on in this chapter.

Investigating and analysing data structures

In order to get accustomed to the investigative technique required to
understand UNIX, the reader is encouraged to follow the steps outlined in this section which confirm the basic information that was
related earlier.

```
3069 crw-rw-rw- 2 root other 10, 0  Oct 26 12:26 /dev/rct0
3069 crw-rw-rw- 2 root other 10, 0  Oct 26 12:26 /dev/rmt/0b
```

Figure 2.3 Output from the command ls -il /dev/rct0 /dev/rmt/0b.

```
0000220    00011   25714   12337   14133   27745   00108   00000   00000
           013 \0    r   d   1   0   5   7   a   1   1  \0   \0  \0   \0  \0
0000240    00025   28515   29550   27759   00101   00000   00000   00000
           031 \0    c   o   n   s   o   l   e  \0   \0  \0   \0  \0   \0  \0
0000260    00026   29285   28530   00114   00000   00000   00000   00000
           032 \0    e   r   r   o   r  \0   \0  \0   \0  \0   \0  \0   \0  \0
0000300    00027   25702   12592   13619   29540   14385   00000   00000
           033 \0    f   d   0   1   3   5   d   s   1   8  \0  \0   \0  \0
```

Figure 2.4   Selected output from the command od -dc /dev | more showing the directory entries for /dev.

The same data as obtained using the ls -i command can be retrieved by examining the directory file directly, using the octal dump program od(C). You can do this by typing

```
$ od -dc /dev | more
```

This will display the contents of the /dev directory file with the position or offset in octal in the leftmost column and the contents listed in decimal and character notation (see Figure 2.4). In order for one to make sense of numeric data like this it is necessary to understand the structure declaration that is used by the operating system to manipulate the data. The format of the directory entry for the original System V filesystem is held in one of the header files used to build the kernel ⟨sys/fs/s5dir.h⟩ (see Figure 2.5).

od(C) displays the position of the data in the file in its first column. In this case (Figure 2.4) the console entry starts at the (octal) 240th byte (160 decimal). The inode number is octal 031 or decimal 25. The first two characters are of the file name and are displayed by od(C) as decimal 28515. This is equal to binary 0110 1111 0110 0011. The Intel iX86 processor is byte swapped and word swapped, so the two bytes need to be reversed and then translated to 8-bit character codes if they are to be viewed in the correct order. Hence 01100011 equals octal 0143 which equals the ASCII character 'c'. 01101111 equals octal 0157 or the character 'o'. The rest of the characters in the string can be translated in the same way.

```
#define   DIRSIZ    14
struct direct
{
      ushort d_ino;
      char d_name[DIRSIZ];
};
```

Figure 2.5   Directory structure declared in ⟨sys/fs/s5dir.h⟩.

```
25 /dev/console
```

Figure 2.6   Output from the command ls -i /dev/console.

The command ls -i /dev/console (Figure 2.6) confirms the information we gleaned using od(C).

Other types of filesystem (such as Berkeley and the Extended Acer Filesystem (EAFS) offered with SCO UNIX) have a slightly more complex directory structure. The Berkeley filesystem incorporates other fields, including one that stores the number of characters in each file name so that longer file names can be stored.

2.3.2   From inode to device driver code

The structure of the inode as held on disk is declared in ⟨sys/ino.h⟩, part of which is shown in Figure 2.7. (The types such as ushort used in this and other kernel header files are declared in ⟨sys/types.h⟩.) Through this structure the kernel can invoke the device driver routines associated with the special device file. The di_mode member indicates whether the inode relates to a regular data file or a special device file. The permissible types are defined in ⟨sys/inode.h⟩. A subset of these is shown in Figure 2.8.

If the IFREG bit is set, read and write system calls are routed through to the regular file handling code in the kernel. Alternatively, if the

```
/*
 *      Inode structure as it appears on a disk block.
 */
struct      dinode
{
        ushort      di_mode;        /* mode and type of file */
        short       di_nlink;       /* number of links to file */
        ushort      di_uid;         /* owner's user id */
        ushort      di_gid;         /* owner's group id */
        off_t       di_size;        /* number of bytes in file */
        char        di_addr[39];    /* disk block addresses */
        char        di_gen;         /* file generation number */
        time_t      di_atime;       /* time last accessed */
        time_t      di_mtime;       /* time last modified */
        time_t      di_ctime;       /* time status last changed */
};
/*
 * The 40 address bytes:
 *    39 used as 13 addresses of 3 bytes each.
 *    40th byte is used as a file generation number.
 */
```

Figure 2.7   Lines from the file ⟨sys/ino.h⟩.

```
#define       IFDIR      0x4000     /* directory */
#define       IFCHR      0x2000     /* character special */
#define       IFBLK      0x6000     /* block special */
#define       IFREG      0x8000     /* regular */
```

Figure 2.8   Lines from the file ⟨sys/inode.h⟩.

IFCHR or IFBLK bits are set, system calls are routed so that they result
in device driver routines being called. In this case they will transfer
data to and from the device rather than a regular file.

The device driver calls are routed through two arrays of structures,
which contain pointers to functions. These functions are the routines
inside the device driver that have been created by the device driver
writer. The array bdevsw, otherwise known as the block device switch
table, is used for calling block device driver routines. The other array
cdevsw, or the character device switch table, contains pointers to the
character device driver routines. These data structures are defined in
⟨sys/conf.h⟩. The relevant section is shown in Figure 2.9. The arrays
cdevsw and bdevsw are indexed by the major device number, which is
obtained from the inode of the special device file being accessed.

```
/*
 * Declaration of block device switch. Each entry (row) is
 * the only link between the main unix code and the driver.
 * The initialization of the device switches is in the file conf.c.
 */
struct bdevsw {
      int   (*d_open)();
      int   (*d_close)();
      int   (*d_strategy)();
      int   (*d_print)();
      char  *d_name;
      struct iobuf   *d_tab;
};
extern struct bdevsw bdevsw[];
/*
 * Character device switch.
 */
struct cdevsw {
      int   (*d_open)();
      int   (*d_close)();
      int   (*d_read)();
      int   (*d_write)();
      int   (*d_ioctl)();
      struct tty *d_ttys;
      struct streamtab *d_str;
      char  *d_name;
};
extern struct cdevsw cdevsw[];
```

Figure 2.9   Lines from the file ⟨sys/conf.h⟩.

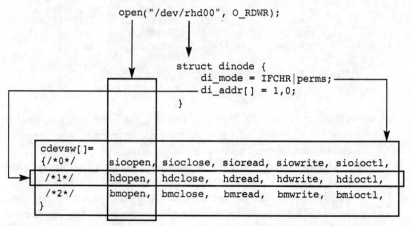

The open(S) of the character device file /dev/rhd00 results in the call to driver routine hdopen

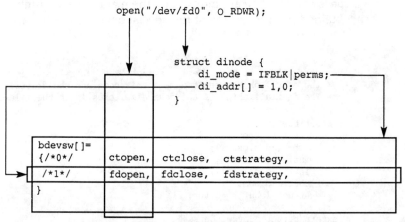

The open(S) of the block device file /dev/fd0 results in the call to driver routine fdopen

Figure 2.10   Diagram showing relationship between the inode and an entry in cdevsw and bdevsw.

The di_addr array, which is a member of the dinode structure, is normally used to store pointers to the data blocks of regular files. In the case of special device files, the first three bytes of di_addr are used to store the major and minor numbers associated with the device in question. Figure 2.10 demonstrates how a combination of the identity of the system call being executed, plus the information held in the inode being operated on, is used to access the required device driver routine.

In summary, the kernel uses a combination of the IFCHR or IFBLK bits along with the major device number (all found in the special device file's inode) and the type of operation which is being performed (for example read(S) or write(S)), to locate the correct device driver function to call.

The kernel is able to invoke the selected function through use of a statement such as:

```
(*cdevsw[major(dev)].d_write) (dev);
```

The dev variable is taken from the di_addr member of the inode for the special device file being accessed. Since cdevsw is indexed by the major number, the macro major (defined in ⟨sys/sysmacros.h⟩) is used to mask and shift out the lower order bits which make up the minor device number.

This mechanism allows calls to device driver routines to be independent of the device driver name. As a result, kernel routines which access devices can be made device independent. The device drivers for these devices can be substituted without affecting the code that calls them. An example of this is the kernel code which implements the UNIX virtual memory system. The routines within this code implement swapping and paging. In doing this they need to write memory pages directly out to disk. The disk device driver can be varied using this calling mechanism without modifying the virtual memory code in the kernel, thus allowing a modular approach to the development of the operating system.

Both the major and minor numbers are passed on to the device driver code as a parameter. The major number selects which device driver is to be called. The minor number is often used to modify the device driver's behaviour. Typical examples are:

- Indicating which partition on a disk is being mapped by the special device file.
- Indicating which line on a terminal controller is being accessed.
- Specifying whether a tape unit needs to rewind when the device is closed.

The interpretation of the minor device number is at the device driver writer's discretion.

A special device file needs be created for each value of the minor number that is understood by the device driver. In this way it is possible for all valid minor number values to be passed to the device driver. Using the last example, there would be a special device file that causes the tape to be rewound when it is closed and an alternative special device file, with the same major number but a different minor number, which would not initiate the rewind upon closing.

To summarize, it is the major device number that controls which device driver is invoked and the minor device number which modifies its behaviour. The device driver is independent of any file system, file name, or inode number.

2.4   The device driver/kernel interface

The device driver/kernel interface consists of both the device driver routines that are called by the kernel and the kernel support routines that are called by the device driver.

The kernel expects certain routines to be provided by the device driver writer. The identity of the routines that need to be provided depends primarily upon whether the device requires a character interface and/or block interface.

Each device driver model has a set of kernel support routines which it can use. For instance, serial device drivers which are used to interface to terminal lines can make use of kernel support routines that implement the command line editing facilities expected by terminal users.

2.5   Routines within a device driver

Certain routines must be present to enable the device driver to be called by the kernel. These routines are the entry points to the device driver. The device driver model dictates which entry points are required. From the ⟨sys/conf.h⟩ file, listed in Figure 2.9, one can see most of the possible entry points that can be provided for each type of device. These are explained individually later in this section.

It is not always necessary to provide all of the possible entry points for a device driver. The exceptions fall into two classes. One is that the function may be invalid for the hardware being supported, for example, provision of a routine to service write(S) calls as part of a mouse device driver. The second possibility is when the routine does not need to be provided for the device to operate but the operation is still a reasonable one for a user process to request, given that it is not aware of the device-specific requirements. An example of this might be a close routine for a parallel printer driver. It might well be that no operation is required by the hardware when a process has finished sending output to the printer.

In both cases no routines need to be written for these functions. Stub routines to fill in the bdevsw and cdevsw entries are provided automatically by SCO's link_unix(ADM) script when the kernel is built. The procedure for doing this is explained in Appendix A, Section A.3.

The device driver writer must decide upon a common prefix for all of the key device driver routines (for our purposes this is denoted as XX). The prefix should be from two to four characters long. The remainder of the routine name depends upon the function that the routine provides to the operating system.

A brief summary of the function of the routines that need to be written for block, character and raw devices follows. More detailed explanations are provided in the following chapters.

2.5.1   Character device drivers

Character device drivers should provide some or all of the following routines:

XXinit

Performs hardware and memory initialization at system initialization time.

XXopen

Performs checks and initialization when the special device file is open(S)ed.

XXclose

Performs any operations necessary when the device becomes inactive.

XXread, XXwrite

Called as a result of a user's read(S) or write(S) system call. They verify the requests, program the controller and transfer the data.

XXioctl

Invoked following an ioctl(S) system call to implement functions not possible through the system call interface used with regular files.

XXhalt

Called when the system is halted in order to implement any shutdown functions necessary for the peripherals.

XXintr
> Called following an interrupt generated by a peripheral device. Interrupts will be fully explained in Chapter 4.

2.5.2 Block device drivers

The block device driver should provide some or all of the following routines:

XXinit, XXopen, XXclose, XXintr, XXhalt
> These routines have the same role as their character device namesakes.

XXstrategy
> This routine is central to the operation of block and raw device drivers and must be provided. It is called indirectly as a result of both read(S) and write(S) requests, as well as by other parts of the operating system when it needs to access disk (for example, the virtual memory system, when paging is performed). It should validate a request and sort it into a queue of other requests waiting to be sent to the device.

2.5.3 Raw device drivers

The raw device driver supplements the routines provided for the block device driver with the following:

XXread, XXwrite
> These routines perform some basic checks and then indirectly call the XXstrategy routine written for the block interface to the same device.

XXioctl
> Invoked following an ioctl(S) system call. In the context of raw device drivers, the device-specific functions that this implements are often concerned with the formatting of disks and tapes or writing of partition tables to disks.

2.6 Guidelines for writing device drivers

So far, we have established an approach to take when writing device drivers, explained how device driver routines are called and outlined the basic function of the principal routines. We will now cover some fundamental guidelines to follow when writing these routines.

2.6.1 Virtual and physical memory

Virtual memory (VM) systems offer two main features:

(1) Locational independence of a process' instructions and data.

(2) A pageable address space.

Most UNIX implementations use VM when accessing kernel and user memory. It is useful to be aware of the way VM management operates when working at the device driver level.

For applications programmers VM management is transparent. However, since the VM system is controlled by the kernel, this facility is not completely transparent to the device driver writer. Although the bulk of the VM management is done by other kernel modules, device drivers, by virtue of the fact that they are part of the kernel, must cooperate with the VM system.

One of the features of VM is locational independence. This allows code to be written without hard-wiring the physical addresses that are used to store data and instructions in RAM. There is a virtual to physical address translation performed by the Memory Management Unit (MMU) associated with, or built into, the CPU, as in the case of the i386/i486 processors.

The i386/i486 processors have a sophisticated memory management system which makes a distinction between three types of address:

(1) Logical or virtual.

(2) Linear.

(3) Physical.

User processes use logical addresses which are expressed as offsets from the start of a memory segment. Memory segments are used by the operating system to separate different types of memory (instructions, data, stack, shared data, kernel and user memory). These segments form the basis of the protection mechanisms used by the processor and the operating system. Their properties are defined by segment descriptors. The base address of a segment is added to a offset portion of a logical address to produce the second type of address, a linear address. This is translated into a physical address using the data structure depicted in Figure 2.11. This translation allows the memory that a segment uses to be distributed throughout the system, but to appear to user processes as if it were contiguous.

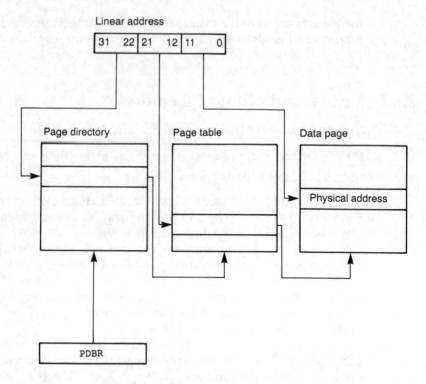

Figure 2.11   Linear to physical address translation.

The linear to physical address translation also allows for sections of the memory space to be held on disk rather than in RAM. This enables the sum of the address spaces of processes in the system to exceed the amount of available RAM.

The three main structures used in the linear to physical address translation are the page directory base register (PDBR), which on SCO UNIX points to a single page directory, the page directory itself and the page tables. A page directory can contain up to 1024 pointers to page tables and each page table can contain up to 1024 pointers to pages, otherwise known as page frames. Page frames, tables and directories are all 4 K in size. A 32-bit linear address consists of three parts. The most significant ten bits index into the page directory to select a page table to access. The next ten bits index that page table, to select a page frame to access. The last twelve bits provide the offset into the page to point to the byte which is being addressed.

This system allows support for a maximum of four gigabytes of virtual address space. The data structures themselves are initialized by software, but the translation is performed automatically by the

MMU hardware. The hardware mechanisms that perform the translation are fully described in Intel's *i486 Programmer's Reference Manual.*

The initial page tables and segment descriptors are set up for the kernel when it is read into memory at the time the system is bootstrapped. Once the system is running, page directory entries are remapped to include the address space of the currently running process.

One important difference between user and kernel virtual addresses with SCO UNIX is that kernel code and data are permanently resident in RAM, whereas only a subset of a user process will normally be resident. User processes themselves are not aware of this. Whenever they access a page that is not resident in RAM their execution is suspended, the relevant code or data is then read in from disk by the kernel and the program is restarted without any knowledge of this activity. This page fault recovery is implemented through a combination of MMU hardware and kernel software.

The kernel support routines used to copy data between peripherals, kernel and user memory take account of this added complexity and ensure that the user memory of the currently executing process is accessible.

Other implementations of UNIX such as IBM's AIX allow portions of the kernel to be paged in on demand. This is a more complex solution but does enable larger kernels to run without using up so much physical memory.

As mentioned earlier, although the VM accessed by user processes appears to be contiguous in memory, this is not the case when dealing with the same data at the physical level. The memory pages containing a 16 Kb array might physically reside out of sequence and with gaps in between them. This is not something that we normally need to worry about when writing device driver code unless the virtual addressing mechanism is bypassed, using, for example, a DMA controller. DMA controllers don't use the CPU and its MMU when transferring data directly from peripherals to physical memory. This potential problem is normally resolved either by using kernel support routines to allocate physically contiguous memory buffers or by breaking up DMA requests into smaller transfers that do not cross page boundaries. The SCO kernel provides a number of support routines to allocate both physical and virtual memory; these are described in the next section.

If a device driver needs to access physical memory, the device driver writer must arrange for a given virtual address to map onto the desired physical location in memory, for example a video buffer. This is because all addresses used by device drivers must be virtual addresses. This is enforced by the i386/i486 CPU when it operates in protected mode. In other words, all memory references use the segment and page table translation mechanisms described above. The mapping of a virtual address to a physical address can be done using the sptalloc(K) routine described in the following section.

2.6.2 Memory management routines

When writing user programs, memory is allocated either automatically or explicitly by the programmer. This section deals with the mechanisms available for explicitly controlling memory within a device driver. Chapter 4's section on the system stack deals with the issues relating to automatic allocation of memory.

One of the key differences between writing device drivers and writing application programs is the lack of the familiar system call facilities with which to manage memory. When writing device drivers, the brk(S) system call and its associated libraries (malloc(S)) are not available. In their place are a number of other routines.

SCO UNIX uses the following routines, which are summarized here in order for you to gain an initial idea of the facilities available.

memget

Syntax:

```
memget(npages)
     int npages;
```

- Allocates npages of physically contiguous memory, suitable for DMA transfers.
- Provides storage which is not at a predetermined position in memory.
- Should be called at initialization time from XXinit.
- Memory cannot be deallocated.

db_alloc

Syntax:

```
#include (sys/devbuf.h)
db_alloc(dv)
     struct devbuf *dv;
```

- Provides storage which is not at a predetermined position in memory.

- Provides physically, contiguous storage suitable for use with DMA.
- Cannot be called from XXintr.
- Memory can be deallocated.
- devbuf.count is used to specify how many bytes are required. The other pointers in devbuf describe the start and end point of the memory allocated and the current positions in the buffer for reading and writing.

db_free

Syntax:

```
#include ⟨sys/devbuf.h⟩
db_free(dv)
    struct devbuf *dv;
```

- Returns memory allocated by db_alloc(K) to a pool.

db_read

Syntax:

```
#include ⟨sys/devbuf.h⟩
db_read(dv, va, count)
    struct devbuf *dv;
    caddr_t va;
    unsigned count;
```

- Used to transfer count bytes from physical memory (allocated with db_alloc(K) and described by dv) into user virtual address location va.

db_write

Syntax:

```
#include ⟨sys/devbuf.h⟩
db_write(dv, va, count)
    struct devbuf *dv;
    caddr_t va;
    unsigned count;
```

- Used to transfer data from a user virtual address to a physical address.

sptalloc

Syntax:

```
sptalloc(pages, mode, base, flag)
    int pages, mode, base, flag;
```

- Used to allocate pages of temporary kernel virtual storage.
- Can be used to address physical memory at a specific location (base) for memory mapped I/O.
- Cannot be called from XXintr.
- The addresses returned are accessible to the kernel and all user programs.

sptfree

Syntax:

```
sptfree(va, npages, freeflg)
    char *va;
    int npages, freeflg;
```

- Returns the npages of memory allocated at address va by sptalloc(K) to a pool.

These SCO-specific routines are documented in the *SCO UNIX Device Driver Writer's Guide*. There is an explanation of how these functions operate in the context where they are used in later chapters. Different UNIX versions tend to vary in the routines that they provide to implement memory management.

2.6.3 Programming in a multi-tasking environment

This topic is one of the more challenging areas to understand, so we will introduce it at this early stage so that you have a chance to think about it at some length. It will be covered in greater detail in Chapter 4 when interrupts are discussed.

Programmers do not have to consider how UNIX achieves multi-tasking when writing user application code. This is because at the user level they have no direct control over how multi-tasking is performed. Despite the fact that their processes coexist with many others on the system they are prevented from corrupting other processes' memory space. This is not the case when writing code at the kernel level.

Time-sharing

The CPU has a number of processes to execute. Details of these processes are held on a run queue. The CPU executes each process in the run queue one at a time. It cycles between each of them so rapidly that all users gain the impression that they are being given dedicated access to the CPU. This impression is maintained provided the run queue does not get too long and so long as other significant delays are not incurred, such as waiting for a large number of disk accesses to complete.

If there is a substantial amount of processing work to do in order to complete the execution of a process, the CPU runs it for a fixed period of time. The process will continue to run until the end of this period or until it needs to wait for I/O. Following this, the CPU suspends execution of the current process and continues execution of the highest priority process in the run queue. The CPU returns later on to resume execution of the original process, if this is required, repeating this cycle continuously. Most UNIX systems implement time-sharing in a way similar to this.

Complications become apparent when one considers scheduling algorithms, prioritization of processes and their order on the run queue.

Context switching

A process' context consists of all the data structures required to record its state so that it can be restarted at a later time. It includes, among other things a copy of the CPU's registers, the kernel stack, an entry in the process table and a data structure called the U-area.

The process table structure is defined in ⟨sys/proc.h⟩. It contains an entry for every active process on the system, holding key details such as process ID, user ID, CPU time consumed, pointers to other key structures relating to the process and all the information necessary for scheduling. The process table is permanently resident in memory. The U-area, which may not always be memory resident, contains additional per-process information which is used whilst the process is running. The U-area is defined in ⟨sys/user.h⟩.

When the CPU moves from executing the code of one process to another this is known as a context switch. At this time details of the current process' context are replaced by those of the process about to be run. The act of context switching consumes CPU time; this is known as the context switching overhead.

Data integrity

When executing in user mode a process can normally only reference variables that are in its own address space. When a process is executing in system mode this is not the case. The kernel will update many variables which are shared by all processes and occur only once in the system. An example of this is the linked list structure that is used to manage the buffer cache. This data structure is shared by all processes. Another example would be the list of vacant swap locations on disk. If the kernel partially modifies one of these structures and does not complete the operation before moving on to something else (because the end of a time-slice occurs), these structures would be corrupted. As a result the kernel is written with the assumption that it will only give up control voluntarily. In other words, the operating system will only allow a context switch to occur when the kernel is ready, once all the data structures are coherent.

Device drivers for real-time and multi-processor systems require the use of more complex techniques in order to ensure the integrity of shared data structures. These centre around use of atomic locks and semaphores to guard access to all shared data structures. This can be extremely complex. Device drivers for multi-processor systems are often run by a single processor in order to simplify their development.

Sleep(K) and wakeup(K)

A context switch will occur when a process in system mode relinquishes control of the CPU voluntarily. This is performed by calling the sleep(K) kernel support routine (not to be confused with the sleep(S) system call). A sleep(K) is usually called by a process when it is waiting for an event to occur and is therefore unable to continue to run. This could be a physical event such as a character being received from a keyboard or a resource such as memory space becoming available.

When giving up control of the CPU, sleep(K) sets a field in the process table entry for the current process to enable it to be woken up at some future time. This field is known as the Wait Channel (p_wchan in ⟨sys/proc.h⟩). Although its value can be arbitrary, typically it is equal to the address of a global data structure which relates to the pending event. An example might be the address of a buffer that is being filled by DMA from a disk.

The kernel routine wakeup(K) is used to put all the processes sleeping on a given Wait Channel back on the run queue. Once back on the run queue a process is ready to continue execution. The Wait Channel that a process is sleeping on can be seen under the WCHAN heading of a ps -1 listing.

```
# crash
dumpfile = /dev/mem, namelist = /unix, outfile = stdout
> proc
PROC TABLE SIZE = 100
SLOT ST PID   PPID  PGRP    UID PRI CPU   EVENT    NAME        FLAGS
   0 s     0     0     0      0   0   0 d00a51dc sched        load sys nwak
   1 s     1     0     0      0  39   0 e0000000 init         load
   2 s     2     0     0      0   0   0 d004e108 vhand        load sys nwak
   3 s     3     0     0      0  20   0 d0048170 bdflush      load sys nwak
   4 s   174     1   174      0  30   0 d007d378 sh
   5 s 15162   173     0      0  39   7 e0000000 sleep        load
   6 s   173     1     0      0  30   8 d007d628 sh           load
   7 s    40     1     0      0  26   0 d006be48 logger       load
   8 s   148     1   148      0  26   0 d00965f2 cron         load
   9 s   176     1   176      0  30   0 d007da30 sh
  10 s   156     1   156      0  26   0 d0096dd4 lpsched      load
  11 s  6257     1  6257      0  28   0 d006bfb4 getty

...

> trace 11

STACK TRACE FOR PROCESS 11:
STKADDR    FRAMEPTR   FUNCTION  POSSIBLE ARGUMENTS
e0000cd0   e0000cf4   swtch     (d006c154,1c,d006c154,d006c160)
e0000cfc   e0000d24   canon     (d006c154,d006c154,d008a3f4,d0095f60)
e0000d2c   e0000d4c   ttread    (d006c154,d008ffac,64013)
e0000d54   e0000d60   vidread   (d008ffac,d0099ae8,60d84,d0010fc2)
e0000d68   e0000d78   cnread    (6,1,d008a3f4,d0099ae8)
e0000d80   e0000db4   s5readi   (d0099ae8,e0000e38,d0073838,0)
e0000dbc   e0000de8   rdwr      (1)
e0000df0   e0000df4   read      (d0069314,402360,0,4031c8)
e0000dfc   e0000e2c   systrap   (e0000e38)
           e0000e38   sys_call  from 00004ed8
ax:       3 cx:       0 dx:    737c bx:       0 fl:    202 ds: 1f fs:   0
sp:e0000e68 bp:7ffffba4 si:  401fa0 di:  402360 err:      3 es: 1f gs:   0
> quit
#
```

Figure 2.12 Output from crash showing getty(M) sleeping.

sleep(K) gives up its thread of execution by calling the process scheduler, a routine called swtch. This can best be seen by running the diagnostic tool crash(ADM). The process table can be inspected and a slot in the table can be used as a reference point to examine the system stack of any process. Figure 2.12 gives an example of a session where the stack trace of one of the getty(M)s on the system is examined.

The output from this stack trace shows a variety of functions that are currently on getty(M)'s system stack. At the base of the stack is the routine that handles the entry point into the system through the system call interface (systrap). The getty(M) process made a read(S) system call on one of the console's multiscreens. The cn console device driver's read routine (cnread) has been called. This then called

the video-adaptor keyboard read routine (vidread), which in turn
called the routine ttread(K). This called the routine canon(K) which
waited for characters to arrive. As there were no characters to be read
the process then slept, using the address of a data structure that
related to the input buffer of the console device as its Wait Channel.
When the characters arrive, the kernel will wakeup(K) all processes
that are sleeping using that address. Chapter 5 will deal more fully
with the operation of terminal drivers, but this example serves to
illustrate the way in which control of the CPU is relinquished by the
device driver.

Process priority

Sleep(K) has a second parameter which specifies the priority level at
which the process will sleep (p_pri in ⟨sys/proc.h⟩). This sets the
process' priority relative to other processes on the system. This priority is used when the process is competing for the CPU, once it has
been woken up. The priority of a process is shown in the PRI column
of the output from ps -l.

One implication of the design of the standard UNIX kernel is that if
device drivers do not relinquish the CPU whilst waiting for events,
the time-sharing system will not function correctly. An example of
this would be the implementation of long delays using spin loops,
where a process stays on the CPU for many milliseconds preventing
other processes from running. The appropriate action is to sleep(K)
rather than to spin in these cases.

A context switch can occur in the following cases:

- Whenever a process calls sleep(K), waiting for an event or a
  resource.

- Whenever the CPU returns from system mode to user mode (at the
  end of exceptions, interrupts and system calls).

Critical sections of code

Having described the circumstances under which a context switch
can occur we can apply that knowledge to provide a facility which is
key when writing operating system code, that of guarding critical
code and data structures.

Often there are operations that need to be atomic or indivisible.
These operations are often centred on objects such as:

- Shared data structures
- Variables used in test-and-set operations
- Device registers.

```
{
        static int no_entry=0;

        while (no_entry)
              sleep(&no_entry, WDPRI);
        no_entry = 1;
        /* START Critical Code which sleeps */
        /* read disk */
        /* compute change */
        /* update structure on disk */
        /* END Critical Code */
        no_entry=0;
        wakeup(&no_entry);

}
```

Figure 2.13   Example of guarding critical code.

These can potentially be manipulated by other parts of the same device driver, executing in the context of another process. The two basic types of critical section are:

(1)   Code containing a sleep(K) which allows other processes to execute and potentially access shared objects.

(2)   Code which accesses objects which are manipulated by an interrupt routine. Guarding these critical sections will be discussed in Chapter 4.

An example of the first situation is the update of a partition table on disk. This may require several operations: a read, some computation and a write to update the structure. This series of operations is likely to result in the process sleeping. If another process then attempts to perform the same operation, corruption may well occur. The solution is to guard critical sections of code like this with flags. An example is shown in Figure 2.13. Despite the fact that the test and set of no_entry is spread over two statements it is still indivisible. This is because the code is executed in system mode and therefore cannot be pre-empted by another process.

There is potential for a context switch in this critical code section, since the reading of the disk could involve a call to sleep(K). Any other process that tried to invoke this code whilst the update was being done would sleep on the address of the no_entry variable. The Wait Channel shown by ps(C) would be equal to the address of the no_entry variable. The sleeping process or processes would be rescheduled once the update was completed. In this way the device driver writer can control the execution of critical sections of the device driver code.

2.7   Summary

This chapter has described how to understand the operation of the kernel through use of software tools and header files and how device driver routines are invoked. We then detailed the main routines that need to be written for character, block and raw device drivers and covered some guidelines to follow when writing operating system code. These included:

- Memory allocation
- Use of sleep(K) and wakeup(K)
- Process priority
- Guarding critical code.

Our next step will be to look at a specific type of device driver, the simple character device driver.

QUIZ

To test your understanding of this chapter, try to answer the following questions.

2.1   Can character device drivers be used to transfer blocks of data?

2.2   What are the first three bytes of the di_addr array used for in the inodes of special device files?

2.3   Which pieces of information are required in order to locate the device driver routine that is required to service a system call?

2.4   What is the major device number used for?

2.5   What is the minor device number used for?

2.6   What are the two circumstances under which a context switch can take place?

EXERCISE

Write a simple device driver.

The objective of this exercise is for you to write your first device driver. All the device driver needs to do is to print messages to the console announcing when each of its functions has been called.

It should be a character device driver made up of a number of short routines (one line each). There should be a routine to service the open(S), close(S), read(S), write(S) and ioctl(S) system calls. Each of the routines should be named using the three letter prefix dum.

The routines should announce that they have been called through use of the kernel support routine cmn_err(K) which is fully documented in the *SCO UNIX Device Driver Writer's Guide*. For this exercise, only two arguments need to be supplied. The first might be the symbol CE_CONT. This is defined in ⟨sys/cmn_err.h⟩. The second should be the string that you want printed when the routine is called. The cmn_err(K) routine is similar to the routine printf(K) which is commonly available on most systems.

Test the device driver by using simple UNIX commands with I/O redirection from the shell. These commands should read from and write to the special device file which corresponds to your device driver. The stty(C) command can be used to test the XXioctl routine.

For hints and further detailed guidance on how to link device driver routines into a kernel and how to reboot using this new kernel, refer to Appendix A.

There is a sample answer in 'Answers to Exercises' along with a set of shell commands that will cause the device driver routines to be called.

3

Simple character device drivers

3.1 Overview

The objective of this chapter is to guide readers to a position where they can write simple character device drivers. These drivers provide the basic facility of transferring small amounts of data between a user process and a device.

Character device drivers are used to support devices that accept variable amounts of data and that do not support filesystems. The simple character device drivers we will be looking at in this chapter do not use the more complex kernel data structures and support routines which are described later in the book. We will be concentrating on the basics of passing small amounts of data between the user process and the device and leaving the development of higher performance, buffering techniques, data flow control and interrupt handling until later. As a result, the examples we will use are simpler than production device drivers.

This approach will allow us to concentrate on the following topics:

- The principal routines within simple character device drivers.

- The way in which user requests are specified to the device driver and the way in which the success or failure of the operation is reported back.

- Transferring data between the user and the device driver.

- Transferring data between the device driver and the device.

- Some of the mechanisms available to schedule the execution of device driver code: polling, delays and timeouts.

Most of the techniques covered in this chapter are applicable when writing the other types of device drivers discussed later in this book. This chapter includes a parallel printer driver which we will use as a working example. The exercise is to write a device driver for a mouse.

3.2   The character device driver kernel interface

Our first step towards writing a simple character device driver is to gain an understanding of the principal functions that form the basis of the code that needs to be written. This section describes these routines, expanding upon the outline given in Chapter 2. Most of the routines are invoked by the kernel from the cdevsw table.

3.2.1   XXinit

Syntax:

```
XXinit()
```

This routine is called by the operating system at boot time. This is the point at which the peripheral hardware is initialized or reset. No operations that require user processes to be present should be performed at this stage. It should display a message on the console confirming that the hardware is present. This can be done by checking for a 'signature' value or magic number which some devices guarantee to have set at a given address. Alternatively, known bit patterns can be checked in peripheral registers following a command that is written to the device.

Memory can be requested by the device driver at this point. If contiguous memory is required, this is a suitable time to request it (before it is fragmented by user process activity). No operations that require interrupts can be performed at this stage as interrupts are not enabled when this routine is called.

3.2.2   XXopen

Syntax:

```
XXopen(dev, flag, id)
    dev_t dev;
    int flag, id;
```

This routine is called by the operating system every time the device is open(S) ed. The dev parameter specifies the major and minor device number of the device file used to invoke the driver. It is passed to many of the other driver entry points. flag is used to record the values used with the open(S) call. The values are defined in ⟨sys/file.h⟩. These include values such as FAPPEND which corresponds to the O_APPEND parameter used with open(S). The id flag is set by the kernel to indicate how the device is being used by the kernel. The values are defined in ⟨sys/open.h⟩; for example, OTYP_CHR indicates that the XXopen routine is being called as a result of an open(S) on a character device file.

XXopen is a suitable place to code:

- Error and status checking (for example, is the floppy disk inserted?)

- Hardware initialization that requires interrupts in order to complete.

- Exclusivity, where only one open(S) of the device is allowed.

- Validation of minor device numbers passed as a parameter.

3.2.3 XXclose

Syntax:

```
XXclose(dev, flag, id)
    dev_t dev;
    int flag, id;
```

Whereas the XXopen routine is called whenever a user performs an open(S) system call on the device, XXclose is called only when the last close(S) system call is made on the special device file. The only exception to this is when an XXclose routine has been called by another layered XXclose routine (for instance, by a software driver to implement disk mirroring). If this is the case XXclose calls will be paired with XXopen calls and id should be set to OTYP_LYR by the driver invoking the XXclose routine.

The value of flag corresponds to that of the flag passed to the XXopen routine.

This is a suitable place to code any clean-up operations that are required. These might include flushing buffers, deallocating dynamic resources which have been previously claimed, disabling the device or shutting down a motor drive.

3.2.4 XXread

Syntax:

```
XXread(dev)
      dev_t dev;
```

This routine is called as a result of a user's read(S) system call.
The routine should:

- Validate the feasibility of the request, bearing in mind the hardware constraints.

- Wait for the device to become ready and then send the required bytes to the device's control register in order to request the data from the device.

- Wait for the data to arrive. When the data arrives from the device XXread should transfer it into the user process' address space. Alternatively, if there has been a hardware error this needs to be passed back to the process which made the read(S) request.

3.2.5 XXwrite

Syntax:

```
XXwrite(dev)
       dev_t dev;
```

This routine is called whenever a user makes a write(S) system call.
The routine should:

- Likewise validate the feasibility of the request, bearing in mind the hardware constraints.

- Copy the data from the user process.

- Wait for the device to become ready and program the device's control registers in order to initiate the transfer.

- Write the data to the device in question. If there is a hardware error this should be passed back to the process which made the write(S) request.

3.2.6   XXioctl

Syntax:

```
XXioctl(dev, cmd, arg, mode)
        dev_t dev;
        int cmd, mode;
        caddr_t arg;
```

This routine is used to implement hardware-specific functions. cmd is used to specify a device driver-specific command. arg can hold either the address of the argument passed to the system call or a single integer argument. The value of mode corresponds to the value of the flag passed to the open(S) system call.

Given the simple open(S)/close(S)/read(S)/write(S) interface that is available for all files, the I/O control system call ioctl(S) was introduced as a 'catch all' system call to control any idiosyncrasies of the device being controlled. This call is often used by application writers who wish to control the behaviour of a serial line. For example, the baud rate is modified by the stty(C) command using ioctl(S) requests. However, it can be used to do almost anything. The device driver writer needs to document the parameters for his or her particular device driver so that users understand the significance of any parameters that are passed to this routine, as these will be device driver specific.

3.2.7   XXhalt

Syntax:

```
XXhalt()
```

The halt routine is called by the kernel when the system is shut down. It allows the device driver to leave the hardware in a state where it can be re-initialized without a power cycle.

3.2.8   XXintr

Syntax:

```
XXintr(irq)
       int irq;
```

This routine is called following an interrupt from the device. irq indicates which interrupt request line generated the interrupt.

Many devices generate interrupts. They can occur when the device has completed an operation such as a read or a write or when there is a change in the device's status, such as when the carrier signal drops on a communications line.

3.2.9   XXstart

Syntax:

```
XXstart()
```

This routine is not a kernel entry point, it is private to the device driver. It is conventionally used to interact directly with the device's hardware, setting up commands in a controller's register in order to start a transfer. XXstart is often called from the XXread, XXwrite and XXintr routines.

3.2.10 XXpoll

Syntax:

```
XXpoll(ppl)
     int ppl;
```

When interrupts from a device are either not available or not reliable this routine can be written and used to service the device. It is called by the kernel following a clock tick. The frequency of the clock is defined by HZ in ⟨sys/param.h⟩ (HZ is defined as 100 in SCO UNIX 3.2 v4). The interrupt priority of the system before the clock tick is supplied in ppl.

3.3   The U-area and simple character devices

Having looked at the routines that provide the entry points into a device driver, we will now look at a key data structure that many of these routines use to communicate with the user process. When an XXread or an XXwrite routine is called as a result of a read(S) or write(S) system call, the only parameter that is passed to these functions (under SCO UNIX) is the device number which corresponds to the device file being accessed. The specification of the

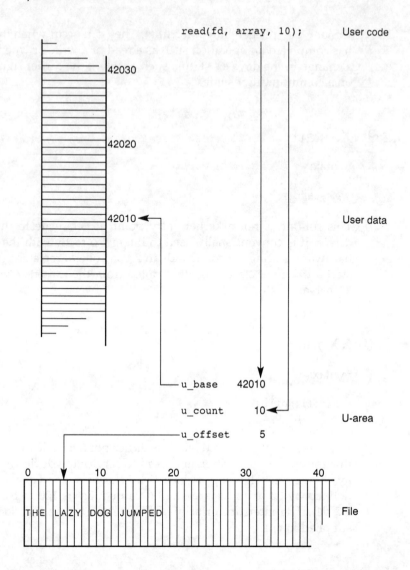

Figure 3.1 The u_base, u_count and u_offset fields in the U-area before a read(S).

transfer that is required is communicated via a data structure called the U-area.

The U-area is a data structure maintained by the kernel. Each process has its own U-area. It contains information that describes the read and write operations which the user application has requested and which the device driver has to implement. The U-area is also used to communicate back to the user process the status of the requested transfer following its execution. The U-area is defined in

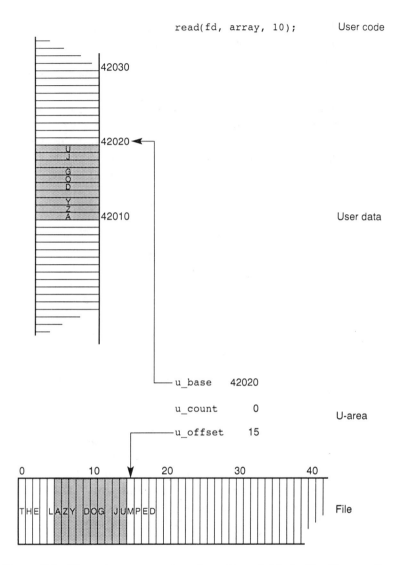

Figure 3.2 The u_base, u_count and u_offset fields in the U-area after a read(S).

the header file ⟨sys/user.h⟩ and is described in greater detail in Chapter 4. In this section we will look at a small part of it.

When a read(S) or write(S) system call is made, its parameters specify:

- The descriptor number of the file to be read or written.
- Where it is to be transferred to or from in the process' memory.
- The amount of data to be transferred.

Following the system call, the kernel copies these parameters from the user process' stack into the appropriate variables in the process' U-area held in kernel space. The current offset in the file which is being read or written is copied from the system file table into the U-area.

These values should be updated by the device driver following the transfer of data from the device.

The following three entries are taken from the U-area structure defined in ⟨sys/user.h⟩. They are used to store the values discussed above:

```
caddr_t   u_base;    /* base address for I/O */
unsigned  u_count;   /* bytes remaining for I/O */
off_t     u_offset;  /* offset in file for I/O */
```

The types used here are defined in the header file ⟨sys/types.h⟩. This is used to hold the type definitions commonly used within kernel source code. caddr_t is defined as char * and is described as being a pointer to a core address. off_t is a long.

The following example shows how these fields are used if a read(S) is performed on a storage device. Figure 3.1 shows values in the U-area before the read(S), Figure 3.2 shows them afterwards. In this example ten bytes are to be transferred by the device driver, starting at byte 5 in the device, into an array which starts in memory at user virtual address 42010. Initially the kernel would set u_base to 42010, u_count would be set to 10 and u_offset would be set to 5. At the end of the successful call the U-area fields should be updated by the device driver so that u_base holds 42020, u_count is set to zero and u_offset should equal 15. The return value that the user gets from the read(S) call is calculated by subtracting the value left in u_count by the device driver from the original byte count.

In this example we have seen how the U-area is used to confirm how much data has been transferred. The U-area is also used to communicate back to the user process the nature of any errors that might have occurred as a result of the request. This is done in the form of an error code which is stored in the u_error member of the u structure. The possible error codes are defined in ⟨sys/errno.h⟩. Setting this field will result in the corresponding value being copied into the errno external variable in the user process. Currently it is possible to set u.u_error with the following: u.u_error = EFAULT; however, it is good practice to use the SCO kernel support routine seterror(K) (which does the same thing), for example, seterror(EFAULT). This ensures forward compatibility if error handling changes in future versions of SCO UNIX.

The errors that should be reported can result from a number of causes including kernel resource shortage, incorrect parameters

Table 3.1 Commonly used error codes.

Code	Description
EAGAIN	Kernel resources not available (e.g. memory space or a table entry)
EBUSY	Device busy (e.g. used in XXopen when enforcing exclusive access)
EFAULT	Invalid memory address passed (e.g. ioctl(S) arg parameter or a memory address is referenced that is outside permitted areas)
EINVAL	Invalid argument passed (e.g. ioctl(S) cmd parameter)
EIO	An error was detected by the device following a valid I/O request (e.g. a bad block on a disk is detected)
ENXIO	Attempting to access beyond the boundaries of a device (e.g. writing beyond the end of a disk) or attempting to access a non-existent device (e.g. an invalid minor device number was used)

passed to device driver entry points or peripheral hardware failures. When selecting an error code you should consult the *SCO UNIX Programmer's Reference Manual* (Volume 2) entry for the system calls that use the device driver function being written and (if possible) choose from the codes listed for that system call. A summary of the meaning of commonly used error codes is given in Table 3.1.

3.4 Transferring data between user and device driver

So far in this chapter we have established the main routines that make up character device drivers, the way requests are specified and the way status is returned. Now we will look at the process of transferring data between the user and the device driver.

Data transfer between kernel and user space cannot be achieved using the same constructs as would be used in application programs. Code such as

```
while (data_to_be_copied) {
    *u.u_base++ = *kernel_data++;
}
```

should not be used to transfer data between kernel and user memory.

Kernel support routines are provided to implement the transfers between kernel address space and user address space. These routines improve the portability of device driver code and relieve the device driver writer of having to understand fully the operation and constraints of the memory management model that is in use. SCO UNIX provides the routines copyout(K) and copyin(K) which are also found in other implementations of UNIX. These support routines are often used in XXread/XXwrite functions to transfer data between user and kernel space. They are also frequently used in XXioctl routines to copy ioctl(S) arguments to and from the user's memory.

copyin(K) copies data from a user's virtual address to a kernel virtual address. It takes three arguments. The first is the address of the user's data, the second is the address of the destination data structure in kernel memory. The last argument specifies how many bytes need to be copied. copyout(K) works the other way around, with the first argument being the kernel address which is being copied from.

XXread routines generally make use of copyout(K), whereas XXwrite routines use copyin(K). Here is an example of how they would typically be used within an XXioctl routine:

```
struct dev_param d_p;

XXioctl(dev, cmd, arg, mode)
        dev_t dev;
        int cmd, mode;
        caddr_t arg;
{
        switch (cmd) {

        case SET_PARAMETER:
            if (copyin(arg, &d_p, sizeof(d_p)) == -1) {
                    seterror(EFAULT);
                    return;
            }
            break;

        case GET_PARAMETER:
            if (copyout(&d_p, arg, sizeof(d_p)) == -1) {
                    seterror(EFAULT);
                    return;
            }
            break;

        default:
            seterror(EINVAL);
            break;
        }
}
```

The parameter arg is the virtual address in user space of the structure containing the device driver parameters that the user wants to be read or written. The d_p parameter is the structure which has been allocated to store these parameters for the device driver code to access. If SET_PARAMETER has been passed as the value of the cmd parameter, copyin(K) will copy the values from user space into the d_p structure in the kernel. If the ioctl(S) call is made with an unknown value in cmd then the XXioctl routine will return, setting the u_error field in the user process' U-area so that the ioctl(S) system call fails.

Both copyin(K) and copyout(K) perform bounds checking on the range of user virtual addresses involved. They do not update the u_base, u_count and u_offset fields held in the U-area. When they are used in XXread and XXwrite routines these fields must be updated explicitly by the device driver.

3.5 Transferring data between device driver and device

This section describes how to pass data between the device driver software and the input/output registers of the physical device.

3.5.1 I/O mapped devices

If a device is I/O mapped you will need to establish what are the addresses of the I/O ports required to operate it. This can often be configurable and depend on the position of switches or placement of 'jumper' connectors on the device controller. Generally the standard 'User Guides' for peripherals do not contain this information and a 'Programmer's Guide' or detailed hardware specification is required.

The Intel iX86 instruction set contains machine code instructions that transfer data to or from an I/O mapped device. The assembly code mnemonics for the main instructions are IN and OUT. These instructions transfer data between a register and an I/O port. They are privileged instructions and are normally only available to the kernel.

SCO UNIX provides a series of assembly language macros defined in ⟨sys/inline.h⟩ which allow these instructions to be used in order to transfer 32-bit (ind(K), outd(K)), 16-bit (inw(K), outw(K)) and 8-bit (inb(K), outb(K)) values to I/O ports.

This is an example of how a device driver might use these routines:

```
#define REG_ADDR   0x1234
mywrite()
{
      char c;

      get_data_from_user(&c);
      outb(REG_ADDR, c);
}
```

In this example the peripheral has an I/O port mapped at address 0x1234. The device driver writer has written a routine get_data_from_user which may use copyin(K) to load a value into the variable c. This value is output to the I/O port using the macro outb(K) which in turn uses the OUTB assembly language instruction.

3.5.2   Memory mapped devices

A memory mapped controller will interpret all reads and writes to memory addresses within its address space as input and output to the device. Memory within this chosen range cannot be used for the normal purpose of Random Access Memory storage.

The device driver writer must establish the start and end locations in physical memory where the peripheral is mapped. Having done this, a mechanism is required to establish a usable pointer to this address so that the device driver can read from and write to it.

SCO UNIX provides a kernel support routine called sptalloc(K) which allocates a virtual address that the device driver writer can use. This can be used for peripherals such as video adaptors where bits written to memory mapped addresses are translated into patterns on the screen.

An example of how sptalloc(K) could be used with a hypothetical video controller follows:

```
#define DEV_ADDR    (caddr_t) 0xB8000
#define DEV_SIZE    4096

{
      caddr_t va;
      int i;

      va = sptalloc(1, PG_P | PG_RW, btoc(DEV_ADDR), 1);
      for (i = 0; i < DEV_SIZE; i++)
            *va++ = 0;
}
```

DEV_ADDR is the physical start address of the memory mapped device. DEV_SIZE, the size of the device, is equal to a single (4K) page. The variable va is assigned the virtual address at which the physical memory is mapped. The first parameter to sptalloc(K) specifies that a single page be mapped. The page is marked present (PG_P) and is made writable (PR_RW). The physical memory address is specified using the macro btoc to convert the byte address DEV_ADDR to a page frame address. The final parameter (1) stipulates that sptalloc(K) should not sleep if a page is unavailable.

The body of the for loop sets the contents of the memory map to zero. With our hypothetical video device it would have the effect of clearing the display.

3.6   Mechanisms to schedule execution of device drivers

Device drivers often have to interface with electro-mechanical devices (such as printers and disks) and other peripherals (such as communications devices) that operate significantly more slowly than the CPU of the main system. In these situations, controlling the time when parts of the device driver are executed becomes important and an extra layer of complexity is introduced. The device driver must be able to wait for events, to execute routines at regular intervals and to give up the CPU to allow other processes to use processor time that would otherwise be wasted. This section describes the kernel support routines that provide these facilities.

All of these functions rely on interrupts that originate from the system's hardware clock. A full discussion of the mechanisms behind this and the wider topic of using interrupts generated by peripherals will be postponed until the next chapter.

3.6.1 Polling

Polling is a simple way of regularly passing data to or from a relatively slow device. Polling is a useful mechanism to use when the device either does not generate interrupts at all or does not generate them in a reliable way. It has been used as a mechanism to service the parallel printer device on IBM AT clones, some of which do not reliably deliver the hardware interrupts that indicate when a character has been printed.

Once interrupts are enabled on the machine, a driver's XXpoll function will be repeatedly called by the kernel, after every clock interrupt, HZ times a second. This system clock is a source of regular interrupts which are used and controlled by software. It is separate from the processor clock which regulates the speed at which the CPU fetches, decodes and executes machine code instructions. The processor clock operates at a much higher speed, typically measured in MHz.

Calls to XXpoll will occur irrespective of which process is running, or whether the device corresponding to the XXpoll routine has been opened. As a result of this, the data structures that are accessed by the XXpoll routine should not relate to any particular user process. Accessing the U-area or copying data back to user process' address space should not be attempted as there is no guarantee which process will be running when the XXpoll routine is called. Following the execution of all the XXpoll routines the kernel increments the system clock, performs process ageing and initiates the routines that implement process scheduling.

By virtue of the fact that the XXpoll routines are called frequently, time spent within XXpoll routines should be brief. One simple way to help achieve this is for XXpoll routines to check to see if their device is open before commencing any work. They can do this by testing a flag set by the driver's XXopen routine.

Although polling is simple and reliable, there are two main disadvantages to using this technique to service a device:

(1) **Performance** The XXpoll routine is called at a constant rate. There may be periods between calls when the device is ready to read or write data, but has to wait until the next clock tick. It remains idle during these times. This limits the device's throughput which may unnecessarily delay the user process which is accessing it.

(2) **Data loss** Devices which have minimal 'on-board' buffering space may lose data if the device driver does not empty their buffers before more data arrives. Most dumb serial cards only have a single character buffer. Data can arrive very rapidly when serial cards are supporting communications lines or lots of users are typing quickly. If data arrives faster than the device driver copies from the character buffer it will be lost. In the case of the communications line, this may be detected and corrected by the communications protocol being used. However, it is not reasonable to expect a user to retype commands if the system loses characters from the keyboard.

In summary, polling is a simple, reliable technique for servicing slower devices that do not generate interrupts reliably.

3.6.2 Delays

When reading from or writing to a slow device it is often useful to insert delays in device driver code which allow the peripheral to complete an operation. These delays will be necessary when the device waits before accepting any more data, pausing until the current data has been dealt with (printed, transmitted or stored). This happens when the controller has no buffering space for outgoing data or it may be that the buffer is full. Alternatively it could be that the controller itself is slow to react when being written to. This often becomes apparent as the speed of CPUs overtakes the speed of the embedded processors in hardware controllers.

One way of implementing such delays is to write a spin loop to slow down the device driver. This has a number of disadvantages. One is that the CPU is locked into executing this rather wasteful code loop when it could be used for some more productive work. Another problem is that if the device driver is run on a faster CPU, the delay loop can be executed faster and as a result of this shorter delay, the device driver code can stop working. This can occur if code is moved from a machine with an i386 CPU to an i486 CPU.

An alternative to using spin loops is to use a kernel support routine called delay(K). This routine is implemented using a sleep(K) call and consequently should not be used within routines called from XXintr or XXpoll. The length of the delay is specified in clock ticks. As mentioned earlier, there are HZ clock ticks a second. Providing that the delay required is not less than one clock tick, then the delay(K) routine can be used. Using this function relinquishes control of the CPU and allows the processing of other work on the system.

There is a processing overhead involved as a result of the context switch which follows use of delay(K) (or sleep(K)). So in some cases very short delays are implemented with spin loops.

Another drawback with using delay(K) is that the length of the delay is approximate. This is because the process only becomes 'runnable' at the end of the specified delay period and therefore cannot be guaranteed to run immediately. The danger of this happening increases when using delay(K) if other jobs do not give up the CPU or are scheduled at a higher priority. When this happens the other jobs will be executed first and the length of the delay will be extended beyond what was anticipated. As with XXpoll, if the peripheral is ready before the delay period expires, time is wasted and data may be lost.

For these reasons this technique is not ideal, especially if data loss will occur if the device is not serviced quickly. In this case, interrupts and an interrupt service routine are normally used. However the delay(K) routine has the benefit of simplicity and can be used when the peripheral is not capable of generating interrupts.

Here is an example which uses the delay(K) routine to help inter-face to a relatively slow device where data loss will not occur if the delay is extended, a parallel printer.

```
lpwrite()
{
        char c;
        while (there_is_data) {
                while ((inb(PSTATUS) & READY) == 0)
                        delay(HZ/25);
                get_data_from_user(&c);
                outb(PDATA, c);
        }
}
```

The outer while loop continues whilst there is data to be sent to the printer. The second while loop is used to pause until the printer is ready to receive more data. It detects that the device is busy by reading the printer's status register at address PSTATUS. The inb(K) function reads the printer's hardware status byte. The C language bitwise-AND & operator is used to check the relevant bit, whilst ignoring other bits in the status byte by using the mask READY. Bit 8 is used to indicate whether the controller is ready for more data while the remaining bits are used to indicate other information (such as whether the printer is on-line). READY is therefore defined as the value 128 (10000000 in binary). Whilst the READY bit is held at 0, the while condition evaluates to true and the delay(K) function is called, paus-ing for at least four clock ticks. Once the printer is ready to receive more data the READY bit is set to 1. The device driver then gets the character from the user and outputs the data held in the variable c to the data register of the printer controller, at which point the loop repeats.

3.6.3   Timeouts

The timeout(K) function allows for a designated routine to be sched-uled for execution after a given time period. In the meantime, the device driver can continue to operate. The timeout(K) mechanism is useful in device drivers when waiting for an event that is not guaran-teed to happen. It allows the device driver to wait an amount of time for an event and then schedule a course of action if the event fails to occur. Its functionality is comparable with what is achieved using the signal(S) and alarm(S) system calls within application programs.

timeout(K) is used within the terminal driver to implement the VTIME functionality. When VTIME is set using an ioctl(S), a read(S) on a serial line will return after a given time, whether or not any characters have been received.

timeout(K) is also used in combination with sleep(K) and wakeup(K) to implement the delay(K) function described above.

3.7 An example parallel printer driver

This section describes the operation of a simplified but working parallel printer driver. The device driver was developed to work with the IBM AT on-board parallel printer port. As a result of its simplification, this device driver is not optimally efficient. The code will be developed further and made more efficient in the following chapter. This version uses most of the concepts and facilities discussed in this chapter. It can be configured into the system using the command:

```
# ./configure -a lpinit lpwrite -c -m MAJOR
```

First we will discuss the preamble.

```
1    #include ⟨sys/errno.h⟩
2    #include ⟨sys/types.h⟩
3    #include ⟨sys/dir.h⟩
4    #include ⟨sys/param.h⟩
5    #include ⟨sys/user.h⟩
```

The file errno.h is included so that the standard error code definitions can be used when reporting error conditions in the device driver. This device driver references the u_count, u_base and u_offset fields which make up part of the U-area. As a result of this, the user structure must be included into the source code for this module. All of the other include files are necessary to satisfy structures, typedefs and defines used within ⟨sys/user.h⟩.

```
6
7    #define   PBASE     0x378
8    #define   PDATA     (0 + PBASE)
9    #define   PSTATUS   (1 + PBASE)
10   #define   PCNTRL    (2 + PBASE)
11
12   #define   SELECT    0x08
13   #define   PRIME     0x0c
14   #define   READY     0x80
15   #define   STROBE    0x01
```

Lines 7 to 10 define the addresses of the I/O mapped registers for the parallel printer controller interface. The PDATA register is written to by the device driver. It holds the ASCII code of the character to be printed. PSTATUS indicates whether the device is busy printing or not. The control register, PCNTRL, is used to initialize the controller and to indicate when a new character has been written to the PDATA register.

SELECT and PRIME are written into PCNTRL in order to initialize the printer. The READY value is used to mask bit 8 in PSTATUS. This is set to 1 by the printer controller when the printer has space in its buffer to receive another character. STROBE is used to mask bit 0 in PCNTRL which is toggled between 1 and 0 by the device driver, to signal the presence of a new character in the PDATA register.

```
16      #define    RESET_DELAY 1000000
17
18      lpinit()
19      {
20              int i;
21
22              outb(PCNTRL, SELECT);
23              for (i = 0; i < RESET_DELAY; i++);
24              outb(PCNTRL, PRIME);
25              printcfg("lp", PBASE, 2, -1, -1,
                        "Simple Parallel Driver");
26      }
27
```

The lpinit routine sets up the printer controller and displays the device driver configuration message. Line 22 writes the SELECT value out to the control register. Line 23 implements a delay so that the controller can reset before the second part of the initialization sequence is performed on line 24. A busy loop is used on line 23 because at the time the XXinit routines are executed, interrupts have not been enabled on the system and as a result, delay(K) will not work. The printcfg(K) call displays on the console the name of the device driver ("lp"), the base address of the control registers (PBASE), along with the range of registers occupied by the registers (PBASE through to PBASE+2). Since the device driver does not use DMA or interrupts, −1 is supplied as the value for the next two parameters, followed by a comment describing the device driver.

```
28      lpwrite()
29      {
30              char c;
31
32              while (u.u_count) {
33                      while ((inb(PSTATUS) & READY) == 0)
34                              delay(HZ/25);
```

```
35              if (copyin(u.u_base, &c, 1) == -1) {
36                      seterror(EFAULT);
37                      return;
38              }
39
40              u.u_count--;
41              u.u_base++;
42              u.u_offset++;
43
44              outb(PDATA, c);
45              outb(PCNTRL, PRIME | STROBE);
46              outb(PCNTRL, PRIME);
47          }
48      }
```

lpwrite is called once for every write(S) system call made to the parallel printer device file. The outer while loop (from line 32 through to 47) is executed once for each character written to the printer. The number of characters remaining that have been transferred by write(S) is held in the U-area variable u.u_count. Lines 33 and 34 are used to wait until the controller is ready to receive the next character. If the 8th bit in PSTATUS is low, then the device driver requests a delay(K) for four clock ticks, enough to introduce a short pause and to allow another process to be scheduled if necessary.

Line 35 copies a character from the user process' address space (u.u_base) into the device driver's address space. If the address were illegal, the copyin(K) routine would return −1, the device driver routine would return and the system call would fail with errno set to EFAULT.

On lines 40 to 42, the appropriate U-area variables are updated to reflect the fact that data has been transferred from the user.

On line 44, the character is written to the hardware. In order for the device to understand that a new character has been passed to it, bit 1 of the printer's control register is toggled from high to low, whilst bits 2 and 4 are maintained high by the outb(K) calls on lines 45 and 46.

3.8   Summary

In this chapter we have looked at all of the basic techniques required to write a simple device driver. We have described the entry points into the device driver, the principal routines that govern its structure. The mechanism used to specify the parameters of requests was detailed in the section which introduced the U-area. We have also seen how data is transferred between the user and the device driver, and from there to the hardware. All of these techniques, when combined with some simple scheduling mechanisms, have allowed us to write our first device driver for a printer.

QUIZ

To test your understanding of this chapter, try to answer the following questions.

3.1   If ten processes concurrently open a device file and then close it, how many times will the XXopen and XXclose routines be invoked?

3.2   Following a read(S) of 20 bytes, how should the variables u.u_base and u.u_count be changed?

3.3   Why should spin loops be avoided when implementing delays in device drivers?

3.4   What kernel support routine can be used to transfer data between user space and an XXread routine?

3.5   What kernel support routine can be used to transfer data between user space and an XXwrite routine?

EXERCISE

Write a device driver for the Microsoft InPort Bus Mouse. Your device driver should use polling in order to read the data from the mouse controller. You should provide XXinit, XXpoll and XXread routines.

The device driver should maintain a data structure defining the state of the mouse. This should be copied out to any user process which is reading the appropriate device file following movement of the mouse or any of the buttons on it.

Format of returned data

It is often the case that the data returned by a device driver is simply an unformatted byte stream terminated by an end of file. This is true for data read from devices such as disks or terminal lines. However for a device such as a mouse where the data is more structured, the data which is copied back to the user from the device driver has to be held in an agreed format. This is normally defined in a header file used by both the device driver writer and the programmer accessing the device.

The format of the data returned by the mouse is defined by the following structure which should be placed in a header file used by your device driver and the application used to test the device driver.

```
/*
 * Structure of the data passed back to applications
 * reading the mouse device file
 */
struct bmouse {
     char buttons;
     char x, y;
};
```

If bmouse.x is a negative value this indicates that the mouse is being moved towards the left. If bmouse.y is a negative value then this indicates the mouse is being moved upwards.

The application program needs to allocate the storage for this structure within its process space so that the device can be read with a statement such as:

```
main()
{
     struct bmouse mouse;
     ...
     cc = read (fd, &mouse, sizeof(struct bmouse));
...
}
```

The source code to two programs designed to test your device driver is provided in 'Answers to Exercises' along with a model answer.

Description of the device

The mouse controller has two I/O mapped registers. The first, which we will refer to as BM_CTL, is only written to and is mapped to address

Table 3.2   Description of the values written to BM_CTL.

Value	Description
0x00	When BM_CTL is set to 0 BM_DATA will contain a bit map which will indicate whether the mouse has moved, whether the mouse buttons have changed position since the register was last read, as well as the state of the buttons on the mouse. See Table 3.3 for details.
0x01	BM_DATA will contain the value of the X counter. This indicates how much the mouse has just moved in the X axis. This is not an absolute X coordinate; it is a delta value, recording the amount of movement relative to the last time the hardware was read.
0x02	BM_DATA will contain the value of the Y counter. This indicates how much the mouse has just moved in the Y axis. This is not an absolute Y coordinate; it is a delta value.
0x80	This resets the mouse. The value should be written as the first part of the initialization of the device.
0x07	BM_DATA will act as a control register which may be written with one of two control values. The value 0 configures the correct mode of operation for this exercise. It should be written to BM_DATA as the second part of the initialization sequence. The value 0x20 freezes the X/Y movement counters. This should be set before the X/Y counters are read and then cleared afterwards.

0x23c; the second, which we will refer to as BM_DATA, is both written to and read from. It is mapped to address 0x23d.

BM_CTL is used to reset the device as well as to provide a means to select which of the four alternative internal registers is accessed through BM_DATA. Table 3.2 describes the values written to BM_CTL.

BM_DATA provides data on whether the mouse has moved, whether any of its buttons have been moved, the state of each button and the amount the mouse has moved in the X and Y axes. The meaning of the BM_DATA bit map is shown in Table 3.3.

Hints

Here is the pseudo code for the working device driver:

```
bminit()
{
      Reset the mouse controller.
      Set the mouse for the correct mode of operation.
      Print the configuration message on the console.
}
```

Table 3.3 Meaning of the BM_DATA bit map.

Bit	Description
0–2	Set high if the corresponding button is pressed down. If bit 0 is set to 1 then the right hand button is being held down. If bit 2 is set to 1 the left hand button is down.
3–5	Set high if the corresponding button has been moved up or down since the register was last read. If these bits are set, then update bits 0–2 in the bmouse structure, copy it out to the user address space and wake up the user process.
6	Indicates whether the mouse has moved on the X or Y axis. If this is set, it is worth reading the other mouse registers to obtain the data on how far the mouse has moved.

```
bmpoll ()
{
        Freeze the mouse X/Y counters.
        Check to see if the mouse has moved or the buttons have been
        pressed.
        If so:
                Copy the state of the buttons to the bmouse structure.
                Select the X counter and copy its value into the bmouse
                structure.
                Select the Y counter and copy its value into the bmouse
                structure.
                Set a flag in the driver indicating that data has been
                received from the mouse.
                Wake up the bmread routine.
        Release the X/Y counters.
}

bmread ()
{
        While the flag indicates there is no new data, sleep.
        Copy the bmouse structure out to the user.
        Set the flag back to indicate there is no new data.
}
```

4

Interrupts

4.1 Overview

This chapter will describe interrupts. We shall explore what an interrupt is, where interrupts come from, and how to deal with them. We shall also review the definition of a process' context, discuss why we might want to arrange for context switches to occur at the end of interrupt routines, and how to do this. Some parts of this chapter assume a reasonable amount of knowledge about the i386 CPU.

In the previous chapter, we wrote a device driver for a mouse which relied on the XXpoll routine being called at each clock tick, from the clock's own interrupt routine. An XXpoll routine is a very good way of managing slow devices that either cannot generate their own interrupts, or that interrupt so infrequently that it might be a good idea to poll the device regularly to make sure that it is still working properly.

However, relying exclusively on the XXpoll mechanism means that the maximum throughput of the device is dependent on the speed of the clock, rather than on the speed of the actual device. By using interrupts, a device can run at its maximum speed, and only receives attention from the kernel when it is required.

In the exercise at the end of this chapter, we shall add an interrupt routine to our mouse device driver.

4.2 What is an interrupt?

An interrupt is a request for service or attention from a device or a controller. A device sends an interrupt (sometimes we say that a device raises an interrupt) to indicate that something has happened and that the kernel should do something about it. Here are some examples of why devices interrupt:

- A disk controller raises an interrupt to indicate that it has finished dealing with a request or command that has been issued to it. For example, it has finished transferring a block of data between the kernel's memory and a disk.

- A dumb serial card raises interrupts to indicate that new data has arrived on one of its ports (a user may have typed a character), that data has been transmitted successfully from its output port, or that the carrier has been lost or restored on the modem control lines.

- A mouse raises an interrupt to indicate either that it has been moved or that one of its buttons has been pressed.

- A lineprinter raises interrupts to indicate that its on-board buffer has emptied and that it is now ready to receive some more data from the kernel.

- The real-time clock raises an interrupt 100 times a second so that the kernel can measure time and reschedule processes.

- Some devices raise interrupts to warn the kernel of hardware failure.

When the device driver handles the interrupt, it should check the controller's status by reading the status register. Assuming all is well, the driver can then read the data from the device, or write some more data to the device, and issue the next I/O request.

In the period when the kernel is handling an interrupt, we describe the system to be at **interrupt-time**. All interrupts are handled in system mode, and any routines which execute at interrupt-time should not do certain things, such as making references to the U-area.

The system is said to be at **task-time** at all other times, when it will be either in user mode or system mode.

4.3 Process contexts

Each process that executes has a context. A process' context describes the process' state, and the environment in which it is running. A process' context is set up initially by the fork(S) system call, and is changed by the kernel and the CPU as the process executes instructions, makes system calls, opens files, grows its stack, and so on. The following list describes some of the components of a process' context:

- The contents of all of the registers, including the instruction pointer CS:EIP[1] and the stack pointer SS:ESP.

- File table entries for the process' open files, inode table entries for the current and root directories, and so on.
- The process' segments, including its text, data and stack segments.
- The process' page tables.
- The process' entry in the process table.
- The process' U-area, including its system stack and Local Descriptor Table (LDT).

Each of the components of the process' context falls into one of two categories:

(1) Information used by the kernel to manage the process, such as the process table entry, the U-area and file table entries.

(2) Information used by the CPU to manage the process, such as the register contents and the LDT.

The kernel and the CPU access the components of the current process' context through a set of variables and registers. For example, the kernel variable curproc points to the process' entry in the process table, and the kernel variable u is the process' U-area. The Local Descriptor Table Register LDTR points to the process' LDT, and the Page Directory Base Register PDBR[2] points to the current page directory.

The CPU is shared amongst the many processes that are competing for it by a mechanism called a context switch, which saves the register values of the current process in a context save area, loads a new set of register values from the context save area of the new process and establishes new values for curproc and u. When context switching occurs many times a second, a system appears to be able to run processes simultaneously, and this is the basis of a multi-tasking operating system.

The i386 CPU provides some special instructions and data structures for saving and restoring contexts. A process' registers are saved in a structure called a Task State Segment (TSS), which is pointed to by the Task Register TR. See Figure 4.1. The TSS also contains three read-only stack pointers for privilege levels 0, 1 and 2, which are automatically loaded into SS:ESP by the CPU whenever there is a corresponding change of privilege level. For example, when a process makes a system call and switches from privilege level 3 to privilege level 0, a new privilege level 0 stack pointer is loaded from the process' TSS, and the old stack pointer is saved on the new stack.

SCO UNIX switches contexts by making an indirect jump through a task gate (a single machine instruction), which saves the context of the current process in the TSS indicated by TR, and loads the context

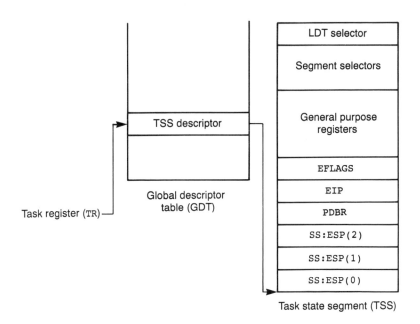

Figure 4.1 A process' TSS is pointed to by the Task Register (TR).

of the new process from the TSS indicated by the task gate. The next instruction to be executed is the one immediately following the indirect jump, but it will be executed in the context of the new process. Context switches are described in more detail in Section 4.8.

4.4 The system stack

In many implementations of UNIX, including SCO UNIX, each process has its own private system stack at the beginning of its U-area. Whenever the i386 CPU switches to privilege level 0 to handle system calls, exceptions and interrupts, it also switches from the process' user stack to the process' system stack. Stack frames for function calls and auto variables are created and removed from the system stack in the same way as they are on the user stack. On return to user mode, the system stack is emptied (see Section 4.5.5), and execution continues on the user stack. The fork(S) system call establishes a new U-area for the child process, and sets up the privilege level 0 stack pointer in the child's TSS to point to the base of the new system stack. See Figure 4.2.

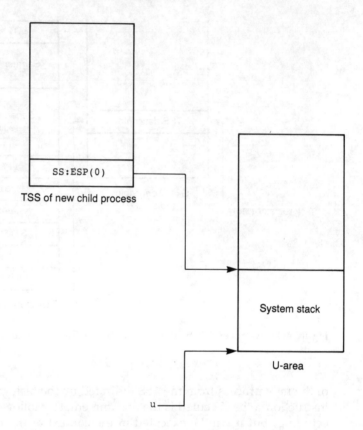

Figure 4.2 Fork(S) sets the child's SS:ESP(0) to point to the base of the system stack in the new U-area.

SCO UNIX handles all exceptions and interrupts in the context of the process that is running at the time of the exception or interrupt.[3] This means that interrupts are dealt with on the system stack of a process which in most cases is not the one which is waiting for the interrupt.[4] We shall discuss the implications of this in Section 4.6.

You may want to re-examine the header file ⟨sys/user.h⟩ and look for the space reserved for the system stack. The system stack is a fixed size – approximately 3.7 Kb, and this has one very important implication:

- All functions in the kernel, including interrupt routines, must be written so that they do not overflow the system stack by declaring too many auto variables.

If a kernel function does declare too many auto variables, the U-area will be corrupted and eventually the kernel will panic.

In summary, each process has its own fixed-size system stack in its U-area, which is used by that process whenever it is in system mode. Exceptions and interrupts are handled in the context of whichever process is running at the time of the exception or interrupt.

4.5   How interrupts arrive in a device driver

In the ISA and MCA architectures, the interrupt request lines (IRQs) of devices that generate interrupts are connected to one of two i8259A Programmable Interrupt Controllers (PICs), which are cascaded together as shown in Figure 4.3, giving a total of 15 different IRQs available for devices to use. The output pin of the slave PIC is connected to line 2 of the master PIC, and the output pin of the master PIC is connected to the Interrupt Request (INTR) line on the i386 CPU. In the simplest case, different controllers or devices are

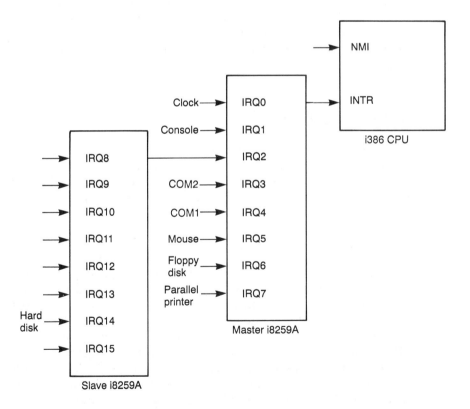

Figure 4.3   Master and slave i8259A PICs.

Table 4.1 Responding to exceptions and interrupts.

Priority level	Exceptions and interrupts
High priority	Debug breakpoints
	Non-maskable interrupts on NMI
	External interrupts on INTR
Low priority	Faults and exceptions

attached to different lines on the PICs, although it is possible for the IRQ lines to be shared between many controllers and/or many devices. Our explanation assumes that each device has its own IRQ.

Whenever a device raises an interrupt, a complex sequence of firmware instructions and i386 assembly code arranges for the appropriate device driver's XXintr routine to be called. We say that the interrupt is **vectored** to the device driver's XXintr routine.

Although it is not necessary to understand exactly what is going on at the lowest levels of the kernel in order to write device driver interrupt routines, it is useful to be aware of the mechanisms that are being used. If you are not too familiar with the i386 architecture, you may choose to skip Section 4.5.4 which describes the low-level interrupt handling mechanisms.

4.5.1 Interrupt priorities

The PICs have a built-in set of hardware interrupt priorities which provide limited control over the order in which devices can interrupt. UNIX implements an additional set of software priority levels which provides the user with some flexibility when adding new devices to the system.

Hardware priority levels

The i386 CPU responds to exceptions and interrupts in the order shown in Table 4.1. The i386 CPU can only respond to external interrupts at the end of an instruction, although it can respond to some exceptions (for example, a Page fault) at any time.

SCO UNIX programs the PICs to operate in Fully Nested Mode. This means that IRQ lines 0 through to 7 will be assigned interrupt priorities from 0 through to 7, where interrupt priority 0 is the highest.[5] For example, if two devices interrupt at exactly the same time on IRQ 3 and IRQ 7, the master PIC will notify the CPU of the interrupt on IRQ 3 before the interrupt on IRQ 7.

Whilst the interrupt from IRQ 3 is being serviced by the CPU, the PICs automatically inhibit interrupts of the same priority or less. However, hard-wiring the interrupt priorities in this way gives the user less flexibility when adding new devices to the system. Suppose that he wants to add a new device that operates at priority level 6, but IRQ line 6 is already being used by another peripheral? This problem is solved by using software priority levels.

Software priority levels

Most versions of UNIX, including SCO UNIX, support the concept of software priority levels, which is a mechanism used to modify the hardware interrupt priorities imposed by the PICs. UNIX can differentiate between seven different software priority levels, from priority 1 (the lowest) to priority 7 (the highest). An example of a device that runs at a high software priority is the real-time clock (it operates at priority 6), and an example of a device that operates at a low software priority is the parallel printer (it operates at priority 2). The general rule is that faster, high volume devices operate at a higher priority than slower, low volume devices.[6] Whenever a device interrupts, the kernel reprograms the PICs so that only higher software priority devices will be allowed to interrupt until the device's own interrupt routine completes. For example, if the kernel is busy servicing an interrupt from the parallel printer, the real-time clock is still able to interrupt whenever it wants to so that the kernel can keep an accurate record of real time. At any moment, therefore, there may be nestings of different interrupt stack frames on the same system stack, each for a different software priority level.

However, if there are two serial ports attached to the machine, each operating at the same priority level but with different IRQ lines on the PIC, one of them could not interrupt the other. This rule is true for all devices – a device's interrupt routine can only be interrupted by a device of a higher priority. Two side-effects of this rule are that a device cannot overwhelm the kernel with interrupts – it has to wait until its own interrupt routine completes before it is allowed to interrupt again – and that interrupt routines do not need to be re-entrant. Table 4.2 gives an indication of typical software interrupt priorities for a selection of devices and kernel subsystems. Note that these priorities may not be the same on other versions of UNIX or in future releases of SCO UNIX.

It is important to note that this concept of interrupt priorities is implemented in the kernel, and is entirely independent of the actual controllers and devices which do not know what priority they are operating at. They only know whether they are able to interrupt or not.

Table 4.2 Typical software priority levels.

Priority	Device
7	Dumb serial cards
6	Clock, Buffer cache
5	Floppy disk, Hard disk, STREAMS
4	Network cards
3	Unused
2	Parallel printer
1	Console keyboard

Interrupt requests from external devices are always latched by the PICs, and are dispatched to the CPU as soon as the software priority level permits. Providing interrupt requests are dispatched reasonably quickly by the PICs, devices should operate without error. However, if interrupt requests are not dispatched quickly enough by the PICs, the reason that a device requested to interrupt may change (for example, the user types another character). When the XXintr routine finally executes and reads the device's status register, an error condition will be indicated (in this case, an overrun error).

4.5.2   Disabling interrupts

All versions of UNIX provide kernel support routines to disable interrupts at a particular priority level. The routines are called spl0(K), spl1(K), ... spl7(K)[7] (the spl means **software priority level**), and they cause the kernel to reprogram the PICs in the same way as it does when responding to device interrupts, described above. A kernel programmer should use these routines to disable interrupts temporarily, in order to interlock task-time processes and interrupt routines which share data structures. For example, whilst a process is reading data from a buffer, it is necessary to prevent an interrupt routine from writing data to the buffer at the same time, otherwise data could be corrupted.

These spl(K) routines write the specified software priority level out to the PICs, and return the previous software priority level (maintained by the kernel in a variable called picipl).

When the task-time process has finished accessing the shared data structure, it must restore the software priority level to its previous value by using the splx(K) kernel support routine. Typically, the value returned from spl(K) is stored in an integer variable called s:

```
int s;
s = spl6();     /* disable s/w priority level 6 interrupts */
access data structure which is shared with XXintr;
splx(s);        /* enable XXintr */
```

The operation of these spl(K) routines will become clearer in Section 4.5.4.

4.5.3 Kernel data structures

SCO UNIX maintains three tables of data to help it manage software interrupt priorities. The first of these is called intpri, a table of interrupt priority levels, indexed by the IRQ number. The second is called iplmask, a table of 8-bit values which the kernel writes to the PICs' Interrupt Mask Registers to disable interrupts from devices which operate at the current software priority level or less. It is indexed by the software priority level. A third table, ivect, is a table of device driver interrupt routines. It is indexed by the IRQ number, and is used by the kernel to vector interrupts to the correct device driver interrupt routine.

The intpri and ivect tables are filled out whenever the kernel is rebuilt with link_unix(ADM) from information in mdevice and sdevice, supplied by the configure(ADM) command. For example, the following configure(ADM) options add details of an XXintr routine to mdevice and sdevice for a character device with major device number 17. The device operates at priority level 4 (-l 4), uses IRQ line 5 (-v 5), which it doesn't share with any other devices or controllers (-T 1):

```
# ./configure -a XXintr -l 4 -v 5 -T 1 -c -m 17
```

The iplmask table is filled out by the kernel at boot time. Figure 4.4 summarizes the contents of these three tables on a typical SCO UNIX system. The use of the configure(ADM) is described more fully in Appendix A.

4.5.4 Low-level interrupt handling

The PICs are initialized by SCO UNIX to respond to either edge-triggered or level-triggered interrupts, depending on the capabilities of the machine architecture. The ISA architecture requires that peripherals generate edge-triggered interrupts, but the MC architecture requires that peripherals generate level-triggered interrupts.

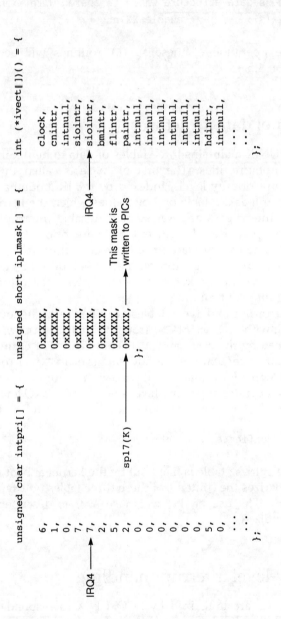

Figure 4.4 Interrupt tables.

Level-triggered interrupts are more reliable, as the PIC is less likely to be triggered by noise on the IRQ line and trigger timing accuracy is not so critical.

The i386 CPU can recognize up to 256 different interrupt IDs (or vectors). The first 32 are reserved for exceptions (such as Invalid opcode, Page fault, and so on), and the remaining 224 are available for external interrupts. SCO UNIX programs the PICs to generate vectors 64 through 79 for interrupts arriving on IRQ line 0 on the master PIC through IRQ line 7 on the slave PIC. The vector is used to index the Interrupt Descriptor Table (IDT), a table of task gates, interrupt gates and trap gates which indirectly point to the kernel's exception and interrupt handling routines. IDT entries 0 through 63 are all trap gates, except for entry 2 (an interrupt gate to deal with non-maskable interrupts) and entry 8 (a task gate to deal with Double faults). IDT entries 64 through 79 are all interrupt gates, so that SCO UNIX will handle interrupts in the context of the process that is running at the time of the interrupt.

When any of the devices attached to the PICs wants to interrupt, it raises its IRQ line high. If the bit corresponding to the IRQ line in the PIC's Interrupt Mask Register is 0, the PIC raises the INTR line on the CPU. The CPU examines INTR at the end of each instruction, and if it is set, it will acknowledge the interrupt by lowering the Interrupt Acknowledge (INTA) line. On the next clock cycle, the CPU lowers INTA again, and the PIC responds by loading the interrupt ID onto the data bus. The interrupt ID is read from the data bus by the CPU, and control jumps through the appropriate interrupt gate in the IDT into the kernel's interrupt handler. Figure 4.5 shows the interrupt gate mechanism for an interrupt from IRQ 4 on the Master PIC.

The jump through the interrupt gate causes the CPU to perform several actions before it starts to execute kernel text:

- If the interrupt happens whilst the CPU is executing user code at privilege level 3, the CPU must switch to privilege level 0 to handle the interrupt. It loads a new privilege level 0 stack pointer from the user's TSS, and pushes the old level 3 stack pointer onto the system stack.[8]

- The EFLAGS register and the instruction pointer are pushed onto the system stack.

- The Interrupt Enable (IF) flag is cleared, so that external interrupts are disabled. This is to prevent the current interrupt handler being interfered with by other interrupts.

- A new instruction pointer is loaded from the interrupt gate, and the CPU starts to execute kernel text.

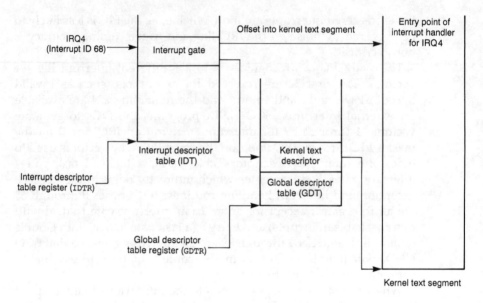

Figure 4.5 The i386 interrupt gate mechanism.

Figure 4.6 shows the contents of the system stack on entry to the kernel's interrupt handler from privilege level 3 (user mode).

Each of the IRQ vectors enters the kernel at a different point – the kernel pushes a dummy error code and the IRQ number onto the system stack,[9] and then jumps to a common interrupt handler. The common interrupt handler does the following:

(1) Pushes all of the general purpose registers onto the system stack.

(2) Pushes the DS, ES, FS and GS segment selectors onto the system stack.

(3) Copies the ESP register into the stack-frame base pointer register, EBP.

(4) Saves the current software priority level on the stack, by copying it into the space occupied by the dummy error code.

(5) Uses the IRQ to index the table of software priorities, intpri, to determine the new software priority level corresponding to the device on this IRQ.

(6) Uses the new interrupt priority level to index the table of PIC masks, iplmask, and writes out the contents to the PICs' Interrupt Mask Registers so that interrupts from all devices at this priority or less are disabled.

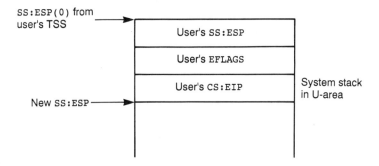

Figure 4.6 The system stack on entry to the kernel from user mode (privilege level 3).

(7) Sends an End-Of-Interrupt command to the PICs, so that they can now accept further interrupts.

(8) Sets the IF flag so that external interrupts are now enabled again. Interrupts can now arrive, but only from higher priority devices (see step 6, above).

(9) Pushes the old software priority level onto the system stack.

(10) Pushes the IRQ onto the system stack.

Finally, the IRQ is used to index the table of device driver interrupt routine names, ivect, and control jumps to the device driver's XXintr routine. The IRQ is passed to XXintr, so that if more than one piece of hardware is sharing the same device driver, the device driver can establish which device actually interrupted. For example, COM1 and COM2 on IRQs 4 and 3 (Figure 4.3) share the same serial I/O device driver:

```
XXintr(irq)
     int irq;
```

Figure 4.7 shows the contents of the system stack on entry to an XXintr routine from user mode (privilege level 3).

4.5.5 Returning from interrupts

The device driver's interrupt routine eventually returns to the low-level common interrupt handler, which does the following:

(1) Clears the IF flag, to disable all interrupts.

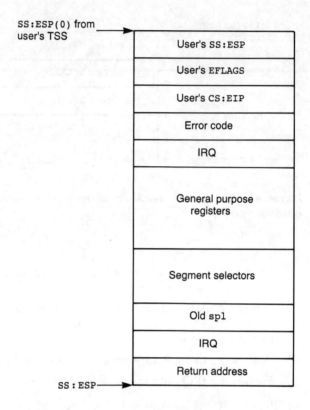

Figure 4.7   The system stack on entry to XXintr.

(2)   Uses the old software priority level (saved at the top of the stack) to index the table of PIC masks, iplmask, and writes out the contents to the PICs' Interrupt Mask Registers so that interrupts from all devices at this priority or less are re-enabled.

(3)   Checks the CS segment selector that was saved on the stack to see whether the interrupt occurred in user mode or system mode.

If the Table Index (TI) bit of the selector is 0, the selector points into the GDT, and therefore the interrupt occurred in system mode. If the TI bit is 1, the selector points into an LDT, and therefore the interrupt occurred in user mode.

(4)   If the interrupt occurred in user mode, the common interrupt handler calls a kernel routine to deal with rescheduling and signal dispatching. If the scheduling flag runrun was set during the interrupt routine, a context switch is likely to occur, and the remaining actions of the common interrupt handler, including signal dispatching, will execute in the context of the new process.

Section 4.7 describes how to use the wakeup(K) routine to reschedule the CPU at the end of an interrupt.

(5) For both user mode and system mode interrupts, the GS, FS, ES and DS segment selectors are popped off the system stack.

(6) The general purpose registers are popped off the system stack.

(7) The IRQ and the previous interrupt priority level (the dummy error code) are removed from the system stack.

Finally, an IRET instruction is executed, which pops CS:EIP and EFLAGS from the system stack. Note that popping EFLAGS will set IF, enabling interrupts as soon as the IRET instruction completes. If the CS segment selector indicates that IRET is returning to a less privileged segment (that is, returning from system mode to user mode), IRET also pops SS:ESP, leaving the system stack empty.

Execution now continues in either user mode or system mode, at the first instruction after the one that was interrupted by the PICs. If there was a context switch at the end of the interrupt, the IRET will have returned into a process that is different from the one that was running before the interrupt.

4.6   Writing an XXintr routine

Writing an XXintr routine is not as difficult as you may think, providing that you follow some basic rules. The key points to remember are:

• Keep your interrupt routines as short (and therefore as fast) as possible.

• Do not make any assumptions about which process is currently executing.

The basic job of an interrupt routine is to respond to a device's request for attention. In the majority of cases, a device interrupts because either it has some data to give to the system or it has finished outputting data and is now ready to do some more work.

The following pseudo-code can be used as the basis for all interrupt routines:

```
XXintr(irq)
    int irq;
{
    if (the device has data to give us) {
        copy data from device into the kernel;
```

```
        } else {
            copy data from kernel to device;
            tell device to start outputting again;
        }
    }
```

Not all interrupt routines will be as simple as this:

- Different devices on the same controller may be sharing an IRQ, so the first thing that the interrupt routine must do is to check the controller's status register to determine which device actually interrupted.

   A similar technique should be used if different controllers are also sharing an IRQ.

- The controller's status register must be checked for any errors. If the device does interrupt with an error, the kernel must inform the relevant user process that its system call has failed.

   In some cases, the driver may need to initiate further I/O operations. For example, after a disk read or write error, the disk heads are recalibrated (returned to cylinder 0) and the transfer is retried.

- Not all devices are capable of doing input and output. For example, a lineprinter only outputs data. A mouse only inputs data. Some devices, such as the clock, don't input or output – they just provide a constant source of regular interrupts.

- The kernel must be able to inform the user process which made the I/O request that new data has now arrived in the kernel, or that the device is now ready to accept more data.

- The kernel must also provide some storage space to buffer the data that is arriving from the device, as the user process may not be able to read(S) all the data each time the device interrupts (or may not want to). Storage space for buffering output data is also desirable, as this will maximize the overall throughput of the system. Buffering data is fully described in Section 4.9.

4.6.1 Informing the user process of errors

As described in Chapter 3, task-time errors that occur during I/O (such as an invalid read(S) request, detected by the XXread routine) are flagged to the user by calling the seterror(K) routine to set u_error in the process' U-area.

The seterror(K) routine must *not* be used at interrupt-time, as we have already explained that UNIX handles interrupts in whichever context is valid at the time of the interrupt. If you do call seterror(K) from an interrupt routine, u_error might be set in the wrong U-area, and the user process that should have received the error will remain unaware of any problems!

The correct way to pass errors back from an interrupt routine is to use a variable or a structure which is not related to the process' context, but which can be shared between the task-time parts of the device driver and the interrupt routine. The following pseudo-code illustrates this:

```
static XXerror;
XXread(dev)
        dev_t dev;
{
        while (there is no data to read) {
                wait for the device to interrupt;
        }
        if (XXerror != 0) {
                seterror(XXerror);
        }
        ...
        ...
}
XXintr(irq)
        int irq;
{
        if (there was an I/O error) {
                XXerror = EIO;
        }
        ...
        ...
}
```

4.6.2 Synchronizing with the user process

After a user process has made an I/O request to a device, there is nothing else that it can do until the data is available. In general, system calls do not return to the user process until after the device has interrupted, indicating either that new data has arrived, or that all the data has been sent. During this time, well-behaved system calls and device driver routines should call the sleep(K) routine to relinquish control of the CPU by forcing a context switch to another runnable process. When the device interrupts, the interrupt routine should wakeup(K) the user process so that its system call can continue and eventually return to user mode. Sleep(K) and wakeup(K) were introduced in Section 2.6, and will be described in more detail in Section 4.7.

Here is some pseudo-code to illustrate this:

```
XXread(dev)
    dev_t dev;
{
    disable XXintr with spl(K);
    while (there is no data to read) {
        sleep(K);
    }
    copy data from shared buffer out to the user process;
    enable XXintr with splx(K);
    ...
    ...
}
XXintr(irq)
    int irq;
{
    if (this is a read interrupt) {
        copy data from the device into shared buffer;
        wakeup(K) anyone who is asleep;
    }
    ...
    ...
}
```

4.6.3   A list of rules for interrupt routines

By now, you should have a good understanding of some of the principles of writing XXintr routines. Here is a full list of rules which you must *always* follow:

- Never access any context-related data, such as the U-area, from an interrupt routine. Context-related data also includes any part of the user's address space, which may have been either swapped or paged out whilst the process was asleep, waiting for the interrupt.

- Never call sleep(K) inside an interrupt routine, as the wrong process may go to sleep, perhaps forever, and the interrupt routine will not complete.

- Never use spl(K) to lower the software interrupt priority level inside an interrupt routine, unless your interrupt routine is properly re-entrant. An example of a re-entrant XXpoll routine is given in Chapter 5.

- Never declare large amounts of auto storage in any kernel routine. This is particularly true in high priority interrupt routines, whose stack frames are more likely to be towards the end of the available system stack space.

- Postpone as much time-consuming processing as you can until task-time, so that the device is able to interrupt again as soon as possible, reducing the likelihood of data loss.
- Always check the device's status register for errors to establish whether it is safe to read or write any data.

4.7   Sleep(K) and wakeup(K)

The sleep(K) and wakeup(K) kernel support routines should be used to synchronize between the task-time and interrupt-time parts of a device driver. Since UNIX is a multi-tasking, multi-user operating system, processes must relinquish the CPU whenever they have to wait for a resource such as a semaphore, or in our case, an interrupt. For processes in user mode, this is not a problem, as the real-time clock provides a constant source of interrupts which will switch the CPU into system mode 100 times per second. As the system returns from system mode back to user mode, the kernel can make a context switch and schedule a different process to run. However, the same is not true of processes in system mode. Unless a process in system mode voluntarily relinquishes control of the CPU by calling sleep(K), there is no way that UNIX can force a context switch. We say that UNIX is not pre-emptive, which means that it cannot arbitrarily decide to make a context switch in system mode whenever it wants to. This has two important implications:

- All UNIX system code is atomic. This means that all system calls will always run to completion, without being context switched, unless they explicitly call sleep(K). They are of course liable to be interrupted, but interrupts are handled in the context of the system mode process that is running at the time of the interrupt.
- UNIX is not a real-time operating system. Real-time operating systems are pre-emptive, and are able to force context switches away from processes that are running in system mode. UNIX cannot do this.[10]

4.7.1   Sleep(K)

A process calls sleep(K) with two arguments:

```
sleep(wchan, priority)
    caddr_t wchan;
    int priority;
```

The calling process is taken off the CPU and put onto a queue of other sleeping processes, called the sleep queue, and a context switch occurs. When the process is eventually woken up, it is returned to the run queue, and eventually switched back onto the CPU, and sleep(K) returns 0 to the calling process.

The wchan (wait channel) parameter is a key which will be used by the wakeup(K) call to identify which processes[11] should be removed from the sleep queue and returned to the run queue. To improve readability of source code, the wait channel is usually associated with the reason for going to sleep. For example, the mouse XXread routine might sleep on the address of the data structure containing the mouse X and Y coordinates. It is essential that the wait channel is known to both the sleep(K) and wakeup(K) calls, so do not use the addresses of either auto or static data.

The priority parameter determines the process' scheduling priority after it has been returned to the run queue by wakeup(K). Whenever the dispatcher examines the run queue, it always selects the process which has the highest priority (a high priority is a low numeric value). A process that sleeps at a higher priority will be chosen in preference to a process that sleeps at a lower priority, if they are both woken up and returned to the run queue before the next context switch. A process can therefore effect a limited amount of control over its scheduling priority each time that it goes to sleep.

Figure 4.8 shows the priorities used by SCO UNIX. A list of priorities is given in ⟨sys/param.h⟩. Note that processes which wait for more critical resources, such as inodes, sleep at a higher priority than processes which wait for less critical resources, such as character I/O. For example, the system processes sched (the swapper) and vhand (the page stealing daemon) always sleep at priority 0. Thus, whenever one of them is woken up and added to the run queue, it will have the highest priority and will run after the next context switch.

The priority and wait channel are saved in the process' process table entry, and are two of the fields displayed by the command:

```
$ ps -el
```

During the development period of a device driver, it can be useful for the device driver to display the wait channels that it uses to sleep(K), as an aid to debugging. Appendix B gives some useful tips and techniques for debugging device drivers.

4.7.2   Interrupting a sleep(K)

Processes that sleep(K) can choose whether or not they want to be woken up prematurely by the kernel, to receive signals. In some cases

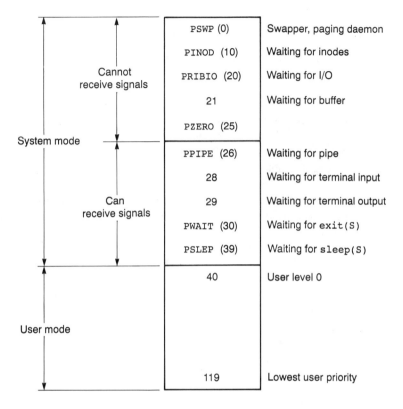

Figure 4.8   SCO UNIX priorities.

this is desirable, but in others it is not. For example, a process that is sleeping as a result of making a wait(S) system call should respond normally to keyboard signals. However, a process that is refilling the inode cache in the superblock and has set the s_ilock semaphore (see ⟨sys/fs/s5filsys.h⟩) to lock the cache, wants to be certain that it cannot be interrupted by any signals until the semaphore is released.

Processes that need to block out signals should sleep(K) at a priority of PZERO or less (that is, between 0 and 25). For example, in Figure 4.8, PINOD is 10. Processes that do not mind receiving signals should sleep(K) at a priority higher than PZERO. For example, in Figure 4.8, PWAIT is 30. Here is an extract from the output of a ps -el command:

```
PID  PPID  C PRI NI    WCHAN  TTY    TIME CMD
  0     0  0   0 20  d014ffdd  ?     0:00 sched
  1     0  0  39 20  e0000000  ?     0:02 init
  2     0  0   0 20  d00ab078  ?     0:00 vhand
  3     0  0  20 20  d00a4e18  ?     0:00 bdflush
```

```
274      1  0   30 20   d00e5660   01         0:02 csh
284      1  0   28 20   d00ca2cc   07         0:01 getty
276      1  1   30 20   d00e5910   02         0:01 sh
233      1  0   26 20   d013d01c   ?          0:00 lpsched
364    276  5   62 20              02         0:00 ps
```

You can see that sched and vhand are sleeping at priority 0 (PSWP), init is asleep at priority 39 (PSLEP), getty is asleep at priority 28 (waiting for terminal input), sh is asleep at priority 30 (waiting for ps to exit(S)), and so on. The sched, vhand and bdflush processes are all asleep at PZERO or less, and therefore are immune to signals.

If a process is asleep and able to receive signals, the usual behaviour when a signal arrives is for the kernel to longjmp(K) the process out of the sleep(K) to the end of the system call, which returns to user mode with the error EINTR. The device driver receives no notification of this activity.

If the device driver wants to be notified of the interrupted sleep(K) (for example, so that it can cancel any pending I/O request on the hardware, clean up data structures, and so on), the process should bitwise-OR the constant PCATCH (from ⟨sys/param.h⟩) into the priority passed to sleep(K). In this way, the sleep(K) will return 1 into the device driver rather than performing a longjmp(K) to the end of the system call when a signal arrives. The device driver now has an opportunity to clean up before setting u_error to EINTR, and returning:

```
XXread(dev)
      dev_t dev;
{
      while (there is no data to read) {
            if (sleep(wchan, priority | PCATCH) == 1) {
                  /*
                   * We have been interrupted by a signal
                   */
                  cancel I/O request;
                  clean up appropriate data structures;
                  seterror(EINTR);
                  return;
            } else {
                  /*
                   * We have been awakened by a wakeup(K)
                   */
                  ...
                  ...
            }
      }
      ...
      ...
}
```

4.7.3   Wakeup(K)

The more usual way of waking up a sleep(K)ing process is to make a call to wakeup(K):

```
wakeup(wchan)
     caddr_t wchan;
```

Wakeup(K) calls are normally issued at interrupt-time, to notify a process that the resource or the event which it was waiting for is now available (for example, a disk I/O request has completed). The wakeup(K) routine searches the sleep queue, looking for processes that are asleep on the specified wait channel. Any that it finds are removed from the sleep queue and put back onto the run queue, and the wait channel in the process table entry is cleared. The last thing that wakeup(K) does is to set the extern variable runrun, which will schedule a context switch to happen before the next IRET to user mode. It is important to note that, unlike sleep(K), wakeup(K) *does not* force a context switch. It merely schedules a context switch to happen at the next opportunity.

When the process is next scheduled to run, the sleep(K) call returns 0, and execution continues normally.

Since wakeup(K) will move all processes with a matching wait channel onto the run queue, regardless of whether they should have been woken up or not, it is extremely important that the task-time process should first check that it has been woken up for the correct reason. If not, it should immediately go back to sleep again. This is most easily accomplished with a while loop. Here is some pseudo-code to illustrate task-time and interrupt-time parts of a device driver synchronizing with sleep(K) and wakeup(K). The next section will explain why an exact implementation of this pseudo-code may cause the kernel to deadlock!

```
static XXflag;
XXread(dev)
     dev_t dev;
{
     while ((XXflag & DATA_READY) == 0) {
          set DATA_WANTED in XXflag;
          sleep(address of shared buffer, priority);
     }
     disable XXintr with spl(K);
     copy data from shared buffer out to the user process;
     enable XXintr with splx(K);
     ...
     ...
}
```

```
XXintr(irq)
    int irq;
{

    if (this is a read interrupt) {
        copy data from the device into shared buffer;
        if (XXflag & DATA_WANTED) {
            clear DATA_WANTED in XXflag;
            set DATA_READY in XXflag;
            wakeup(address of shared buffer);
        }
    }
    ...
    ...
}
```

4.7.4 Avoiding deadlock

In the example pseudo-code above, consider what would happen if the device interrupted immediately after the point that the XXread had tested XXflag & DATA_READY to be 0, and then set DATA_WANTED:

- At interrupt-time, XXintr clears DATA_WANTED, sets DATA_READY and issues a wakeup(K).
- Control returns to XXread at task-time, which immediately calls sleep(K), even though DATA_WANTED is now clear and data is available in the shared buffer.

The process will now sleep indefinitely, as XXintr will never see DATA_WANTED set again, and therefore will never issue another wakeup(K)! To make matters worse, the process may be asleep at a priority of PZERO or less, so it will not be possible to terminate it with a signal.

The solution is to apply the rule that we described in Section 4.5.2, to protect data shared between task-time and interrupt-time routines:

```
static XXflag;
XXread(dev)
    dev_t dev;
{
    disable XXintr with spl(K);
    while ((XXflag & DATA_READY) == 0) {
        set DATA_WANTED in XXflag;
        sleep(address of shared buffer, priority);
    }
    copy data from shared buffer out to the user process;
    enable XXintr with splx(K);
    ...
    ...
}
```

It is now safe to manipulate XXflag at task-time, and deadlock is avoided.

4.7.5　Waking up processes sleeping at PZERO or less

During the early stages of device driver development, particularly for prototype hardware that does not interrupt reliably, processes which sleep at PZERO or less whilst waiting for an interrupt can become locked in the system if the interrupt doesn't arrive. The following pseudo-code shows how to wakeup(K) such a process and report the suspected hardware problem using a timeout(K):

```
#define SLEEPING_EVENT        0x1
#define DID_GET_INTERRUPT     0x2

int flag = 0;
/*
 * hwfail() is called by a timeout(K)
 */
hwfail()
{
    if ((flag & DID_GET_INTERRUPT) != 0) {
        /*
         * The timeout expired after the device
         * has interrupted - so nothing to do
         */
        return;
    }
    /*
     * The timeout has expired before the device
     * has interrupted - so wakeup(K) the process.
     *
     * When the process wakes up, EVENT will be set
     * but INTERRUPT will not be set.
     */
    flag |= SLEEPING_EVENT;
    wakeup(&flag);
}
/*
 * XXfoo() sleeps at <= PZERO, but will be woken up
 * by a timeout(K) after .5 seconds.
 */
XXfoo()
{
    int id, s;
    s=splN(K);
```

```
            while ((flag & SLEEPING_EVENT) == 0) {
                /*
                 * Before we sleep(K), set a timeout(K) to
                 * call hwfail() if we are not woken up
                 * correctly by XXintr() within .5 seconds
                 */
                id = timeout(hwfail, 0, Hz / 2);
                sleep(&flag, at a priority <= PZERO);
                /*
                 * When we wake up, see if INTERRUPT is
                 * still clear. If so, we assume that the
                 * hardware has failed.
                 */
                if ((flag & DID_GET_INTERRUPT) == 0) {
                        untimeout(id);
                        indicate error in u.u_error;
                        cmn_err(CE_WARN, "possible hardware failure");
                        clear up any temporary or inconsistent data
                        structures;
                        splx(s);
                        return;
                }
            }
        splx(s);
        ...
        ...
    }
XXintr(irq)
{
        ...
        ...
        flag |= SLEEPING_EVENT;
        flag |= DID_GET_INTERRUPT;
        wakeup(&flag);
        ...
        ...
}
```

Remember that the timeout(K) call to hwfail will happen at spl6(K), so the usual rules for interrupt routines apply.

4.8   Context switching

In Chapter 2 we listed the different circumstances in which a context switch can occur:

- Whenever the CPU returns from system mode to user mode, at the end of exceptions, interrupts and system calls.

  Note that the regular and frequent source of interrupts from the real-time clock ensures that processes which stay in user mode for relatively long periods will still be subject to context switching.

- Whenever a process in system mode is waiting for an event or resource, such as free memory, or data from a device, and calls sleep(K).

In Section 4.7 above, we described how a call to sleep(K) forces a context switch to occur. We explained that wakeup(K) does not force a context switch – it just sets runrun[12] which schedules a context switch to happen at some point in the future.

In this section, we will describe how a context switch happens as a result of runrun being set.

At the end of every exception, interrupt and system call, the kernel examines the CS selector saved at the bottom of the system stack to determine whether the exception (or interrupt or system call) occurred in user mode or system mode. If the exception occurred in user mode, a routine is called to examine runrun. If runrun is set, the kernel calls qswtch to actually make the context switch. The qswtch routine does the following:

(1) The current process is taken off the CPU and put onto the run queue. Its state is changed from SONPROC to SRUN.

(2) The dispatcher is called to search the run queue for the highest priority process.

(3) The new process is taken off the run queue. Its state is changed from SRUN to SONPROC.

(4) A TSS Descriptor is constructed in the GDT, to point to the new process' TSS.

(5) The kernel executes an indirect jump through a task gate, which selects the TSS Descriptor described above.

  The indirect jump saves the context of the old process in the TSS pointed to by TR, and loads the context of the new process from the TSS pointed to by the TSS Descriptor.[13]

(6) The new U-area is mapped to u.

(7) The CPU's cache (called the Translation Lookaside Buffer, or TLB) is flushed, so that all memory references must be fetched from memory rather than being satisfied by the out-of-date (and therefore incorrect) TLB entries.

Finally, qswtch returns from the system stack in the new U-area, in the context of the new process. The entire context switch operation takes approximately 1000 clock cycles. Most of these are used by the

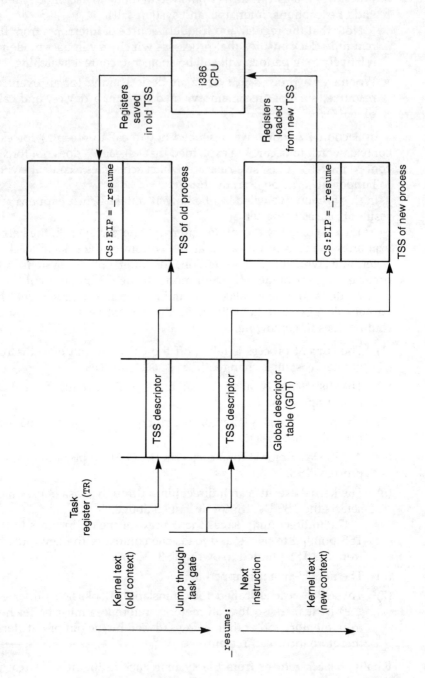

Figure 4.9   An i386 context switch.

indirect jump through the task gate. Figure 4.9 illustrates the fundamental context switch mechanisms.

The common interrupt handler then returns back to user mode, as described in Section 4.5.5, above.

We have now described how an interrupt routine can wakeup(K) a user process which is asleep at task-time. With a reasonable amount of luck, that process will be switched onto the CPU at the end of the current exception. It will return from its sleep(K), and its system call will then be able to run to completion.

4.9   Buffering data

The final area that we need to discuss in order to fully understand interrupts is the buffering of data. Buffering data serves to increase system throughput, and decouples the user process from the device, so that they can operate asynchronously of each other. Buffering increases throughput on all devices, but is particularly effective for low speed, low volume devices. Recall the parallel printer driver from Chapter 3, and consider the following pseudo-code modifications:

```
static char c;
lpwrite(dev)
      dev_t dev;
{
      while (u.u_count) {
            while ((inb(PSTATUS) & READY) == 0) {
                  sleep(K) and wait for lpintr();
            }
            spl(K) to disable lpintr() and protect c;
            if ((c = get next character from user) == -1) {
                  splx(K) to enable lpintr() again;
                  return;
            }
            call lpintr() to start output;
            splx(K) to enable lpintr() again;
      }
}
lpintr(irq)
      int irq;
{
      outb(PDATA, c);
      outb(PCNTRL, PRIME | STROBE);
      outb(PCNTRL, PRIME);
      wakeup(K) anyone asleep in lpwrite();
}
```

Note that we are calling XXintr at task-time to start up output. This is perfectly valid, providing that we interlock correctly with spl(K). Although we are apparently using sleep(K) and wakeup(K) correctly to synchronize between the task-time and interrupt-time parts of the driver, this is probably the least efficient device driver that we could write! In fact, we are no better off than we were at the start of this chapter with XXpoll:

- There will be at least two context switches (at approximately 1000 clock cycles per switch on an Intel CPU) for each byte of data that is written to the printer.

- On a busy system, the user process that has made the write(S) system call and is now asleep will almost certainly not be able to run at the first context switch following the wakeup(K).

- The user process may even get paged or swapped out whilst it is asleep, which will put an even greater load on the system, as the process will have to be swapped back in again after the wakeup(K).

In the meantime, the printer will be idle for most of the time, printing only a few characters per second at best.

4.9.1 Buffering output

We can address these problems by introducing a buffer into the device driver, which is shared between the task-time and interrupt-time parts. We have added some more pseudo-code to our parallel printer driver:

```
static char lpbuf[1024];
lpwrite(dev)
     dev_t dev;
{
     while (u.u_count and space in lpbuf) {
          spl(K) to disable lpintr() and protect lpbuf;
          if (copyin(u.u_base, into lpbuf, 1) == -1) {
               seterror(EFAULT);
               splx(K) to enable lpintr() again;
               return;
          }
          u.u_count--;
          u.u_base++;
          u.u_offset++;
     }
     call lpintr() to start output;
     splx(K) to enable lpintr() again;
}
```

```
lpintr(irq)
     int irq;
{
     while (printer is ready
          && there is data in lpbuf) {
          move byte of data out to printer;
     }
}
```

Our pseudo-code is not quite complete, as we should put the user process to sleep(K) if lpbuf is already full at the start of lpwrite, and then call lpintr. The user process should be woken up from lpintr when lpbuf empties.

We can assume that the printer has its own on-board buffering capability, so that most of the time lpbuf will be emptied on the first call to lpintr. You can see that we have addressed the main problems of the previous driver:

- The user process' write(S) system call can run to completion, without any context switches, assuming that there is enough space in lpbuf to hold all of the data.
- The printer can be serviced directly from lpbuf at interrupt-time, whether or not the user process is actually writing any data.

4.9.2 Buffering input

Similar benefits can be obtained on input. By decoupling the interrupt routine from the task-time process making read(S) system calls, the interrupt routine can fill up a buffer as fast as the device interrupts, whether or not the user process is reading any data.

Using buffers does introduce the added complexity of what to do if the buffer fills up (this is particularly true for input), but this disadvantage is far outweighed by the benefits of increased throughput and overall system efficiency.

4.9.3 Low and high water marks

Device drivers can use low and high water marks to monitor the amount of free space in the buffer, and to further improve throughput. A water mark is simply a threshold value. If the amount of data in the output buffer exceeds the high water mark, the XXintr routine should be called to start up output and the user process should sleep(K). When the amount of data in the buffer falls back

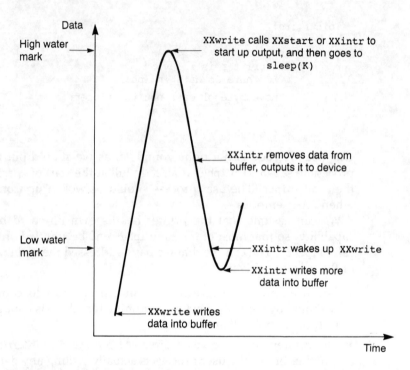

Figure 4.10 High and low water marks.

beneath the low water mark, XXintr should wakeup(K) the user process so that it can start filling the buffer again. The low water mark is
almost always greater than zero, because we know that when a
wakeup(K) is issued, the user process may not get to run immediately
after the next context switch. During this time, the device is still able
to do some work, and it can be kept busy with the last remaining
characters in the buffer. If the wakeup(K) isn't issued until the buffer
empties, the device would go idle and wouldn't start up again until
the user process was next switched onto the CPU.

Low and high water marks can be applied to all buffering schemes.
Figure 4.10 shows them being used to monitor a char array.

4.9.4 Kernel support for buffering data

The kernel provides two major buffering schemes for device drivers
to use, depending on whether they are character device drivers or
block device drivers. Both schemes have been designed to address
the issues that we have discussed in this chapter.

Character device drivers can use buffers called character lists, or
clists. Chapter 5 gives a full account of how clists work. All that we
need to understand for the time being is how to use two new kernel
support routines putc(K) and getc(K) which put data onto and take
data off a clist:

```
#include ⟨sys/tty.h⟩
putc(c, cp)
     int c;
     struct clist *cp;
```

And:

```
#include ⟨sys/tty.h⟩
getc(cp)
     struct clist *cp;
```

Character device drivers are free to use an alternative buffering
scheme, if they so wish.

Block device drivers implicitly use 1K buffers from the kernel's
buffer cache for all their I/O. On output, data moves from the user
process into the buffer cache, and from there out to the device. The
reverse happens on input. A full account of block device drivers is
given in Chapter 7.

We can now complete our modifications to the parallel printer
driver from Chapter 3. The device driver uses a clist to decouple the
user process from the interrupt routine. Note that XXintr is called
indirectly at task-time via XXstart. To aid readability, we have added
a new routine called utok[14] to take care of transferring data between
user space and the kernel. The printer runs at software priority
level 2:

```
/*
 * src/lpintr.c
 *
 * Copyright (c) 1992 Peter Kettle and Steve Statler
 *
 * Interrupt driven parallel printer driver for the onboard
 * printer port of a PC AT compatible.
 *
 * This is based on the simple printer driver discussed in
 * Chapter 3.
 *
 * The enhancements include the use of interrupts, clist
 * buffering, and moving the code which copies from user to
 * kernel into a separate module.
 *
 * ./configure -a lpinit lpwrite lpintr -v VECTOR -1 INTPRI
 * -T 1 -c -m MAJOR
 */
```

```
#include ⟨sys/types.h⟩
#include ⟨sys/dir.h⟩
#include ⟨sys/param.h⟩
#include ⟨sys/user.h⟩
#include ⟨sys/tty.h⟩
#include ⟨sys/errno.h⟩

#define PBASE        0x378
#define PDATA        (0 + PBASE)
#define PSTATUS      (1 + PBASE)
#define PCNTRL       (2 + PBASE)

#define SELECT       0x08
#define PRIME        0x1e
#define STROBE       0x01
#define INTENBL      0x10
#define READY        0x80

#define RESET_DELAY  1000000

#define LPSLEEP      0x1
#define LPACTIVE     0x2

#define LPPRI        (PZERO + 1)

#define LOWAT        50
#define HIWAT        150

struct clist lpq;
int lpflags;
/*
 * lpinit()
 *
 * Initialize printer controller and announce its presence.
 *
 */
lpinit()
{
    int i;
    outb(PCNTRL, SELECT);
    for (i=0; i < RESET_DELAY; i++);
    outb(PCNTRL, PRIME);
    printcfg("lp", PBASE, 2, 7, -1,
            "Interrupt driven printer driver");
};
/*
 * lpwrite()
 *
 * Called by the user process write(S) via cdevsw[] to
 * write to the device.
 *
 * Move characters from the user onto the clist.
 *
 * If the clist fills up, call lpintr() at task-time via
 * lpstart() to start up output, and put the task-time
 * process to sleep.
 */
```

```
lpwrite(dev)
     dev_t dev;
{
     int c, s;
     while ((c = utok()) >= 0) {
          s = spl2();                    /* protect lpq from
                                            lpintr() */
          while (lpq.c_cc >= HIWAT) {
               lpstart();
               lpflags |= LPSLEEP;
               sleep(&lpq, LPPRI);
          }
          putc(c, &lpq);
          splx(s);
     }
     s = spl2();
     lpstart();
     splx(s);
}
/*
 * lpstart()
 *
 * If the driver is already busy (possibly just waiting for
 * an interrupt), return.
 *
 * Otherwise call lpintr() at task-time to start up output.
 */
lpstart()
{
     if (lpflags & LPACTIVE) {
          return;
     }
     lpflags |= LPACTIVE;
     lpintr(0);
}
/*
 * lpintr()
 *
 * Called at task-time from lpwrite() to start up output,
 * and at interrupt-time when the printer's on-board buffer
 * empties.
 *
 * Output characters whilst the printer is idle and the
 * clist isn't empty.
 */
lpintr(irq)
     int irq;
{
     int c;
     if ((lpflags & LPACTIVE) == 0) {
          return;
     }
```

```
            while ((inb(PSTATUS) & READY) && ((c = getc(&lpq)) >=
                   0)) {
                outb(PDATA, c);
                outb(PCNTRL, PRIME | STROBE);
                outb(PCNTRL, PRIME);
            }
            if ((lpq.c_cc < LOWAT) && (lpflags & LPSLEEP)) {
                lpflags &= ~LPSLEEP;
                wakeup(&lpq);
            }
            if (lpq.c_cc == 0) {
                lpflags &= ~LPACTIVE;
            }
            outb(PCNTRL, PRIME | INTENBL);
    }
    /*
     * utok()
     *
     * Use copyin(K) to transfer a byte of data from user space
     * into the kernel, then adjust the U-area I/O fields.
     * Returns -1 on fail, or no more data.
     */
    utok()
    {
            char c;
            int s;
            if (u.u_count == 0) {
                return(-1);
            }
            s = copyin(u.u_base, &c, 1);
            if (s == -1) {
                seterror(EFAULT);
                return(-1);
            }
            u.u_count--;
            u.u_base++;
            u.u_offset++;  /* for completeness */
            return((int)c);
    }
```

4.10 Summary

In this chapter, we have described how interrupts work and why
it is beneficial to use them. We have examined a process' context in
detail, and we have explained what a context switch is and why it is

important to enable context switches to happen in a multi-user, multi-tasking operating system such as UNIX. We have presented a list of rules for use when writing interrupt routines, and we have looked at the benefits of buffering data.

Finally, we have seen that maximum bandwidth to a device can be attained by using interrupts, and by decoupling the task-time and interrupt-time parts of a driver with a buffer.

QUIZ

To test your understanding of this chapter, try to answer the following questions.

4.1 How should a task-time process force a context switch when there is no work for it to do?

4.2 Is a device driver permitted to call wakeup(K) at interrupt-time?

4.3 How many clock cycles (approximately) does a context switch take on an Intel CPU?

4.4 How should a task-time process protect data that is shared with the interrupt routine?

4.5 How should a device driver arrange to receive notification of interrupted sleep(K)s?

4.6 How does the kernel determine whether an interrupt occurred in user mode or system mode?

EXERCISE

Modify the mouse device driver from Chapter 3 so that it is interrupt driven.

Here are some hints:

- Set jumper 2 on the mouse to use a spare IRQ line. Use the hwconfig(ADM) command to find out which IRQ lines are free.
- Use interrupt priority 6.

- Remember to deconfigure your XXpoll routine!
- Remember to specify the -T 1 option to configure(ADM) so that the system knows to expect interrupts.
- A quick, simple solution would be to call XXpoll from XXintr.

Advanced session:

- Modify XXopen to examine the minor device number. If the minor device number is 0, use timeouts. If the minor device number is 1, use interrupts. Remember to create a new entry in /dev with the appropriate minor device number.
  Disable interrupts or timeouts when the device is closed.

A suggested answer is given in 'Answers to Exercises'.

NOTES

1. We use the notation exemplified by CS:EIP to describe segment selector registers (CS is the code segment selector) and offsets into segments (EIP is the 32-bit instruction pointer, used as an offset into the code segment).

2. PDBR is an alternative name for Control Register 3 (CR3).

3. Except for the Double fault exception, which is handled in its own context.

4. The process which is waiting for the interrupt will probably be asleep.

5. This is exactly the reverse of the software priority levels that UNIX uses!

6. An exception to this priority rule is dumb serial cards, which operate at priority level 7. This is to avoid overruns and data loss.

7. We refer to the spl routines generally by using the notation spl(K).

8. If the CPU has to switch from privilege level 3 to privilege 0 to handle the interrupt, the system stack will be empty at this point.

9. The i386 automatically pushes an error code for some exceptions. The interrupt handler pushes a dummy error code so that all exception and interrupt stack frames are the same size.

10. Some implementations of UNIX provide real-time extensions, but do not necessarily provide the guaranteed response time of dedicated real-time operating systems.

11. More than one process can sleep on the same wait channel.

12. The clock interrupt routine sets runrun directly, to force context switches at the end of time-slices.

13. If the dispatcher found the same process on the run queue that had just been taken off the CPU, the actual context switch is bypassed.

14. utok is equivalent to SCO's cpass(K).

5

Line disciplines and serial device drivers

5.1   Overview

In this chapter we shall look at line disciplines and serial device drivers, traditionally the most difficult of all device driver types to understand.

A line discipline is a layer of kernel software between a serial device driver and a user process, and it provides a set of support routines and data structures that can be used by the driver writer. Many of the tasks that a serial device driver has to do, such as handling backspace characters from the user's keyboard and echoing characters, are common for all serial device drivers. A line discipline offloads the responsibility for these common tasks and provides a well-defined interface which can significantly reduce the development time of the device driver.

Line disciplines are identified by a number. In most UNIX systems, line discipline 0 provides the support routines required by device drivers for dumb serial I/O cards. SCO UNIX includes two additional line disciplines, 1 and 2, which provide support for Shell Layers and mouse device drivers. Some manufacturers of intelligent serial I/O cards provide their own specialized line disciplines, which must be installed into the kernel alongside the manufacturer's device driver.

This chapter describes the operation of line discipline 0, and shows how it should be used by a serial device driver for a dumb serial card based on the Intel i8250 Universal Asynchronous Receiver/Transmitter (UART).

The example serial device driver presented in Section 5.7 is the most complex of all device drivers in this book. To ensure that data is

111

never lost, dumb serial cards must operate at software interrupt priority 7 (the highest of all). However, one of the rules for interrupt routines is that they must be as short as possible. This is particularly true of higher priority interrupt routines, so our device driver uses an XXpoll routine (called 100 times per second at software priority level 6) to offload processing from the XXintr routine.

In the exercise at the end of this chapter, we shall write a very simple line discipline for the mouse device driver. The line discipline will manage a queue of events describing each movement of the mouse. We shall modify the mouse's XXread routine so that it calls the line discipline to read an event from the event queue. This will enable processes to track the movement of the mouse closely, which might be desirable in a drawing application.

5.2   An introduction to line discipline 0

Line discipline 0 is used by device drivers for dumb serial I/O cards, and provides all of the functionality required to support asynchronous terminals and serial communications software, such as uucp(C). It includes the following major features:

- Two character buffering schemes to decouple the task-time and interrupt-time parts of the device driver.
- Backspace and Line Kill (Ctrl-u) processing.
- Generation of signals from certain keys (for example, SIGQUIT from Ctrl-\, SIGINT from Del).
- Flow control and Modem control (XON/XOFF, CTS/RTS).
- International keyboard support.
- Echoing.
- Character expansion and translation (for example, tabs to spaces, newline to carriage return and newline).

Figure 5.1 shows the relationship between the user, the serial device driver, line discipline 0 and a user process.

Line disciplines from intelligent serial I/O card manufacturers have more or less identical responsibilities, although the actual implementation is different. Some manufacturers run part of the line discipline on the serial I/O card, using a secondary processor (for example, an i80186) to offload processing from the main CPU.

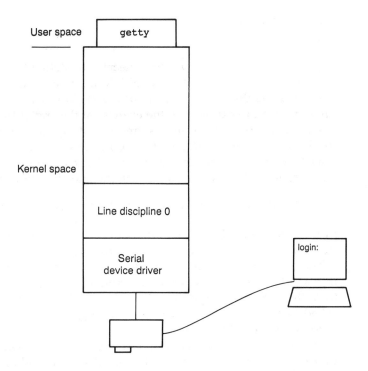

Figure 5.1 The user, the serial device driver, line discipline 0 and a user process.

5.3   Accessing a line discipline

Device driver routines such as XXread and XXwrite call the line discipline routines via entries in a line switch table, in much the same way that the kernel uses the character and block device switch tables to call a device driver's entry points. The line switch table is an array of linesw structures, and is indexed by the line discipline number. The structure is defined in ⟨sys/conf.h⟩:

```
struct linesw {
      int   (*l_open)();
      int   (*l_close)();
      int   (*l_read)();
      int   (*l_write)();
      int   (*l_ioctl)();
      int   (*l_input)();
      int   (*l_output)();
      int   (*l_mdmint)();
};
```

```
extern struct linesw linesw[];
extern int linecnt;
```

The contents of linesw and linecnt are defined in /etc/conf/
pack.d/kernel/space.c. Additional line disciplines can be added to
space.c using the shell script idaddld(ADM). You will have an opportunity to use idaddld(ADM) in the exercise at the end of this chapter.

The line discipline routines are called by the corresponding
routines in the device driver. For example, when the user makes a
read(S) system call, the device driver's XXread routine uses the l_read
entry from the linesw structure to call the line discipline read routine:

```
(*linesw[line discipline number].l_read)(parameters);
```

In the case of line discipline 0, this calls ttread, which transfers data
from the input buffer out to the user process.

The l_input and l_output routines are called at XXpoll-time to
transfer data from the device to the input buffer, and to transfer data
from the output buffer to the device. The l_mdmint routine should be
called to service modem interrupts, although this is a nulldev in the
current release of SCO UNIX.

Figure 5.2 summarizes control flow and data flow between the user
process, the serial device driver, the line discipline and the hardware.

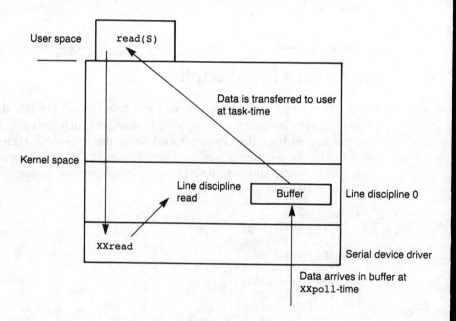

Figure 5.2   Control flow and data flow.

5.4   Serial device drivers

High-performance device drivers for dumb serial I/O cards are perhaps the most difficult of all to write:

- UARTs have eight registers (described in Section 5.7.2) which must be programmed correctly to set the baud rate, character size, number of stop bits, and so on.

- Serial device drivers have three sources of interrupts: one for input, one for output and one for the modem. Dumb serial cards with single-character buffers raise an interrupt each time a byte of data either arrives in the UART or is transmitted from the UART.

- Three separate character buffers are required. Two are used for buffering input data, and one is used for buffering output data. Each buffer is constructed from a clist, introduced in Chapter 4.

  The two input buffers are called the raw and canonical queues. Data arrives on the raw queue at XXpoll-time via a ccblock structure (described in Section 5.4.3), and is moved onto the canonical queue at task-time by the kernel support routine called canon(K), described in Section 5.6.

- The line discipline manipulates the clists with putc(K) and getc(K), which are protected from software priority level 5 interrupts with calls to spl5(K). We have already stated that the XXpoll routine offloads processing from the high priority XXintr routine, but of course XXpoll runs at software priority level 6, not at level 5!

  To ensure that all processing is properly interlocked, an extra buffer decouples XXintr from XXpoll, and XXpoll calls the line discipline only if putc(K) or getc(K) have not already set spl5(K). To further improve performance, XXpoll also calls spl5(K) so that the clock can continue to interrupt whilst the line discipline is processing the clists. This means that XXpoll is re-entrant, and must be protected with a semaphore.

  Figure 5.3 illustrates the relationship between the input buffer, the ccblock, and the raw and canonical clists.

- Serial device drivers must provide XXioctl support for ioctl(S) requests from stty(C) to change the parity, the baud rate, the character size (5, 6, 7, or 8 bits), the number of stop bits, and so on.

- On a multiport card, the XXintr routine must be able to determine which line requires attention. It must also determine why it was called.

- Some applications require characters to be marked with the sequence 0377, 0, X if the received character X has a framing or parity error.

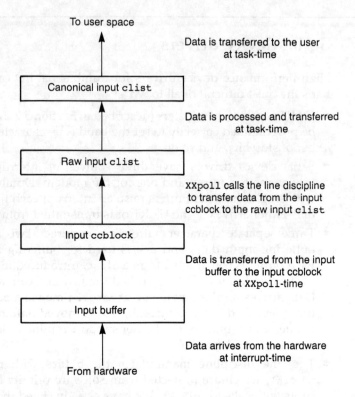

Figure 5.3 The input buffer, `ccblock` and the raw and canonical `clist`s.

The next sections will explain some of the data structures that are used.

5.4.1 Raw and canonical processing

UNIX commands, utilities and applications require that serial lines can be switched, via `ioctl(S)`, to operate in either raw or canonical mode. For example, most text editors, including `vi(C)`, set the line to raw mode. Command interpreters, such as `sh(C)`, set the line to canonical mode. The mode of the line determines how much data will be returned from each `read(S)` system call.

Raw mode

In raw mode, everything that the user types is returned to the application when it makes a `read(S)` system call. The application can specify the minimum number of characters to return, the maximum amount of time to wait for characters after the read(S) is issued, or a combination. The default behaviour is to return however many characters the user asks for, although the application can make ioctl(S) calls to modify this behaviour if necessary. The two parameters to modify are called min and time, and are stored in the t_cc array of special control characters in the tty structure (see Section 5.4.3).

The default values are min = 0, time = 0, which causes a read(S) system call to return however many characters have been asked for, providing that the characters are present in the raw queue (otherwise it will return less).

The other values of min and time and their interactions are fully described in the termio(M) manual pages.

Canonical mode

In canonical mode, the read(S) system call returns only when a delimiter character (newline, end-of-file or end-of-line) is found on the canonical queue.

As well as checking for delimiter characters, the line discipline is also responsible for some intermediate processing of the data, before it is read by the application. For example, each incoming character is checked against the special control characters interrupt, quit and suspend, and appropriate action is taken if one of these characters is detected (a signal is sent to the process group).

Backspace characters are echoed as a backspace followed by space and another backspace, and line kill characters are echoed as a carriage return followed by a newline. Any characters that the user has either erased or killed are removed from the canonical queue, so that they will not be returned by the read(S) system call. Figure 5.4 shows some canonical processing.

It is possible to see the difference between the two modes by setting your terminal line into raw mode, and then resetting it. Type:

```
$ stty raw -echo
```

Your terminal line is now in raw mode. Try typing some characters! Restore canonical mode by first pressing Ctrl-j (Ctrl-j in raw mode is equivalent to carriage return in canonical mode). Your shell will probably complain about all the rubbish characters that you have just typed. Then type:

```
$ stty sane
```

Note that you do not have any echoing enabled, and that you must terminate this line with another Ctrl-j. Sanity should then be restored.

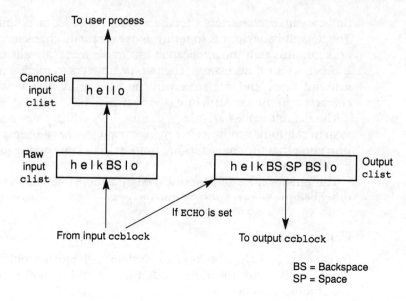

Figure 5.4 Canonical processing.

5.4.2 The clist structure

A clist is an anchor for a linked list of cblock structures, which contain the input and output data. The clist and cblock structures are defined in ⟨sys/tty.h⟩:

```
#include ⟨sys/tty.h⟩
struct clist {
      int  c_cc;              /* character count */
      struct cblock *c_cf;    /* pointer to first */
      struct cblock *c_cl;    /* pointer to last */
};
#define  CLSIZE   64
struct cblock {
      struct cblock  *c_next;
      unsigned char  c_first;
      unsigned char  c_last;
      unsigned char  c_data[CLSIZE];
};
```

The kernel resource NCLIST determines how many cblocks are available for use by the system.[1] To set up a clist, all the device driver has to do is to declare a struct clist variable, and then to begin using putc(K) and getc(K). These two routines automatically obtain new cblocks as they are required, and free them up when they become empty and are no longer being used. All clist manipulations are interlocked from software priority level 5 interrupts with spl5(K).

Line discipline 0 uses low and high water marks (explained in Chapter 4) on the input and output queues to ensure that individual serial lines cannot use up all of the NCLIST resource. The values for each pair of water marks are dependent on the baud rate of the line. For example, a 9600 baud line has a low water mark of 80, and a high water mark of 240. A 1200 baud line has a low water mark of 60, and a high water mark of 180.

Here are the putc(K) and getc(K) routines again. The putc(K) routine adds a character to the end of a clist. It makes its own call to spl5(K):

```
#include ⟨sys/tty.h⟩
putc(c, cp)
      int c;
      struct clist *cp;
```

A character is removed from the front of a clist with the getc(K) routine. It also makes its own call to spl5(K):

```
#include ⟨sys/tty.h⟩
getc(cp)
      struct clist *cp;
```

Figure 5.5 shows a typical clist. Note that the first and last cblocks are partially empty – these are the ones that will be accessed by the next calls to putc(K) and getc(K). Figure 5.6 shows the same clist after some more calls to getc(K). Note that one of the cblocks has now been freed.

5.4.3 The tty structure

Line discipline 0 requires serial device drivers to declare a struct tty for each of the serial lines to be supported. Most serial device drivers do this by declaring an array of tty structures, and reference the appropriate entry using bits from the minor device number. The tty structure contains all of the information needed by the line discipline and a serial device driver. It is defined in ⟨sys/tty.h⟩:

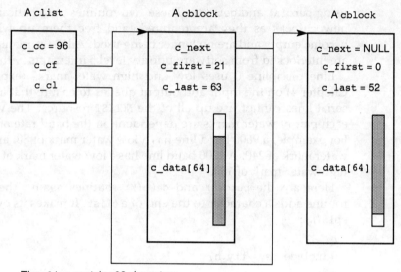

The clist contains 96 characters.
There are 43 characters in the first cblock, from c_data[21] to c_data[63].
There are 53 characters in the second cblock, from c_data[0] to c_data[52].

Figure 5.5 A typical clist.

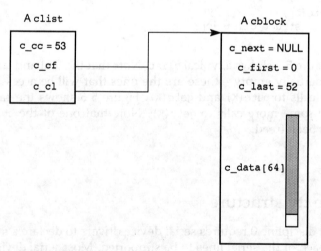

The clist now contains 53 characters.
The first cblock has been emptied by calls to getc(K), and has been returned to the freelist.
There are 53 characters in the remaining cblock, from c_data[0] to c_data[52].

Figure 5.6 The same clist after some calls to getc(K).

```
#define NCC     8
struct tty {
        struct clist    t_rawq;     /* raw input queue */
        struct clist    t_canq;     /* canonical queue */
        struct clist    t_outq;     /* output queue */
        struct ccblock t_tbuf;      /* tx control block */
        struct ccblock t_rbuf;      /* rx control block */
        int   (* t_proc)();         /* routine for device
                                       functions */

        ushort    t_iflag;          /* input modes (stty) */
        ushort    t_oflag;          /* output modes (stty) */
        ushort    t_cflag;          /* control modes (stty) */
        ushort    t_lflag;          /* line discipline modes
                                       (stty) */

        short     t_state;          /* internal state of driver */
        short     t_pgrp;           /* process group ID */
        char t_line;                /* line discipline number */
        char t_delct;               /* delimiter count in t_canq */
        char t_term;                /* terminal type */
        char t_tmflag;              /* terminal flags */
        char t_col;                 /* current column */
        char t_row;                 /* current row */
        char t_vrow;                /* variable row */
        char t_lrow;                /* last physical row */
        char t_hqcnt;               /* number of hi queue
                                       packets on t_outq */

        char t_dstat;               /* used by terminal handlers
                                       and line disciplines */
        unsigned char  t_cc[NCC+5];    /* settable control
                                          chars */

        char t_mstate;              /* emapping state */
        char t_merr;                /* emapping error flag */
        char t_xstate;              /* extended state */
        struct    xmap *t_xmp;      /* ptr to extended tty
                                       struct */
        unsigned char  t_schar;     /* saved timeout char */
        char t_yyy[3];              /* reserved */
};
```

Many of the fields in the tty structure are used by the line discipline, and do not need to be referenced by the serial device driver. The fields that are used by the serial device driver are as follows. You can see some examples in the serial device driver presented in Section 5.7.

t_rawq, t_canq

These are the clist anchors for the raw and canonical queues. Data arrives on t_rawq at XXpoll-time, and is transferred onto t_canq at task-time by the routine canon(K).

t_outq

This is the clist anchor for the output queue. Data arrives on t_outq at task-time from l_write, and at XXpoll-time from l_input, when echoing is enabled.

t_rbuf, t_tbuf

These are the intermediate ccblocks for input and output. For input, XXpoll transfers data from the input buffer onto t_rbuf, and then calls l_input to transfer data from t_rbuf onto t_rawq (see Figure 5.3). For output, XXpoll calls l_output to transfer data from t_outq onto t_tbuf, and then transfers data from t_tbuf to the output buffer.

The ccblock structure is defined in ⟨sys/tty.h⟩:

```
struct ccblock {
        caddr_t   c_ptr;       /* buffer address  */
        ushort    c_count;     /* character count */
        ushort    c_size;      /* buffer size     */
};
```

The c_ptr field is set up to point to the c_data field in a cblock, and is incremented after each character is moved into the buffer. The c_count field records how many characters are in the cblock, and is incremented after each character is moved into the buffer. The c_size field doesn't change – its value is always CLSIZE. Figure 5.7 shows data arriving on t_rbuf at XXpoll-time.

t_proc

This is the address of the serial device driver's XXproc routine. It is used by the line discipline to make calls into the driver. For example, if t_rawq goes above the high water mark, the line discipline will call XXproc to send an XOFF down the line to the transmitter. When t_rawq falls back beneath the low water mark, XXproc is called again to send an XON, so that the transmitter can start sending more data.

The serial device driver fills out the t_proc entry on the first XXopen of the device.

The example serial driver in Section 5.7 includes an XXproc routine.

t_iflag

This is a 16-bit mask of flags defining the input modes of the line, such as whether to ignore parity, whether to strip input characters to 7 bits, and so on. A full list of the different bits is given in ⟨sys/termio.h⟩, and the function of each bit is described in the stty(C) and termio(M) manual pages.

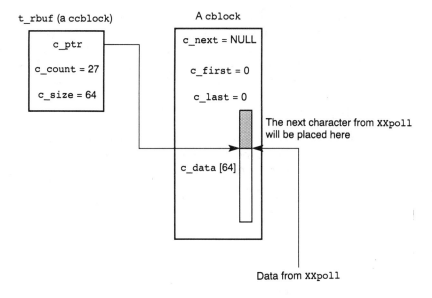

Figure 5.7 Data arriving on t_rbuf.

t_oflag

This is a 16-bit mask of flags defining the output modes of the line, such as whether to map lower case characters to upper case, whether to map newline to carriage return and newline, and so on. Bits in t_oflag also determine whether any delays are inserted after carriage returns, horizontal and vertical tabs, backspaces and formfeeds. Output delay processing is important on devices such as slow, dumb lineprinters, where the print head may take a relatively long time to return back to column 0 from the end of each line. In practice, most modern devices are more intelligent and have on-board buffering capabilities, so output delays are rarely used.

The line discipline takes care of the interpretation of each of the bits in t_oflag. A full list of the different bits is given in ⟨sys/termio.h⟩, and the function of each bit is described in the stty(C) and termio(M) manual pages.

t_cflag

This is a 16-bit mask of flags describing the hardware status of each of the serial lines, including the baud rate, the character size, whether to enable parity generation and checking, the number of stop bits, and so on.

The t_cflag field is maintained by the kernel support routine ttiocom(K), but it is also used by the serial device driver to determine how to program the hardware in response to calls to XXioctl. A full list of the different bits is given in ⟨sys/termio.h⟩, and the function of each bit is described in the stty(C) and termio(M) manual pages.

t_lflag

This is a 16-bit mask of flags used exclusively by the line discipline to control terminal functions, such as whether the line is in canonical mode, whether echoing is enabled, whether to echo a newline on receipt of a line kill character, and so on. A full list of the different bits is given in ⟨sys/termio.h⟩, and the function of each bit is described in the stty(C) and termio(M) manual pages.

t_state

This is a 16-bit mask of flags describing the software status of each of the serial lines. For example, whether the line is open, whether the serial device driver is waiting for the modem carrier, whether an XOFF has been received on the line, and so on. A full list of the possible states is given in ⟨sys/tty.h⟩. Bits in t_state are set, cleared and used exclusively by the serial device driver.

t_line

This is the line discipline number to be used by the serial line. Recall from Section 5.3 that the line discipline number is used to index the line discipline switch table:

```
struct tty *tp = &ttys[UNMODEM(dev)];
(*linesw[tp->t_line].l_read)(parameters);
```

Since each serial line has its own value for t_line, it is possible (although unusual) for the serial lines attached to the same serial I/O card to use different line disciplines. The default is for all serial lines to use line discipline 0, but this can be changed with an appropriate ioctl(S) call.

t_delct

This counts the number of delimiter characters in either the raw or canonical buffers, depending on the mode of the serial line. If the line is in raw mode, t_delct corresponds to the length of the raw buffer. If the line is in canonical mode, t_delct counts the number of newline and end-of-line characters in the canonical buffer. It is set by the line discipline, and is used during the processing of read(S) system calls.

t_cc

This contains the current values for the special control characters interrupt, quit, erase, line kill, end-of-file, end-of-line, end-of-line-2, switch,[2] suspend, start and stop.[3] These default to DEL, Ctrl-\, Ctrl-h, Ctrl-u, Ctrl-d, NUL, NUL, Ctrl-z, Ctrl-z, DC1 (Ctrl-q) and DC3 (Ctrl-s) respectively.

If the line is in raw mode, end-of-file and end-of-line have no meaning, and these locations contain the values for min and time instead.

The contents of t_cc are used by l_input during the processing of t_rbuf (see Section 5.5.6).

t_schar

This is the value used to prime the timeout, in clock ticks, for output delay processing (see the discussion of t_oflag, above). It is set and used exclusively by the line discipline.

5.5   A description of line discipline 0

We now present a description of the routines in line discipline 0. Some readers may choose to skip this section and the next, and go directly to Section 5.7. However, readers who are planning to implement either a new line discipline or a device driver for an intelligent serial card will find this section of particular benefit.

The heading of each section will contain:

- The name of the field in the linesw structure.
- The name of the corresponding entry point in line discipline 0.
- The name of the serial device driver routine that calls the line discipline.

Each section will contain an extract from a working serial device driver to illustrate the interaction between the device driver and the line discipline. The complete device driver is given in Section 5.7.

5.5.1 l_open, ttopen, XXopen

```
int
ttopen(tp)
      struct tty *tp;
```

The l_open routine is called from XXopen, on each open(S) of a serial line. The specific serial line to be opened is indicated by the minor device number.

If the process is not already a member of a process group, and this terminal is not already a controlling terminal, ttopen establishes this terminal as a controlling terminal for a new process group:

```
u.u_ttyp = &tp->t_pgrp;
tp->t_pgrp = u.u_procp->p_pgrp; .
```

This ensures that any keyboard-generated signals (SIGQUIT and SIGINT) received from this terminal will be dispatched to the correct process group.

If the XCLUDE bit is already set in t_lflag, and the user who is making this open(S) request is not root, ttopen returns EBUSY. This will cause the open(S) system call to fail.

Processes should use an ioctl(S) system call, described in the termio(M) manual pages, to set the XCLUDE bit to request exclusive use of the serial line. For example, a communications package such as uucp(C) would set XCLUDE.

After establishing a process group and checking for exclusive use, ttopen calls the kernel support routine ttioctl(K) to allocate an empty cblock to t_rbuf, and to initiate input on the device with a call to XXproc(tp, T_INPUT):

```
ttioctl(tp, LDOPEN, 0, 0);
```

Finally, ttopen clears the WOPEN bit (waiting for open to complete), and sets the ISOPEN bit (open is complete) in t_state.

The line is now open. Here is an extract from a typical XXopen routine showing the call to l_open:

```
XXopen(dev, flags, id)
      dev_t dev;
      int flags, id;
   {
      register struct tty *tp = &XX_tty[UNMODEM(dev)];
      ...
      ...
      /*
       * If we've been asked to do an exclusive open, fail
       * if already open or if user process doesn't belong
       * to root.
       */
      if ((tp->t_lflag & XCLUDE)
            && (tp->t_state & (ISOPEN | WOPEN))
            && (suser() == 0)) {
```

```
        seterror(EBUSY);
        return;
}
/*
 * If not already open, initialize data structures
 * and the hardware. Set CLOCAL (we are assuming no
 * modem control) and CARR_ON, then call the line
 * discipline open.
 */
if ((tp->t_state & (ISOPEN | WOPEN)) == 0) {

        tp->t_proc = XXproc;
        tp->t_xstate |= EXTDLY;
        XXpinit(udev);
        ttinit(tp);
        tp->t_cflag |= CLOCAL;
        XXparam(udev);
}

tp->t_state |= CARR_ON;

s = spl7();
(*linesw[tp->t_line].l_open)(tp);
splx(s);
}
```

5.5.2 l_close, ttclose, XXclose

```
int
ttclose(tp)
        struct tty *tp;
```

The l_close routine is called from XXclose on the last close(S) of a serial line.

Most of the work is done by a call to ttioctl(K), which waits for the contents of t_outq to empty to the device, and then calls ttyflush(K) to free the cblocks from t_canq and t_rawq. Before returning to ttclose, ttioctl(K) also frees the cblocks from t_rbuf and t_tbuf:

```
ttioctl(tp, LDCLOSE, 0, 0);
```

Finally, ttclose clears the ISOPEN bit in t_state, clears the XCLUDE bit in t_lflag, and disassociates the terminal from the process group:

```
tp->t_pgrp = 0;
```

The line is now closed. Here is an extract from a typical XXclose
routine showing the call to l_close:

```
XXclose(dev)
     dev_t dev;
     {
     register struct tty *tp = &XX_tty[UNMODEM(dev)];
     int s;

     dev = UNMODEM(dev);
     /*
      * Call the line discipline close, then turn off
      * interrupts for this device (we have only one).
      *
      * At the end of XXclose(), the line will be in the
      * same state as before XXopen().
      */
     (*linesw[tp->t_line].l_close)(tp);

     outb(RIENABL, 0);
     tp->t_state &= ~(CARR_ON|WOPEN);
     tp->t_cflag &= ~CLOCAL;
     }
```

5.5.3 l_read, ttread, XXread

```
int
ttread(tp)
     struct tty *tp;
```

The l_read routine is called from XXread to transfer data from either
the raw or canonical queue to the user process, in response to a
read(S) system call.

If there are no characters on the canonical queue, ttread must first
call canon(K) to process any data waiting on t_rawq. The canon(K)
routine is responsible for task-time processing in both raw and canonical modes – it is described in Section 5.6.1.

The read(S) system call described in the U-area is then satisfied by
a call to copyout(K), which copies characters from the appropriate
queue out to the user's address space. Either u.u_count bytes or the
entire contents of the queue are copied, whichever is the smaller.

Finally, if the TBLOCK bit is set in t_state, indicating that an XOFF
has been sent down the line to the transmitter, and t_rawq has
drained beneath its low water mark, ttread calls XXproc(tp,
T_UNBLOCK) to send an XON down the line to restart input.

Here is an extract from a typical XXread routine showing the call to
l_read:

```
XXread(dev)
      dev_t dev;
{
      register struct tty *tp = &XX_tty[UNMODEM(dev)];
      (*linesw[tp->t_line].l_read)(tp);
}
```

5.5.4 l_write, ttwrite, XXwrite

```
int
ttwrite(tp)
      struct tty *tp;
```

The l_write routine is called from XXwrite at task-time to copy characters from the user process onto t_outq, in response to a write(S) system call.

It copies all of the characters into temporary cblocks, calling ttxput(K) to transfer the contents of each cblock onto t_outq. If any of the calls to ttxput(K) cause t_outq to go above its high water mark, l_write calls XXproc(tp, T_OUTPUT) to start up output on the device, and then puts the task-time process to sleep. The ttxput(K) routine is described in Section 5.6.10.

When all of the characters have been copied from the user process, l_write calls XXproc(tp, T_OUTPUT) to start up output on the device.

Here is an extract from a typical XXwrite routine showing the call to l_write:

```
XXwrite(dev)
      dev_t dev;
{
      register struct tty *tp = &XX_tty[UNMODEM(dev)];
      (*linesw[tp->t_line].l_write)(tp);
}
```

5.5.5 l_ioctl, ttioctl, XXioctl

```
int
ttioctl(tp, cmd, arg, mode)
      struct tty *tp;
      int cmd, arg, mode;
```

The l_ioctl routine is called from l_open and l_close as described in Sections 5.5.1 and 5.5.2 above, and also indirectly from XXioctl via ttiocom(K). The value of the cmd parameter is one of LDOPEN, LDCLOSE, LDCHG, LDSMAP, LDGMAP or LDNMAP.

The `ttioctl` routine is called with `LDCHG` to deal with the `ICANON` bit (canonical processing on input) when it is set in `t_lflag` by an `ioctl(S)` system call. For example, a process which has been using the line in raw mode may restore the line to canonical mode before the process calls `exit(S)`.

The contents of the raw queue are transferred onto the end of the canonical queue, and then the raw queue is thrown away.

The other three commands `LDSMAP`, `LDGMAP` and `LDNMAP` are for international keyboard support, which is outside the scope of this book.

Here is an extract from a typical `XXioctl` routine showing the call to `ttiocom`, which calls `l_ioctl`:

```
XXioctl(dev, cmd, arg, mode)
    dev_t dev;
    int cmd, mode;
    caddr_t arg;
{
    register struct tty *tp = &XX_tty[UNMODEM(dev)];

    dev = UNMODEM(dev);
    if (ttiocom(tp, cmd, arg, mode)) {
        XXparam(dev);
    }
}
```

5.5.6   l_input, ttin, XXpoll

```
int
ttin(tp, code)
    struct tty *tp;
    int code;
```

The `l_input` routine is called at `XXpoll`-time to transfer characters from `t_rbuf` onto `t_rawq`. It deals with international keyboard mapping, input flow control, keyboard signals and echoing.

The value of code is either `L_BREAK` or `L_BUF`. If the value of code is `L_BREAK`, a hardware break interrupt has occurred on the line (the input was held in the spacing state for longer than the total time of start bit + data bits + parity + stop bits). This condition is indicated by an error bit in the Line Status Register (see Section 5.7.2). The `l_input` routine sends a `SIGINT` signal to the process group, calls `ttyflush(K)` to flush the input and output buffers, then returns to `XXpoll`. The `ttyflush(K)` routine is described in Section 5.6.11.

If the value of code is `L_BUF`, there are characters in `t_rbuf` waiting to be processed and moved onto `t_rawq`.

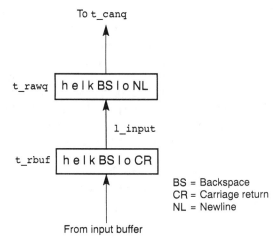

Figure 5.8 l_input transfers characters from t_rbuf to t_rawq. Note processing of ICRNL (map carriage return to newline).

If any of the following bits are set in t_iflag:

- INLCR (map newline to carriage return)
- IGNCR (ignore carriage return)
- ICRNL (map carriage return to newline)
- IUCLC (map upper case to lower case)

l_input does the appropriate mapping before calling putc(K) to copy each individual character from t_rbuf onto t_rawq. Otherwise, l_input calls putcb(K) to copy all of the characters from t_rbuf onto t_rawq in a single operation. The contents of t_rbuf are kept intact for further processing by l_input (see below). Figure 5.8 shows characters being transferred from t_rbuf to t_rawq.

If t_rawq now exceeds its high water mark, l_input calls XXproc(tp, T_BLOCK) to send an XOFF down the line to the transmitter, and then it wakes up any processes that are waiting for input so that t_rawq can be emptied.

If the transmitter does not respond to the XOFF, there is a possibility that t_rawq will continue to grow and eventually consume all of the available cblocks. To prevent this happening, l_input also checks t_rawq against the absolute high water mark TTYHOG (256 characters in SCO UNIX release 3.2v4), and calls ttyflush(K) to flush the input buffers if this limit is reached.

After all the characters have been copied into t_rawq, l_input examines each of the characters in t_rbuf again, looking for keyboard-generated signals, delimiters, and erase and line kill characters.

If the ISIG bit (enable signal processing on input) is set in t_lflag, characters in t_rbuf are checked against the special control characters interrupt (SIGINT), quit (SIGQUIT), suspend (SIGTSTP) and switch. If the character is interrupt or quit, the appropriate signal is sent to the process group, and ttyflush(K) is called to flush the input and output buffers. If the character is suspend, the signal is sent to the process group, but only the input buffers are flushed. If the character is switch, the input and output buffers are flushed, and then XXproc is called with T_SWTCH. No signal is sent.

If the ICANON bit (canonical processing) is set in t_lflag, characters in t_rbuf are checked against the newline and end-of-file delimiters. The value in t_delct is incremented if any are found. Characters are also checked against backspace and line kill. If the character is a backspace, and the ECHOE bit (echo erase) is set in t_lflag, l_input calls ttxput(K) to put a backspace character followed by a space character onto t_outq. If the character is a line kill, and the ECHOK bit (echo line kill as a newline) is set in t_lflag, l_input calls ttxput(K) to put a line kill character onto t_outq.

If ECHO is set, l_input calls ttxput(K) to echo the character onto t_outq,[4] and then calls XXproc(tp, T_OUTPUT) to start up output.

The processing of t_rbuf is now complete. Figure 5.9 summarizes the canonical processing of t_rbuf by l_input.

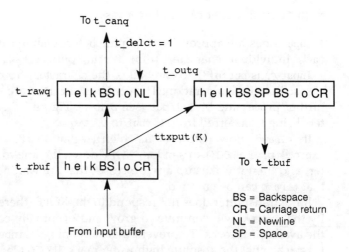

Figure 5.9 l_input does canonical processing of t_rbuf. Note that t_delct has been incremented (there is an NL delimiter on t_rawq).

If the `ICANON` bit is not set in `t_lflag`, `l_input` checks to see whether conditions for raw input can now be met, and sets `t_delct` if they can.

Finally, if `t_delct` is set, indicating that characters are available on `t_rawq` for either canonical or raw input, `l_input` calls `ttiwake(K)` to wake up any processes that are waiting for input.

Here is an extract from a typical `XXpoll` routine showing a call to `l_input`:

```
XXpoll()
{
        register struct tty *tp;
        . . .
        . . .
        for (each port on the serial card) {
                . . .
                . . .
                /*
                 * Copy the received character rchar into t_rbuf,
                 * then call l_input to transfer it onto t_rawq.
                 */
                *tp->t_rbuf.c_ptr++ = rchar;
                if (--tp->t_rbuf.c_count == 0) {
                        tp->t_rbuf.c_ptr -= tp->t_rbuf->c_size;
                        (*linesw[tp->t_line].l_input)(tp, L_BUF);
                }
        }
        . . .
        . . .
}
```

5.5.7   l_output, ttout, XXpoll

```
int
ttout(tp)
        struct tty *tp;
```

The `l_output` routine is called at `XXpoll`-time and at task-time to transfer characters from `t_outq` into `t_tbuf`, and to deal with output delay processing. All characters arrive on `t_outq` from `ttxput(K)`.

The first job of `l_output` is to check for a value in `t_schar`, which indicates that the character that has just been sent to the hardware requires an output delay. The required delay is indicated by two special characters on `t_outq`, placed there by `ttxput(K)`. The first of these is the queue escape character `QESC`, defined in ⟨sys/tty.h⟩. The second character is the required delay in clock ticks, bitwise-OR'd with `QESC`.

Whenever l_output sees a QESC on t_outq, it examines the next character to determine whether any special processing is required. If this character has a value higher than QESC, l_output copies it into t_schar.[5]

If l_output finds a value in t_schar, it sets the TIMEOUT bit (delay timeout in progress) in t_state, and then primes a timeout(K) to call ttrstrt(K) after t_schar clock ticks. When the timeout expires, ttrstrt(K) will call XXproc(tp, T_TIME) to restart output. Since there is nothing to do in the meantime, l_output returns to XXpoll.

If the OPOST bit (output post-processing, that is, output delays) is not set in t_oflag, l_output copies as many characters as possible from t_outq onto t_tbuf. However, if the OPOST bit is set, l_output copies individual characters from t_outq onto t_tbuf, processing any QESC characters as described above. Characters that are not QESC are copied directly onto t_tbuf.

Finally, if t_outq has drained beneath its low water mark, l_output calls ttowake(K) to wake up any processes that are asleep waiting to output.

Figure 5.10 summarizes the operation of l_output.

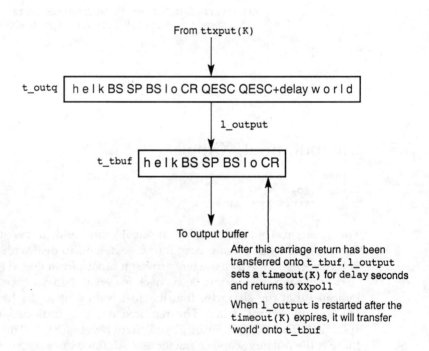

Figure 5.10 l_output transfers characters from t_outq to t_tbuf and deals with output delay processing.

The value returned to XXpoll is either CPRES (defined in
⟨sys/tty.h⟩) or 0. A CPRES indicates that characters were copied from
t_outq onto t_tbuf, and XXpoll should now output some more data
from t_tbuf to the device.

Here is an extract from a typical XXpoll routine showing a call to
l_output:

```
XXpoll()
{
      register struct tty *tp;
      . . .
      . . .
      for (each port on the serial card) {
            . . .
            . . .
            if ((tp->t_tbuf.c_ptr == NULL)
                  || (tp->t_tbuf.c_count == 0)) {
                  if (tp->t_tbuf.c_ptr) {
                        tp->t_tbuf.c_ptr -= tp->t_tbuf.c_size;
                  }
                  if (((*linesw[tp->t_line].l_output)(tp) &
                        CPRES) != 0) {
                        /*
                         * CPRES tells us that data was
                         * transferred onto t_tbuf.
                         */
                        if ((tp->t_state & BUSY) == 0) {
                              XXstart(0);
                        }
                  }
            }
      }
}
```

5.6   Additional kernel support for serial device drivers

The SCO UNIX kernel provides some additional support routines for
line disciplines that can be used by third party device driver writers.
The routines are fully described in the *SCO UNIX Device Driver
Writer's Guide*, but are included here for completeness.

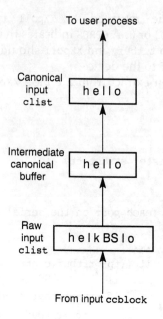

Figure 5.11   The operation of canon(K).

5.6.1   canon(K)

```
int
canon(tp)
     struct tty *tp;
```

The canon(K) routine is called at task-time from l_read. It processes data on either the raw or canonical queues.

In canonical mode, canon(K) processes data on t_rawq and places the results into an intermediate buffer called canonb, before copying the results onto t_canq. The intermediate buffer is used so that the number of unnecessary calls to putc(K) and getc(K) is minimized (for example, whilst processing a backspace). Each character is checked against backslash (the escape character), backspace, line kill and end-of-file, and the contents of t_canq are modified accordingly. Figure 5.11 summarizes the operation of canon(K).

In raw mode, canon(K) manages the min and time processing described in Section 5.4.1 above, sets timeouts if necessary, and returns when the appropriate conditions for raw input are met.

5.6.2   ttiocom(K)

```
int
ttiocom(tp, cmd, arg, mode)
    struct tty *tp;
    int cmd, arg, mode;
```

The ttiocom(K) routine is a general purpose ioctl(S) routine for use by serial device drivers. It is called at task-time from XXioctl, and is a convenient way of responding correctly to ioctl(S) calls from programs such as stty(C). It takes care of managing most of the fields in the tty structure, including all of the bits in the t_cflag, t_iflag, t_lflag and t_oflag.

The ttiocom(K) routine returns 1 to the device driver if the requested change should also be passed out to the hardware, such as a change to the baud rate, parity checking, and so on.

5.6.3   ttinit(K)

```
int
ttinit(tp)
    struct tty *tp;
```

This is called at task-time from XXopen to establish reasonable default values for most of the tty structure members. It assumes that line discipline 0 will be used.

5.6.4   ttiwake(K)

```
int
ttiwake(tp)
    struct tty *tp;
```

This is called at XXpoll-time from l_input to wake up any processes that are asleep on t_rawq, waiting for input.

5.6.5   ttowake(K)

```
int
ttowake(tp)
    struct tty *tp
```

This is called at XXpoll-time from l_output to wake up any processes that are asleep on t_outq, waiting to output.

5.6.6   ttrdchk(K)

```
int
ttrdchk(tp)
     struct tty *tp;
```

This is called at task-time via the rdchk(S) and select(S) system calls
to determine whether there is data waiting to be read on either t_canq
or t_rawq. The rdchk(S) system call is provided for backwards compatibility with SCO XENIX serial device drivers.

5.6.7   ttrstrt(K)

```
int
ttrstrt(tp)
     struct tty *tp;
```

This is called to restart output after an output delay timeout expires.
Its only task is to call XXproc(tp, T_TIME). See the discussion of
l_output in Section 5.5.7, above.

5.6.8   ttselect(K)

```
void
ttselect(tp, rw)
     struct tty *tp;
     int rw;
```

This is called at task-time via the select(S) system call to ensure that
a subsequent one-byte read(S) or write(S) system call will be able to
complete without blocking. The rw parameter is either SELREAD or
SELWRITE (see ⟨sys/select.h⟩).

5.6.9   tttimeo(K)

```
tttimeo(tp)
     struct tty *tp;
```

This is called at task-time from canon(K), or at XXpoll-time from
l_input to manage min and time processing for raw mode.

5.6.10 ttxput(K)

```
ttxput(tp, ucp, ncode)
    struct tty *tp;
    union {
        ushort ch;
        struct cblock *ptr;
    } ucp;
    int ncode;
```

This is called at XXpoll-time from l_input (for echoing characters), and at task-time to put characters onto t_outq. It is responsible for functions such as adding output delays, expanding tabs to spaces, mapping lower case to upper case and mapping newline to carriage return newline, and also for international keyboard support.

It is passed either as a single character (ncode is 1), or a pointer to a cblock of ncode characters.

5.6.11 ttyflush(K)

```
ttyflush(tp, cmd)
    struct tty *tp;
    int rdwr;
```

This is called at XXpoll-time and at task-time to flush the input and output queues. The rdwr parameter is a mask of FREAD and FWRITE (see ⟨sys/file.h⟩).

If FREAD is set, ttyflush(K) throws away the contents of t_canq and t_rawq, returns all the cblocks to the freelist, and then calls XXproc(tp, T_RFLUSH) to empty the hardware's input buffer. If FWRITE is set, ttyflush(K) throws away t_outq and calls XXproc(tp, T_WFLUSH) to empty the hardware's output buffer.

5.6.12 ttywait(K)

```
ttywait(tp)
    struct tty *tp;
```

This is called at task-time via XXclose to wait for characters to drain from t_outq to the device. It then calls delay(K) to allow the hardware's output buffer to empty.

5.7   An example serial device driver

In Sections 5.5 and 5.6, we presented a detailed description of the operation of line discipline 0. In this section, we present an example high performance serial device driver for a dumb serial card. Although it is not a fully tested production device driver, it illustrates many of the principles that we have been discussing in this chapter, including the use of XXpoll to offload clist processing from XXintr. For clarity, we shall assume that only a single serial line is supported by the hardware, and we have omitted all code relating to modem control.

5.7.1 Serial I/O chips

We shall begin with a description of the actual serial I/O chip that our device driver controls.

The i8250 UART and the i8251A USART both implement asynchronous communication in a functionally identical manner. Each has separate single character buffers for input and output, where data is assembled and converted to/from parallel/serial format. The chips generate an interrupt either when the input buffer contains a complete character or when the output buffer empties and is ready to accept another character from the CPU. They incorporate full modem control (clear to send, request to send, data set ready, data terminal ready, ring indicator and carrier detect). They can generate 5-, 6-, 7- or 8-bit characters with odd or even parity, and 1, 1.5 or 2 stop bits. The on-chip baud rate generator allows the chips to operate at speeds of up to 9.6 Kbaud (19.2 Kbaud for the i8251A USART).

The NS16550 serial I/O chip has a similar specification, but features on-chip buffers, or FIFOs, for input and output which can each contain a maximum of 16 characters. The NS16550 chip can be programmed to generate an interrupt when the input FIFO contains 1, 4, 8 or 14 bytes. A transmit interrupt is generated each time the output FIFO empties. If required, the FIFOs can be disabled so that the NS16550 chip will behave similarly to the i8250 and i8251A chips. However, enabling the FIFOs reduces the number of interrupts and makes the NS16550 chip more suitable for use in dumb multiport cards, where higher volumes of data must be managed.

5.7.2 Programming the serial I/O chips

The serial I/O chips described above each have a set of eight registers which controls the operations of the serial lines and provides access to the receive and transmit buffers. All dumb serial cards which have ports conforming to the original IBM Personal Computer Type 1 Serial Adaptor can be programmed identically through these registers. Manufacturers fix the base address in I/O space for their particular card, and the different registers are at the same offsets on all cards. You will see the registers being used in the example serial device driver, below. The register definitions are as follows.

Base address + 0, Transmitter Holding register

The Transmitter Holding register contains the character to be sent. If the register is read rather than written, it is called the Receiver Holding register, and contains the received character. If the chip has FIFOs, the FIFOs are also written and read through this same register.

If the Divisor Latch Access Bit of the Line Control register is 1, this register is used to read or write the low byte of the Divisor Latch, which is used to program the baud rate generator.

Base address + 1, Interrupt Enable register

The Interrupt Enable register is used to specify when the chip will generate an interrupt on its single interrupt output pin. Four separate interrupts can be enabled by setting the appropriate bits in this register:

(1)   Modem Status Interrupt.

(2)   Receiver Line Status Interrupt.

(3)   Transmitter Holding Register Empty Interrupt.

(4)   Received Data Available Interrupt.

If the Divisor Latch Access Bit of the Line Control register is 1, this register is used to read or write the high byte of the Divisor Latch, which is used to program the baud rate generator.

Base address + 2, Interrupt Identification register

When an interrupt arrives, this register can be read to indicate what kind of interrupt it is.

If this register is written, it is called the FIFO Control register and is used to program the FIFO registers. Bits 6 and 7 of this register program the trigger level for the FIFO receive interrupt to be 1, 4, 8 or 14 bytes.

Base address + 3, Line Control register

This register is used to set the format of asynchronous communications, including parity generation and checking, word length and the number of stop bits.

Base address + 4, Modem Control register

This register controls the handshaking with the modem, including the Request to Send (RTS) and Data Terminal Ready (DTR) signals.

Base address + 5, Line Status register

This is the status register, and includes bits which indicate framing errors, parity errors and overrun errors.

Base address + 6, Modem Status register

This register indicates the status of the control lines from the modem, including Carrier Detect, Data Set Ready (DSR) and Clear to Send (CSR) signals.

Offset 7, Scratch register

This register is not used by the chip and is available as a scratch register for the Operating System to use.

Here is the complete serial device driver. It controls a single I/O port at base address 0x3f8. Its operation is summarized in Figure 5.12. If you want to test the device driver, deconfigure the existing sio driver from the kernel as follows:

```
$ ./configure -d -Y -m MAJOR -c
```

First, the header file "extt.h":

```
/*
 * src/extt.h
 *
 * Register definitions for UART at 0x3f8.
 *
 * Copyright (c) Peter Kettle and Steve Statler, 1992
 */
/*
 * UART registers
 */
#define    RBASE      0x3f8
#define    RTDATA     (RBASE + 0)  /* Transmitter holding
                                      reg (W) */
```

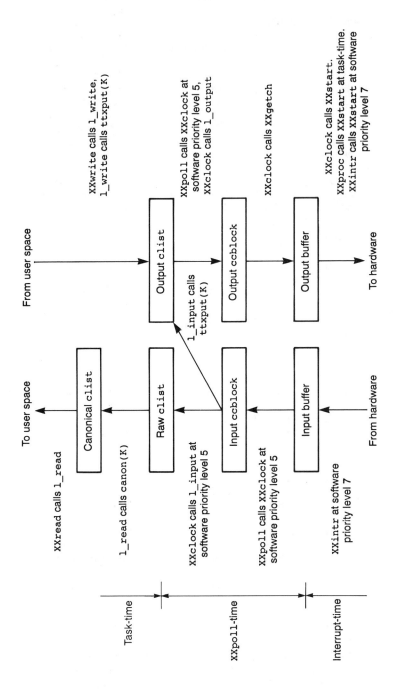

Figure 5.12 A high performance serial device driver.

```
#define   RRDATA    RTDATA        /* Receiver holding
                                     reg (R) */
#define   RLSBLAT   RTDATA        /* LSB of Divisor
                                     latch (W) */
#define   RIENABL   (RBASE + 1)   /* Interrupt enable
                                     reg (W) */
#define   RMSBLAT   RIENABL       /* MSB of Divisor
                                     latch (W) */
#define   RIIREG    (RBASE + 2)   /* Interrupt
                                     identification reg (R) */
#define   RFCNTRL   (RBASE + 2)   /* FIFO control
                                     register (W) */
#define   RLCNTRL   (RBASE + 3)   /* Line control
                                     reg (W) */
#define   RMCNTRL   (RBASE + 4)   /* Modem control reg (W) */
#define   RSTATUS   (RBASE + 5)   /* Line status reg (R) */
#define   RMODEM    (RBASE + 6)   /* Modem status reg (R) */
/*
 * Bits in Interrupt enable reg
 */
#define   ERxEINT   0x01          /* Enable receive intrs */
#define   ETxEINT   0x02          /* Enable transmit intrs */
#define   ERxSTAT   0x04          /* Enable receive line
                                     status intrs */
#define   EMoEINT   0x08          /* Enable modem
                                     interrupts */
/*
 * Bits in Interrupt identification reg
 */
#define   INOINTP   0x01          /* No interrupt pending */
#define   ITxINTR   0x02          /* Transmitter intr */
#define   IRxINTR   0x04          /* Receive intr */
#define   IRxERRO   0x06          /* Receive error intr */
/*
 * Bits in Line control reg
 */
#define   CCHAR8    0x03          /* 8 bit character */
#define   C2STOP    0x04          /* 2 stop bits if set,
                                     else 1 */
#define   CPARON    0x08          /* Enable parity */
#define   CEVENP    0x10          /* Even parity */
#define   CBREAK    0x40          /* Generate a break
                                     condition */
#define   CDIVLB    0x80          /* Divisor latch access
                                     bit */
/*
 * Bits in Line status reg
 */
#define   SRxCHAR   0x01          /* Received character */
#define   SRxOVER   0x02          /* Overrun error */
#define   SPARERR   0x04          /* Parity error */
#define   SFRMERR   0x08          /* Framing error */
```

```
#define   SBRKINT   0x10        /* Break interrupt */
#define   STxEMPT   0x20        /* Transmitter holding
                                   reg is empty */
/*
 * Bits in Modem control reg
 */
#define   MCRDTR    0x01        /* Data Terminal Ready */
#define   MCRRTS    0x02        /* Request To Send */
#define   MCRBIT2   0x04
#define   MCRBIT3   0x08        /* Interrupt control for
                                   8250 level 4 */
#define   LOBYTE(x) ((x) & 0xff)
#define   HIBYTE(x) (((x) >> 8) & 0xff)
/*
 * How many serial ports
 */
#define NEXTT  1
/*
 * Intermediate buffers between XXintr() and XXpoll()
 *
 *    q_rxbuf[] and q_erbuf[] contain received characters
 *    and corresponding error values (from RSTATUS), and
 *    behave as circular lists indexed by q_rxtsrt (front)
 *    and q_rxend (end).
 *
 *    q_txbuf[] contains characters waiting to be output.
 */
#define NQCHRS32
struct extt_queue {
        char q_rxbuf[NQCHRS];        /* Received characters */
        char q_erbuf[NQCHRS];        /* Received errors */
        int q_rxstrt, q_rxend;
        char q_txbuf[NQCHRS];        /* Output characters */
        int q_txstrt, q_txend;
} extt_queue[NEXTT];
#define QDELAY 0x100
```

And finally, the device driver itself:

```
/*
 * src/extt.c
 *
 * An example serial device driver.
 *
 * Copyright (c) Peter Kettle and Steve Statler, 1992
 *
 * This driver defers clist processing to XXpoll(), in a
 * similar way to SCO's sio.c
 *
 * Supports a single UART port at 0x3f8 to 0x3ff.  Modem
 * control is not shown.
```

```
 *
 * ./configure -a exttinit exttopen exttclose exttread
 *   exttwrite exttioctl exttpoll exttintr -l 7 -v 4 -T 1 -I
 *   3f8 3ff -c -m MAJOR
 */
#include ⟨sys/types.h⟩
#include ⟨sys/param.h⟩
#include ⟨sys/conf.h⟩
#include ⟨sys/dir.h⟩
#include ⟨sys/file.h⟩
#include ⟨sys/user.h⟩
#include ⟨sys/termio.h⟩
#include ⟨sys/tty.h⟩
#include ⟨sys/errno.h⟩
#include ⟨sys/cmn_err.h⟩
#include "extt.h"

int exttopen(), exttclose(), exttread(), exttwrite(),
exttioctl();
void exttintr();

/*
 * exttbauds[] are used as divisors of the UART's
 * clock frequency.
 */

unsigned short exttbauds[] = {
    0x00,
    0x900,          /* 50 baud */
    0x600,          /* 75 baud */
    0x417,          /* 110 baud */
    0x359,          /* 134 baud */
    0x300,          /* 150 baud */
    0x240,          /* 200 baud */
    0x180,          /* 300 baud */
    0x0c0,          /* 600 baud */
    0x060,          /* 1200 baud */
    0x040,          /* 1800 baud */
    0x030,          /* 2400 baud */
    0x018,          /* 4800 baud */
    0x00c,          /* 9600 baud */
    0x006,          /* 19200 baud */
    0x003           /* 38400 baud */
};

/*
 * The tty structure for the single (NEXTT) serial port.
 */

struct tty extt_tty[NEXTT];

/*
 * Synchronize exttintr() and exttpoll().  Set exttwork if
 * there is work for exttpoll() to do.
 */

int exttwork = 0;
```

```
/*
 * Synchronize exttpoll() and exttclock().  Set exttblock
 * whenever we are inside exttclock().
 */
int exttblock = 0;

/*
 * exttinit()
 *
 * Announce our presence with printcfg(K).
 */
exttinit()
{
    printcfg("serial", 0x3f8, 7, 4, -1,
            "unit=0 type=EXTT nports=1");
}

/*
 * exttpinit()
 *
 * Initialize a port.
 * Turn off interrupts and disable any FIFOs.
 *
 * Called from exttopen().
 */
exttpinit(udev)
    int udev;
{
    outb(RIENABL, 0);
    inb(RRDATA);
    inb(RSTATUS);
    inb(RMODEM);
    outb(RMCNTRL, MCRDTR | MCRRTS | MCRBIT3);
    outb(RFCNTRL, 0);
}

/*
 * exttopen()
 *
 * Open the device and set the initial state of the serial
 * card, including baud rate and parity
 */
exttopen(dev, flags, id)
    dev_t dev;
    int flags, id;
{
    register struct tty *tp;
    struct extt_queue *qp;
    int s, udev, exttproc();

    udev = UNMODEM(dev);
    tp = &extt_tty[udev];
    qp = &extt_queue[udev];
```

```
            if ((tp->t_lflag & XCLUDE)
                && (tp->t_state & (ISOPEN | WOPEN))
                && (suser() == 0)) {
                seterror(EBUSY);
                return;
            }
            if ((tp->t_state & (ISOPEN | WOPEN)) == 0) {
                qp->q_rxstrt = qp->q_rxend = 0;
                tp->t_proc = exttproc;
                tp->t_xstate |= EXTDLY;
                exttpinit(udev);
                ttinit(tp);
                tp->t_cflag |= CLOCAL;
                exttparam(udev);
            }
            tp->t_state |= CARR_ON;
            outb(RMCNTRL, MCRBIT3 | MCRDTR | MCRRTS);
            s = spl7();
            (*linesw[tp->t_line].l_open)(tp);
            splx(s);
}
/*
 * exttclose()
 *
 * Close the device.
 *
 * Most of the work is done by the line discipline.  We just
 * turn off all interrupts.
 */
exttclose(dev)
        dev_t dev;
{
        register struct tty *tp;
        int s;
        dev = UNMODEM(dev);
        tp = &extt_tty[dev];
        (*linesw[tp->t_line].l_close)(tp);
        outb(RIENABL, 0);
        tp->t_state &= ~(CARR_ON|WOPEN);
        tp->t_cflag &= ~CLOCAL;
}
/*
 * exttread()
 *
 * Call the line discipline to return data to the user.
 */
exttread(dev)
        dev_t dev;
{
        register struct tty *tp;
```

```
        tp = &extt_tty[UNMODEM(dev)];
        (*linesw[tp->t_line].l_read)(tp);
}
/*
 * exttwrite()
 *
 * Call the line discipline to read data from the user.
 */
exttwrite(dev)
        dev_t dev;
{
        register struct tty *tp;
        tp = &extt_tty[UNMODEM(dev)];
        (*linesw[tp->t_line].l_write)(tp);
}
/*
 * exttparam()
 *
 * Called from exttopen() and exttioctl() to change the
 * state of the line.
 */
static
exttparam(udev)
        int udev;
{
        register struct tty *tp;
        int flags, intr = 0, lctrl = 0, s;
        tp = &extt_tty[udev];
        flags = tp->t_cflag;
        /*
         * Set up the Line control reg
         */
        if (flags & PARENB) {
            lctrl |= CPARON;              /* Turn on parity */
            if ((flags & PARODD) == 0) {
                lctrl |= CEVENP;     /* Even parity */
            }
        }
        lctrl |= (flags & CSIZE) >> 4;   /* Character size */
        if (flags & CSTOPB) {
            lctrl |= C2STOP;             /* 2 stop bits */
        }
        /*
         * Now write out the baud rate and Line control
         */
        s = spl7();
        intr = inb(RIENABL) & EMoEINT;
```

```
            outb(RLCNTRL, CDIVLB);            /* Divisor latch */
            outb(RLSBLAT, LOBYTE(exttbauds[flags&CBAUD]));
            outb(RMSBLAT, HIBYTE(exttbauds[flags&CBAUD]));
            outb(RLCNTRL, (char)lctrl);
            /*
             * Finally, allow the device to interrupt
             */
            intr |= ETxEINT;
            if (flags & CREAD) {
                  intr |= (ERxEINT|ERxSTAT);
            }
            outb(RIENABL, (char)intr);
            splx(s);
}
/*
 * exttioctl()
 *
 * Call general purpose ttiocom(), and then exttparam()
 * if the hardware must change too.
 */
exttioctl(dev, cmd, arg, mode)
      dev_t dev;
      int cmd, mode;
      caddr_t arg;
{
      register struct tty *tp;
      dev = UNMODEM(dev);
      tp = &extt_tty[dev];
      if (ttiocom(tp, cmd, arg, mode)) {
            if (tp->t_cflag & CLOCAL) {
                  tp->t_state |= CARR_ON;
            }
            exttparam(dev);
      }
}
/*
 * exttintr()
 *
 * Determine whether this is a receive or transmit
 * interrupt, and behave accordingly.
 *
 *    o For receive, add the received character and error
 *      status to q_rxbuf[], doing X-Off processing as
 *      necessary.
 *    o For transmit, call exttstart() to outb() the next
 *      character from q_wxbuf[].
 *
 * NOTE THAT WE CANNOT CALL THE LINE DISCIPLINE OR ACCESS
 * t_rbuf OR t_tbuf AS WE ARE AT SPL7().
 */
```

```
void
exttintr(irq)
    int irq;
{
    register struct tty *tp;
    register int iir;
    unsigned char rxchar, status;
    struct extt_queue *qp;
    int udev;

    if (irq == 4){

        udev = 0;
    } else {
        cmn_err(CE_WARN, "Stray interrupt from IRQ %d",
                irq);
        return;
    }

    tp = &extt_tty[udev];
    qp = &extt_queue[udev];

    /*
     * Tell XXpoll() that there is some
     * work to do
     */

    exttwork = 1;

    /*
     * Find out why we were interrupted, and then loop
     * dealing with all pending interrupts
     */

    iir = inb(RIIREG);

    do {
        iir &= (ITxINTR | IRxINTR);

        if (iir & IRxINTR) {

            /*
             * This is a receive interrupt.  Get the
             * character and the status from the hardware.
             *
             * Do X-Off processing here, then transfer
             * the character(s) onto q_rxbuf.
             *
             * We have already set exttwork so that
             * XXpoll() will move data from q_rxbuf
             * to t_rbuf.
             */

            status = inb(RSTATUS);
            rxchar = inb(RRDATA);

            /*
             * Check that there is room in q_rxbuf.
             */
```

```
                    if (((qp->q_rxend + 1) % NQCHRS) !=
                            qp->q_rxstrt ) {
                        unsigned xchar = rxchar & ((tp->t_iflag
                                            & ISTRIP) ?
                                        0x7f : 0xff);
                        if ((xchar == CSTOP)
                                && (tp->t_iflag&IXON)
                                && ((tp->t_state & TTSTOP) == 0)) {
                            (*tp->t_proc)(tp, T_SUSPEND);
                        } else {
                            qp->q_rxbuf[qp->q_rxend] = rxchar;
                            qp->q_erbuf[qp->q_rxend] = status;

                            qp->q_rxend++;
                            qp->q_rxend %= NQCHRS;
                        }
                    }
                    /*
                     * If STxEMPT is set, (transmitter holding
                     * register empty), set iir to ITxINTR so that
                     * it will appear that we have a transmit
                     * interrupt as well as this receive
                     * interrupt.
                     */
                    if (status & STxEMPT) {
                        iir = ITxINTR;
                    } else {
                        continue;
                    }
                }
                if (iir & ITxINTR) {
                    /*
                     * Transmit interrupt.  Call exttstart() to
                     * output the next character from q_txbuf.
                     */
                    exttstart(udev);
                }
        } while (((iir = inb(RIIREG)) & INOINTP) == 0);
        /*
         * This inb() is required to fix a peculiar glitch
         * on some cards.
         */
        inb(RSTATUS);
}
/*
 * exttproc()
 *
 * Respond to requests from exttintr(), exttclock(), and
 * the line discipline.
```

```
     *
     * Set udev = tp - extt_tty to determine which line we've
     * been called to service.
     */
exttproc(tp, cmd)
     register struct tty *tp;
     int cmd;
{
     extern int ttrstrt();
     struct extt_queue *qp;
     int udev, s;

     udev = tp - extt_tty;
     switch (cmd) {

     case T_OUTPUT:
          /*
           * Send more data to the device.  Set exttwork to
           * be picked up by XXpoll() then return.
           */
          exttwork = 1;
          break;

     case T_SUSPEND:
          /*
           * We've received an X-Off.
           */
          tp->t_state |= TTSTOP;
          break;

     case T_RESUME:
          /*
           * We've received an X-On
           */
          s = spl7();
          tp->t_state &= ~TTSTOP;
          exttwork = 1;
          exttstart(udev);
          splx(s);
          break;

     case T_BREAK:
          /*
           * Send a hardware break and then timeout(K) for
           * .25 second
           */
          s = spl7();
          tp->t_state |= TIMEOUT;
          outb(RLCNTRL, inb(RLCNTRL) | CBREAK);
          splx(s);
          timeout(ttrstrt, (caddr_t)tp, HZ/4);
          break;
```

```
        case T_TIME:
                /*
                 * The hardware break initiated by T_BREAK has
                 * expired, so clear the CBREAK bit from the
                 * line control register.
                 */
                s = spl7();
                outb(RLCNTRL, inb(RLCNTRL) & ~CBREAK);
                tp->t_state &= ~TIMEOUT;
                exttstart(udev);
                splx(s);
                break;
        case T_WFLUSH:
                /*
                 * Throw away the contents of t_tbuf, then call
                 * l_output to empty t_outq into t_tbuf.
                 */
                qp = &extt_queue[udev];
                if (tp->t_tbuf.c_ptr) {
                        tp->t_tbuf.c_ptr -= tp->t_tbuf.c_size -
                                            tp->t_tbuf.c_count;
                }
                (*linesw[tp->t_line].l_output)(tp);
                s = spl7();
                qp->q_txstrt = qp->q_txend;
                tp->t_state &= ~TTSTOP;
                exttstart(udev);
                splx(s);
                break;
        case T_RFLUSH:
                /*
                 * Flush the device's input buffer.
                 * If input is blocked, unblock it by falling
                 * through this case into T_UNBLOCK
                 */
                qp = &extt_queue[udev];
                s = spl7();
                qp->q_rxstrt = qp->q_rxend;
                splx(s);
                if ((tp->t_state & TBLOCK) == 0) {
                        break;
                } /* else fall through to T_UNBLOCK */
        case T_UNBLOCK:
                /*
                 * Called from l_input when t_rawq falls below
                 * its low water mark.  Call exttstart() to
                 * send an X-On down the line.
                 */
```

```
                s=spl7();
                tp->t_state &= ~(TBLOCK|TTXOFF);
                tp->t_state |= TTXON;
                exttstart(udev);
                splx(s);
                break;

        case T_BLOCK:

                /*
                 * Called from l_input when t_rawq goes above
                 * its high water mark.  Call exttstart() to
                 * send an X-Off down the line.
                 */

                s=spl7();
                tp->t_state &= ~TTXON;
                tp->t_state |= (TBLOCK|TTXOFF);
                exttstart(udev);
                splx(s);
                break;

        case T_PARM:

                exttparam(udev);
                break;

        default:
                break;
        }
}
/*
 * exttstart()
 *
 * Called at spl7() from XXintr(), XXproc(), and XXclock()
 * to start output on the device.
 *
 * The port parameter is an UNMODEM'd minor device number.
 */

exttstart(port)
        int port;
{
        register struct tty *tp;
        struct extt_queue *qp;
        char txchar;
        tp = &extt_tty[port];
        qp = &extt_queue[port];

        /*
         * If we are blocked or waiting for a timeout(K)
         * to expire, return immediately
         */

        if (tp->t_state & (TIMEOUT|TTSTOP)) {

                return;
        }
```

```
/*
 * If we should be responding to X-On X-Off
 * on input ...
 */
if (tp->t_iflag & IXOFF) {
    /*
     * ... and XXproc() has asked us to send
     * an X-Off, send a CSTOP to the device.
     */
    if ((tp->t_state & TTXOFF)
        || (tp->t_state & TBLOCK)) {
        tp->t_state |= BUSY;
        tp->t_state &= ~TTXOFF;
        outb(RTDATA, CSTOP);
        inb(RSTATUS);

        return;
    } else {
        tp->t_state &= ~TTXOFF;
    }
    /*
     * ... and XXproc() has asked us to send
     * an X-On, send a CSTART to the device.
     */
    if ((tp->t_state & TBLOCK)
        || (tp->t_state & TTXON)) {
        tp->t_state |= BUSY;
        tp->t_state &= ~TTXON;
        outb(RTDATA, CSTART);
        inb(RSTATUS);

        return;
    } else {
        tp->t_state &= ~TTXON;
    }
}
/*
 * Get the next character from q_txbuf, and send
 * it to the device.
 */
if (qp->q_txstrt == qp->q_txend) {
    tp->t_state &= ~BUSY;
    if (tp->t_state & TTIOW) {
        tp->t_state &= ~TTIOW;
        exttwork = 1;
    }
    return;
}
txchar = qp->q_txbuf[qp->q_txstrt++];
qp->q_txstrt %= NQCHRS;
```

```
        /*
         * We have a character in txchar to send to the
         * device.  Check for output delay processing.
         */
        if (txchar & QDELAY) {
                tp->t_state |= TIMEOUT;
                timeout(ttrstrt, (caddr_t)tp, (txchar & 0x7f) +
                        HZ/10);
                return;
        }
        /*
         * Output txchar, and then return
         */
        outb(RTDATA, (char)txchar);
        tp->t_state |= BUSY;
        inb(RSTATUS);
}
/*
 * exttpoll()
 *
 * Called at spl6() by the clock interrupt routine.  If the
 * system was NOT already at spl5() or higher when the clock
 * ticked, and there is something for us to do (exttwork is
 * not 0), call exttclock().
 */
exttpoll(ps)
        int ps;
{
        int s;

        if (ps >= 5) {

                return;
        }
        if (exttblock) {

                /*
                 * We are already in exttclock at spl5()
                 * from a previous exttpoll(), so don't
                 * go there again on this clock tick.
                 */

                return;
        }
        if (exttwork) {

                /*
                 * We are allowed to spl5() because we know that
                 * the system was at LESS than spl5() before the
                 * clock tick.
                 */
```

```
                exttwork = 0;
                exttblock++;
                s=spl5();
                exttclock();
                splx(s);
                exttblock = 0;
        }
}
/*
 * exttclock()
 *
 * Called at spl5() from XXpoll() whenever there is any work
 * to do:
 *
 *    o For receive, transfer characters from q_rxbuf to
 *      t_rbuf, and then to t_rawq, handling all errors
 *      and also X-On.
 *    o For transmit, transfer characters from t_tbuf to
 *      q_txbuf, and then call exttstart().
 */
exttclock()
{
        register struct tty *tp;
        struct extt_queue *qp;
        int flg, i, c, status, s, lcnt, qlen, rflag, xflag;
        char lbuf[3];

        for (i = 0; i < NEXTT; i++) {
                tp = &extt_tty[i];
                qp = &extt_queue[i];

                /*
                 * Deal with input first of all.  Transfer
                 * characters from q_rxbuf to t_rbuf (if there's
                 * space), and then call l_input to move them onto
                 * t_rawq.
                 *
                 * Set rflag as soon as we know there is some
                 * data.
                 */
                rflag = 0;
                while (qp->q_rxstrt != qp->q_rxend) {
                        if (tp->t_rbuf.c_ptr == NULL) {
                                break;
                        }
                        rflag = 1;
                        c = qp->q_rxbuf[qp->q_rxstrt];
                        status = qp->q_erbuf[qp->q_rxstrt];
                        lcnt = 1;
                        if (tp->t_iflag & IXON) {
                                if (tp->t_state & TTSTOP) {
```

```
            if ((c == CSTART)
                || (tp->t_iflag & IXANY)) {
                (*tp->t_proc)(tp, T_RESUME);
            }
        } else {
            if (c == CSTOP) {
                (*tp->t_proc)(tp, T_SUSPEND);
            }
        }
        if ((c == CSTART) || (c == CSTOP)) {
            goto out;
        }
    }
    flg = tp->t_iflag;
    if ((flg & INPCK) == 0) {
        status &= ~SPARERR;
    }
    if (status & (SRxOVER | SPARERR | SFRMERR |
                SBRKINT)) {
        if (status & SBRKINT) {
            if (flg & IGNBRK) {
                goto out;
            }
            if (flg & BRKINT) {
                (*linesw[tp->t_line].l_input)
                (tp, L_BREAK);
                goto out;
            }
            c = 0;
        } else {
            if (flg & IGNPAR) {
                goto out;
            }
        }
        if (flg & PARMRK) {
            lbuf[2] = 0xff;
            lbuf[1] = 0;
            lcnt = 3;
        } else {
            c = 0;
        }
    } else {
        if (flg & ISTRIP) {
            c &= 0x7f;
        } else {
            c &= 0xff;
```

```
                    if ((c == 0xff) && (flg & PARMRK)) {
                            lbuf[1] = 0xff;
                            lcnt = 2;
                    }
              }
          } /* if (status & ... */
          lbuf[0] = c;
          while (lcnt) {
                *tp->t_rbuf.c_ptr++ = lbuf[--lcnt];
                if (--tp->t_rbuf.c_count == 0) {
                        tp->t_rbuf.c_ptr -=
                                        tp->t_rbuf.c_size;
                        (*linesw[tp->t_line].l_input)(tp,
                        L_BUF);
                }
          }
out:
          if (qp->q_rxstrt == qp->q_rxend) {
              break;
          }
          qp->q_rxstrt++;
          qp->q_rxstrt %= NQCHRS;
      } /* while */
      if (rflag) {
          if (tp->t_rbuf.c_count != tp->t_rbuf.c_size) {
              tp->t_rbuf.c_ptr -= tp->t_rbuf.c_size -
                                  tp->t_rbuf.c_count;
              (*linesw[tp->t_line].l_input)
              (tp, L_BUF);
          }
      }
      /*
       * Now deal with output.  Determine how much space
       * there is in q_txbuf, and then transfer that
       * many characters from t_outq, via calls to
       * exttgettch.
       */
      if (tp->t_state & BUSY) {
          continue;
      }
      xflag = 0;
      if ((qlen = (qp->q_txstrt -
          qp->q_txend - 1)) < 0) {
          qlen += NQCHRS;
      }
      while (--qlen >= 0) {
          if ((c = exttgettch(tp)) < 0) {
                break;
          }
```

```
                        xflag = 1;
                        if ((c == QESC) && (tp->t_oflag & OPOST)) {
                                if ((c = exttgettch(tp)) > QESC) {
                                        c |= QDELAY;
                                } else {
                                        if (c < 0) {
                                                break;
                                        }
                                }
                        }
                        qp->q_txbuf[qp->q_txend++] = c;
                        qp->q_txend %= NQCHRS;
                } /* while */
                if (xflag) {
                        tp->t_state |= BUSY;
                        s = spl7();
                        exttstart(i);
                        splx(s);
                }
        } /* for */
}
/*
 * exttgettch()
 *
 * Called at spl5() by exttclock() to get the next
 * character from t_tbuf.
 *
 * Return -1 if there are no characters present.
 */
exttgettch(tp)
        register struct tty *tp;
{
        register struct ccblock *tbuf = &tp->t_tbuf;

        if ((tbuf->c_ptr == NULL)
            || (tbuf->c_count == 0)) {
                if (tbuf->c_ptr) {
                        tbuf->c_ptr -= tbuf->c_size;
                }
                if (((*linesw[tp->t_line].l_output)(tp) & CPRES)
                    == 0) {
                        return(-1);
                }
        }
        tbuf->c_count--;
        return(*(unsigned char *)tbuf->c_ptr++);
}
```

5.8   Summary

We began this chapter by stating that serial device drivers are the most difficult of all device driver types to understand. We have presented a detailed explanation of SCO's line discipline 0, and we have shown how this can be used by a real serial device driver for a dumb serial card.

The principles that we have described in this chapter are applicable to all serial device drivers, and you should now have at least a conceptual understanding of how they might work.

QUIZ

5.1 How many separate clists are there for each line supported by a serial device driver?

5.2 What is the name of the kernel support routine that does task-time processing of t_rawq?

5.3 What are the names of the routines that add and remove characters to and from clists?

5.4 What is the name of the routine in line discipline 0 that is called at XXpoll-time to transfer data from t_rbuf onto t_rawq?

5.5 What should the line discipline do if t_rawq fills up?

5.6 If the carriage return character requires an output delay of five clock ticks, how would ttxput(K) encode this information in t_outq?

5.7 What should the XXproc routine do when it is called with T_UNBLOCK?

5.8 In the example serial device driver presented in Section 5.7, why can't XXintr access the input and output ccblocks directly?

5.9   How should you add a new line discipline to the kernel?

5.10 Can you think of any additional benefits of having buffers between XXintr and the ccblocks when using an NS16550 chip?

EXERCISE

The mouse device driver from Chapters 3 and 4 does not have any buffering between the hardware and the user. This means that individual mouse movements could be lost if the user process does not read the device often enough or quickly enough. This problem can be solved by storing individual mouse movements, so that the user process can track the exact movement of a mouse. This might be useful in a drawing application, for example.

Write a simple line discipline that manages an event queue.

The event queue will be a linked list of structures which will contain a record of the mouse's movement and buttons, each time the mouse changes state.

Here are some hints:

- Your line discipline should have four routines called l_open, l_close, l_input and l_read.

- Your l_open routine will be called from XXopen to initialize a freelist of mouse event structures. Decide how many event structures to have. A suitable structure would be as follows:

```
struct bmevent {
  struct bmevent *next;
  struct bmouse  bmouse;
};
```

- Declare anchors for the freelist and the event queue.

- Your l_close routine will be called from XXclose and should clear the event queue by returning all the event structures to the freelist.

- Your l_input routine will be called from XXintr to add an event structure to the event queue. It should remove a structure from the freelist, copy the mouse data into the structure, and then add the structure to the event queue.

- Your l_read routine will be called from XXread to remove the next event structure from the event queue, copy the data to the user, and then return the structure to the freelist.

- Remember to protect the event queue from mouse interrupts.

- Add sleep(K) and wakeup(K) calls to the line discipline so that the user process goes to sleep if the event queue is empty. Wake up the user process when another event arrives on the event queue.

- Decide what to do when the freelist is empty and another mouse event arrives from XXintr.

- Modify your mouse device driver from Chapter 4 to use your line discipline. Make sure that the line discipline number to be used is made available in your device driver.

- Modify idaddld(ADM) to recognize $ROOT, and add details of your line discipline to pack.d/kernel/space.c. Alternatively, use vi(C) to edit space.c and add the appropriate information by hand.

Test your device driver and line discipline using mouse and mousey, which should not require any modifications.

A suggested answer is given in 'Answers to Exercises'.

NOTES

1. The default value is 120 on SCO UNIX release 3.2v4.

2. The switch character is used by SCO's Shell Layers.

3. The suspend, start and stop characters are used for POSIX Job Control.

4. The echoed character is another backspace if a backspace has been received, or a newline if a line kill character has been received.

5. Characters that do not have values higher than QESC are treated as normal characters.

6

STREAMS

6.1 Overview

In this chapter we shall look at STREAMS. The Stream Input–Output System was first described by Dennis Ritchie in the *AT&T Bell Laboratories Technical Journal* Volume 63, Number 8, October 1984. Additional background information for this chapter has been drawn from *The AT&T STREAMS Primer* and *The AT&T STREAMS Programmer's Guide*.

Ritchie developed STREAMS to address two separate issues:

- There was no existing mechanism in the UNIX kernel to facilitate the separation of network protocols into functionally distinct layers (for example, TCP/IP, or the OSI 7-layer model).

- The traditional line discipline solution to character-based I/O was becoming unwieldy and too slow for certain applications. More significantly, it was becoming more difficult to understand and consequently more difficult to maintain and modify (see Chapter 5).

STREAMS first appeared in a commercial product in AT&T's System V Release 3.0 in 1986. It has been available for SCO XENIX and SCO UNIX since 1988 and has been used to implement many of SCO's networking products, including TCP/IP. At present, serial device drivers continue to use the `clist`-based line discipline 0 to support character I/O, as described in Chapter 5.

In the exercise at the end of this chapter, we shall convert the mouse driver to a Stream driver.

165

6.2   What is a Stream?

We shall begin by introducing some of the concepts and terminology
of STREAMS. A Stream is a flexible character-based full-duplex communications path that links a user process to a device driver. The
simplest Stream has a Stream head which is next to the user, and a
Stream driver which controls the hardware. The connection between
the Stream head and the Stream driver is established automatically
when the device is first opened, and a user process can make open(S),
close(S), read(S), write(S) and ioctl(S) system calls in exactly the
same way as for ordinary character device drivers. STREAMS supports three additional system calls getmsg(S), putmsg(S) and poll(S),
which are described later in this chapter.

Data is passed through a Stream in a structure called a message,
which is the basic data type used by a Stream. Messages awaiting
processing are buffered into message queues, similar to clists, which
include high and low water marks for use by the STREAMS flow
control, discussed in Section 6.5.1. A message contains a description
of the message type and any data associated with the message. For
example, messages containing data from a write(S) system call are of
type M_DATA.

A message is constructed from one or more message blocks, and is
passed downstream from the Stream head towards the Stream driver,
or upstream from the Stream driver towards the Stream head. The
downstream and upstream flows of messages are completely independent of each other, so that STREAMS can be full-duplex mechanisms. Figure 6.1 shows the basic architecture of a simple Stream
configuration.

A more complex configuration can have one or more Stream modules between the Stream head and the Stream driver, to carry out
intermediate processing of the messages. For example, SCO TCP/IP
implements the TCP and IP protocol layers in separate Stream modules, with several Stream drivers (Western Digital Ethernet, 3COM
Ethernet, IBM Token Ring, and others) multiplexed onto the bottom
of the IP Stream module (see Section 6.7). Figure 6.2 shows an
example Stream configuration including some Stream modules.

A Stream module consists of two QUEUEs, which are responsible
for processing the respective downstream and upstream messages as
they pass through the module. Stream modules are linked into a
Stream at run time in response to special ioctl(S) system calls to
push or pop Stream modules onto the Stream, which grows upwards
from the Stream driver towards the Stream head. Modules that are
linked in this way are said to be **adjacent** to each other.

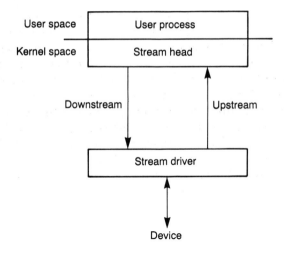

Figure 6.1 A simple Stream configuration.

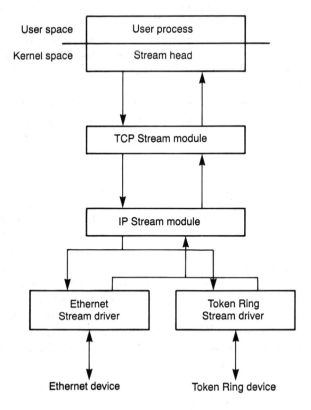

Figure 6.2 A multiplexed Stream configuration.

A Stream driver has the same job as any other UNIX device driver – it provides a uniform interface between the kernel and the hardware. The major differences between a Stream driver and a regular character device driver are the kernel interface and the manner in which data is manipulated. For example, a Stream driver does not have an XXread routine, and the XXwrite routine has been replaced with an XXput routine, called from upstream to receive a message. A Stream driver passes messages upstream by calling the upstream XXput routine of the appropriate Stream module (or the Stream head).

In the remainder of this chapter, we shall indicate downstream routine names, such as XXput, by writing XXwput (the w indicates write), and upstream routine names by writing XXrput (the r indicates read).

6.2.1 A Stream head

A Stream head provides the interface between the user process and the Stream in kernel space. The Stream head converts data from write(S), putmsg(S) and ioctl(S) system calls into messages, which are sent to a downstream module by calling the appropriate XXwput routine. Messages which have travelled upstream to arrive at the Stream head are made available to read(S), getmsg(S) and ioctl(S) system calls.

A Stream head is allocated and initialized by the kernel on the first open(S) system call of the device, and requires no further attention from the STREAMS developer.

6.2.2 A Stream module

A Stream module is pushed into a Stream between a Stream head and a Stream driver, and consists of an upstream QUEUE and a downstream QUEUE which are responsible for manipulating the messages that pass through the module (see Section 6.4). Each QUEUE consists of a set of routines (for example, XXopen, XXput), information such as the high and low water marks used for STREAMS flow control, and an anchor point for the appropriate message queue.

An upstream QUEUE (or the Stream head) passes messages downstream by using the putnext macro to call the downstream QUEUE's XXwput routine:

```
putnext(q, mp)
    queue_t *q;
    mblk_t *mp;
```

The parameters to putnext are the calling QUEUE and the message to be passed. These data structures are described in Sections 6.4 and 6.3 respectively.

The downstream QUEUE's XXwput routine should accept the message and either process it immediately, or defer processing by adding it to a message queue. Similarly, a downstream QUEUE (or the Stream driver) passes messages upstream by using the putnext macro to call the upstream QUEUE's XXrput routine.

If a QUEUE chooses to defer processing until later, the STREAMS scheduler (see Section 6.5) will invoke the QUEUE's XXservice routine to complete the processing of the queued message. A typical XXservice routine will manipulate each message on its message queue (for example, divide each message into 32-byte packets, add checksum bytes and allocate some new message blocks for the new packets) and then pass the new messages either upstream or downstream with putnext.

Note that when a module is pushed into a Stream, all user processes which have that Stream open will be affected. This is comparable to user processes that are sharing a serial line – when any one of them makes an ioctl(S) request to change the line characteristics, they will all be affected.

QUEUEs and flow control are fully described in Sections 6.4 and 6.5 respectively.

6.2.3 A Stream driver

A Stream driver has more or less the same responsibilities as any other device driver. It must provide a uniform interface to the higher level parts of the kernel, and therefore hide the complexities of the underlying hardware from the kernel and user processes. A Stream driver is merely a special instance of a Stream module.

As for all character device drivers, a Stream driver can have XXinit, XXopen, XXclose and XXpoll routines. The write interface to a Stream driver is through the driver's XXwput routine, which is called by the upstream module (or Stream head) to accept messages.

Stream drivers do not have an ordinary character device driver XXread interface. When data arrives on the device, the Stream driver's XXintr routine allocates a message to contain the data and then passes the message upstream by calling the upstream module's XXrput routine. The message eventually arrives at the Stream head, where it can be read by the user process. The STREAMS support software in the kernel protects itself from interrupts where necessary by making calls to spl5(K), so Stream drivers should not be configured to run at spl6(K) or higher.[1]

Ioctl(S) system calls pass down the Stream as messages of type M_IOCTL. Any ioctl(S) that is intended for the Stream driver will arrive via the Stream driver's XXwput routine, where the message type will identify it as an ioctl(S) message. The XXwput routine can either process the message itself or pass it to an optional, private XXioctl routine. Note that an XXioctl routine is not part of the kernel interface, and it should not be specified with the configure(ADM) command.

Finally, a Stream driver can have an XXpoll routine which behaves in the same way as for ordinary character drivers (but see the note regarding spl5(K) above). Note that the XXpoll routine is not related to the new poll(S) system call, described in Section 6.6.4.

6.3   Messages

A message is described by a triplet of data structures. The head of the triplet is a structure of type struct msgb, called a message block. The message block contains a pointer to a second structure of type struct datab, called a data block. The data block describes the message type and contains a pointer to a buffer containing the actual data. These structures are defined in ⟨sys/stream.h⟩:

```
/*
 * Message block descriptor
 */
struct    msgb {
      struct msgb    *b_next;        /* next message on
                                        queue */
      struct msgb    *b_prev;        /* previous message
                                        on queue */
      struct msgb    *b_cont;        /* next message
                                        block of message */
      unsigned char  *b_rptr;        /* first unread byte
                                        in buf */
      unsigned char  *b_wptr;        /* first unwritten
                                        byte in buf */
      struct datab   *b_datap;       /* data block */
};
typedef struct msgb mblk_t;
/*
 *  Data block descriptor
 */
```

```
struct datab {
    struct datab    *db_freep;    /* internal use only */
    unsigned char   *db_base;     /* first byte of buf */
    unsigned char   *db_lim;      /* last byte of buf + 1 */
    unsigned char   db_ref;       /* # messages pointing
                                     to this block */
    unsigned char   db_type;      /* message type */
    unsigned char   db_class;     /* internal use only */
};
typedef struct datab dblk_t;
```

Figure 6.3 shows a simple message of type M_DATA (see below), containing 32 bytes of data.

If a Stream module needs to extend a message beyond the original data buffer, either a new buffer of the correct size can be allocated or further message blocks describing the additional buffer space can be attached to the original message block. Whichever method the module chooses, the final messages are semantically identical. Figure 6.4 shows the same message after it has been extended by an additional eight bytes, using an additional message block attached to b_cont.

Messages awaiting processing are linked onto a message queue using additional pointers in the message block at the head of each message. Figure 6.5 shows two messages on a message queue.

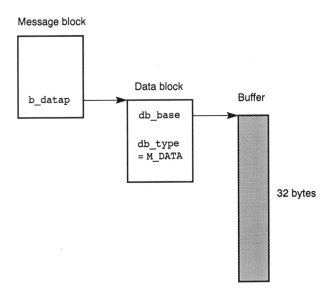

Figure 6.3 An M_DATA message of 32 bytes.

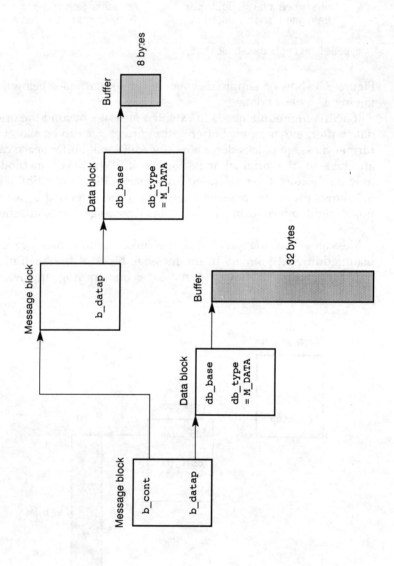

Figure 6.4 An M_DATA message of 40 bytes. The two components of the message are linked on b_cont.

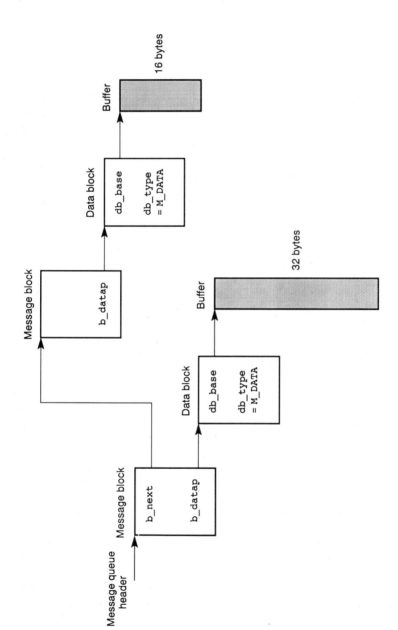

Figure 6.5 Two M_DATA messages on a message queue. The two messages are linked on b_next.

At present, there are 24 different message types supported, and these are divided into two classes called **ordinary messages** and **priority messages**.

6.3.1   Ordinary messages

Ordinary messages are subject to the regular flow control mechanisms of the Stream, as described in Section 6.5. They are linked onto a message queue on a FIFO basis, and receive no special priority processing. The ten different types of ordinary message are M_DATA, M_PROTO, M_BREAK, M_PASSFP, M_SIG, M_DELAY, M_CTL, M_IOCTL, M_SETOPTS and M_RSE. The most common types are M_DATA and M_IOCTL:

- M_DATA messages contain ordinary data. For example, a Stream head would use an M_DATA message to send data downstream from a write(S) system call.

- M_IOCTL messages are allocated by the Stream head in response to ioctl(S) system calls. See Section 6.6.5 below.

The remaining ordinary message types are described in Appendix B of *The AT&T STREAMS Programmer's Guide*.

6.3.2   Priority messages

Priority messages bypass the regular flow control mechanisms of the Stream, and are always placed at the front of a message queue, after any other priority messages that are already present. Figure 6.6 shows a message queue containing priority messages and ordinary messages.

The 14 different types of priority message are M_IOCACK, M_IOCNAK, M_PCPROTO, M_PCSIG, M_READ, M_FLUSH, M_STOP, M_START, M_HANGUP, M_ERROR, M_COPYIN, M_COPYOUT, M_IOCDATA and M_PCRSE. The most common types are M_IOCACK, M_IOCNAK, M_ERROR and M_FLUSH:

- M_IOCACK and M_IOCNAK messages are sent upstream to the Stream head in response to M_IOCTL messages, as described in Section 6.3.1 above.

  An M_IOCACK message indicates positive acknowledgement of a previous M_IOCTL message, and the Stream head will return a non-negative integer through the ioctl(S), as specified by the ioc_rval member of the struct iocblk (see Section 6.6.5).

  An M_IOCNAK message indicates failure of a previous M_IOCTL message, and the Stream head will return −1 through the ioctl(S).

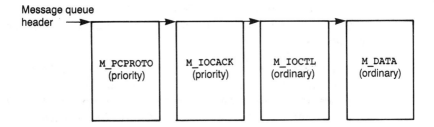

Figure 6.6 Priority and ordinary messages.

- M_ERROR messages are sent upstream to the Stream head to report error conditions from downstream, such as a hardware failure. When the Stream head receives an M_ERROR message, all subsequent system calls on the Stream will fail.

- M_FLUSH messages can originate at the Stream head or in any module or driver, and request that all recipients flush their message queues according to the flags specified in the first byte of the message (FLUSHR to flush the read queue, FLUSHW to flush the write queue, or FLUSHRW to flush both), and then pass the message to their neighbour.

  A message queue is flushed by discarding all of the messages that it contains, using the flushq routine.

  All modules and Stream drivers which queue messages must implement support for M_FLUSH messages, as described in Appendix B of *The AT&T STREAMS Programmer's Guide*.

The remaining priority message types are described in Appendix B of *The AT&T STREAMS Programmer's Guide*.

6.3.3 Message block allocation

Message blocks are allocated by a kernel routine called allocb():

```
mblk_t *
allocb(size, pri)
    int size, pri;
```

The allocb routine returns a pointer to a message block of type M_DATA, with a single data block describing a buffer of at least size bytes attached, or NULL if no message blocks are available. The pri parameter indicates the priority of the allocb request, and can

have one of three values BPRI_LO, BPRI_MED and BPRI_HI (see
⟨sys/stream.h⟩). The priority gives an indication of the urgency of the
request:

- A BPRI_LO priority request is normally used by a Stream head to
  allocate a message block to contain data from a write(S) or a
  putmsg(S) system call. The tunable kernel parameter STRLOFRAC[2]
  determines whether or not a request to allocate a BPRI_LO message
  will fail. If the number of message blocks already allocated is more
  than STRLOFRAC per cent of the total number of message blocks
  available of a particular size (called a class), allocb tries to allocate a
  message block from the next largest class. If this allocation also
  fails, allocb returns a NULL pointer. Section 6.7.3 describes what to
  do if allocb fails.

- A BPRI_MED priority request is the most common request, and is
  used for general purpose messages. For example, a Stream driver's
  XXintr routine would allocate message blocks at BPRI_MED to contain data arriving from a device, before sending the message
  upstream. The tunable kernel parameter STRMEDFRAC[3] determines
  success or failure in the same way as for BPRI_LO messages.

- A BPRI_HI priority is used for urgent control messages such as
  sending an M_ERROR message upstream when the Stream driver
  detects hardware failure. Providing that a message block is available, calls to allocb will always succeed.

The interaction of message priorities and the tunable thresholds tries
to ensure that message buffers are always available for BPRI_HI
requests.

Figure 6.7 shows the result of a call to allocb(32, BPRI_MED).

Once the buffer has been allocated, the module should copy data
into mp->b_rptr, and adjust mp->b_wptr by the number of bytes
copied:

```
if ((mp = allocb(sizeof(buf), BPRI_MED) == NULL) {
    cmn_err(CE_WARN, "Couldn't allocb(%d, BPRI_MED)",
            sizeof(buf));
    return;
}
bcopy(&buf, mp->b_rptr, sizeof(buf));
mp->b_wptr += sizeof(buf);
```

Figure 6.8 shows the data buffer at the end of this operation.

The tunable resources NBLK4 through NBLK4096 determine the number of message blocks, data blocks and buffers in each class. The

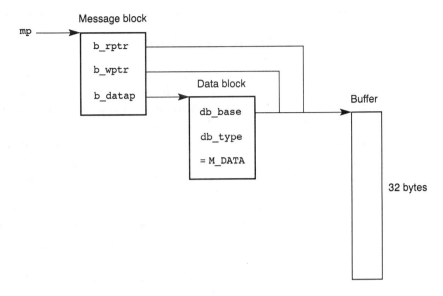

Figure 6.7   The result of calling allocb(32, BPRI_MED).

strstat option of the crash(ADM) utility reports how many buffers of each size are allocated. The column headed FAIL indicates how many times allocb has had to allocate a buffer from the next largest class, and is an indication that STREAMS may need retuning.

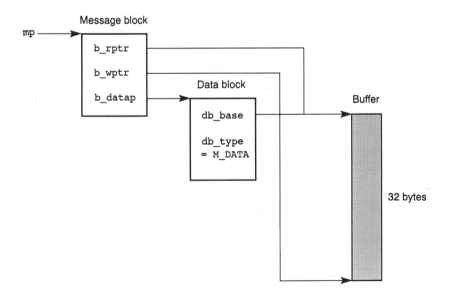

Figure 6.8   After copying 32 bytes and adjusting b_wptr.

6.4   QUEUEs and the kernel interface

Each Stream module (including the Stream head and the Stream driver) consists of two QUEUEs which are responsible for processing the downstream and upstream messages that pass through a module. A QUEUE has four principal components:

- One or more routines to process the messages. A QUEUE must have at least an XXput routine that can be called to accept messages from other modules. It may also have an XXservice routine to carry out some or all of the message processing.

  Additional, private routines can also be provided for local use by the XXput and XXservice routines. For example, an XXioctl routine.

- A set of QUEUE attributes, including high and low water marks for the message queue.

- A message queue, containing the messages that are waiting to be processed by the QUEUE.

- Private data, used to manage the state of the module and the QUEUE. For example, a state transition look-up table.

6.4.1   The QUEUE structure

A QUEUE is defined by a struct queue (see ⟨sys/stream.h⟩):

```
/*
 * The QUEUE structure
 */
struct    queue {
      struct qinit    *q_qinfo; /* routines and limits
                                      for QUEUE */
      struct msgb     *q_first; /* head of message queue */
      struct msgb     *q_last;  /* tail of message queue */
      struct queue    *q_next;  /* next QUEUE in Stream */
      struct queue    *q_link;  /* to next QUEUE (for
                                      scheduling) */
      caddr_t   q_ptr;       /* to private data structure */
      ushort    q_count;     /* number of blocks on QUEUE */
      ushort    q_flag;      /* QUEUE state */
      short     q_minpsz;    /* min packet size
                                 accepted by this module */
      short     q_maxpsz;    /* max packet size
                                 accepted by this module */
      ushort    q_hiwat;     /* message queue high water mark */
      ushort    q_lowat;     /* message queue low water mark */
};
typedef struct queue queue_t;
```

Each module (including the Stream head and the Stream driver) has two QUEUES allocated automatically when the module is first opened.[4]

6.4.2 The kernel interface

The kernel interface to a Stream module (and therefore a Stream driver) is via the routines described by the struct qinit *q_info member of each QUEUE. A struct qinit defines the XXput, XXservice, XXopen, XXclose and XXadmin routines for the QUEUE, and also holds pointers to a struct module_info and an optional struct module_stat:

```
/*
 * QUEUE information structure
 */
struct    qinit {
      int  (*qi_putp)();          /* XXput() routine */
      int  (*qi_srvp)();          /* XXservice() routine */
      int  (*qi_qopen)();         /* XXopen() routine */
      int  (*qi_qclose)();        /* XXclose() routine */
      int  (*qi_qadmin)();        /* for ATT 3bnet only */
      struct module_info *qi_minfo; /* module information
                                       structure */
      struct module_stat *qi_mstat; /* module statistics
                                       structure */
};
/*
 * module information structure
 */
struct module_info {
      ushort    mi_idnum;      /* module id number */
      char      *mi_idname;    /* module name */
      short     mi_minpsz;     /* min packet size accepted */
      short     mi_maxpsz;     /* max packet size accepted */
      ushort    mi_hiwat;      /* hi-water mark */
      ushort    mi_lowat;      /* lo-water mark */
};
struct module_stat {
      long      ms_pcnt;       /* counts calls to XXput() */
      long      ms_scnt;       /* counts calls to
                                  XXservice() */
      long      ms_ocnt;       /* counts calls to XXopen() */
      long      ms_ccnt;       /* counts calls to XXclose() */
      long      ms_acnt;       /* counts calls to XXadmin() */
      char      *ms_xptr;      /* private statistics buffer */
      short     ms_xsize;      /* length of private
                                  statistics buffer */
};
```

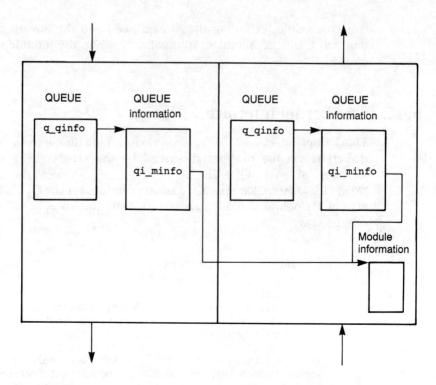

Figure 6.9   A Stream module has two QUEUEs.

Figure 6.9 shows a typical Stream module with two QUEUEs. Note that the two QUEUEs share the same module information structure, and also the absence of a module statistics structure.

Figure 6.10 shows the same Stream module with some messages attached to each of the QUEUEs.

The XXput routine

A QUEUE's XXput routine is always required, and is called via the putnext macro by another module's QUEUE (or the Stream head or Stream driver) to receive a message for processing:

```
XXput(q, mp)
    queue_t *q;
    mblk_t *mp;
```

The q parameter identifies the appropriate read or write QUEUE, and mp points to the message. Any immediate processing that is required should be performed by the XXput routine. In general, all priority

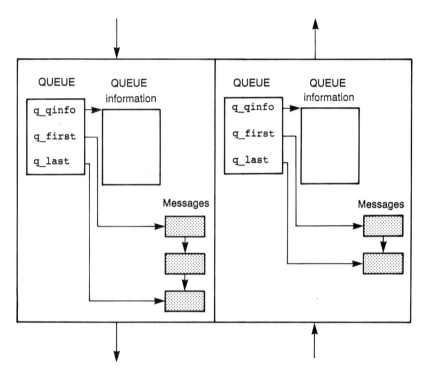

Figure 6.10 Message queues attached to module QUEUEs.

messages (see Section 6.3 above) should be processed immediately by XXput, and/or passed on to the next module. Ordinary messages can also be processed by XXput, although the module designer can provide an XXservice routine so that processing can be deferred. After processing the message, both the XXput and XXservice routines should use putnext to pass the message to the adjacent module's XXput routine.

Therefore, depending on the design of each of the modules in a Stream, a message can flow all the way from the Stream head to the Stream driver (and vice versa) as an atomic operation. Figure 6.11 shows a message flowing downstream to a Stream driver via XXput routines.

There may be times when an XXput routine cannot immediately process the message. For example, a Stream driver's XXput routine may have to wait until a device's output buffer empties before it is able to transmit any more data. A Stream head may be receiving data from downstream, but there may not be any user processes making read(S) system calls. In both of these cases, it is clear that the

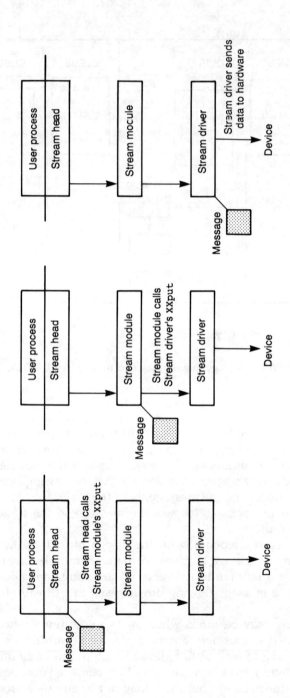

Figure 6.11   A message flowing downstream.

messages must be queued in some way and the actual processing of the message must be deferred until later.

If the XXput routine is unable to process the message, it should call the putq routine to add the message to the QUEUE's own message queue. The putq routine also enables the corresponding QUEUE by adding it to the end of the STREAMS scheduling queue (see Section 6.5 below). After a short period, the STREAMS scheduler will call the QUEUE's XXservice routine to complete the processing.

The XXput routine should return as soon as putq returns.

The XXservice routine

The XXservice routine is responsible for the deferred processing of messages. An XXservice routine is not mandatory, and the module designer (or device driver writer) should determine whether to provide an XXservice routine or not. Generally, if it is likely that XXput may not be able either to start or to complete the processing of a message, an XXservice routine must be provided.

When a QUEUE is enabled as described above, the STREAMS scheduler will call the QUEUE's XXservice routine at the next convenient opportunity:

```
XXservice(q)
    queue_t *q;
```

The q parameter identifies the appropriate read or write QUEUE. The XXservice routine should retrieve the first message from the message queue using the getq routine, process the message and then pass it on to the next module, using putnext. XXservice should repeat these steps until either the queue is empty, or flow control prevents any more messages being passed to the next module.

It is important to note that XXput and XXservice routines do not always run in a valid user context. This is a side-effect of the STREAMS scheduling mechanism, and means that the same care must be taken as when writing interrupt routines:

- Never access any context-related data, such as the U-area, or any part of the user's address space.
- Never go to sleep(K) inside an XXput or XXservice routine.
- Always return to the caller.

Flow control is discussed in Section 6.5 below.

The STREAMS loopback driver in Section 6.10 includes an XXservice routine.

The XXopen routine

The XXopen routine is called on every open(S) system call on the Stream, and also on each push of a Stream module:

```
XXopen(q, dev, flag, sflag)
    queue_t *q;
    dev_t dev;
    int flag, sflag;
```

The q parameter always points to the module's read QUEUE. The dev and flag parameters are the same as for ordinary driver XXopen calls – they contain the major and minor device numbers and a value from ⟨sys/file.h⟩. If this is an XXopen request on a module, dev and flag are both zero. The sflag parameter is the Stream open flag, and has one of three values from ⟨sys/stream.h⟩:

- MODOPEN indicates that this is a normal Stream module open request.

- 0 indicates that this is a normal Stream driver open request.

- CLONEOPEN indicates that this is a clone driver open request (see Section 6.7.1).

Modules should return OPENFAIL if the open request does not complete successfully.

The STREAMS loopback driver in Section 6.10 includes an XXopen routine.

The XXclose routine

The XXclose routine is called on the last close(S) system call on the Stream, and also on each pop of a Stream module:

```
XXclose(q, flag)
    queue_t *q;
    int flag;
```

The flag parameter is the same as for ordinary driver XXclose calls, unless this is an XXclose request on a module, when it will be zero.

The STREAMS loopback driver in Section 6.10 includes an XXclose routine.

The XXadmin routine

The XXadmin routine is used only on the AT&T 3b2 computer. It is not used by SCO UNIX.

The module info structure

The module_info structure contains module identification information and values used by the flow control mechanism which will be discussed in Section 6.5. The two QUEUEs within a Stream module (or a Stream driver) share the same module information structure.

The module ID is used by the STREAMS logging and tracing subsystems, which are described in Section 6.8. The module ID should be unique, although this is not necessary for the correct operation of the module.

The module name is not used currently, but it is recommended that it should be the same as the prefix used for the streamtab structure (see Section 6.4.3).

The minimum and maximum packet sizes limit the size of each message (measured in bytes) passed to the module. These limits are advisory except for the Stream head, which observes the limits of the write QUEUE of the adjacent downstream module. The use of these limits is developer-dependent in all other modules. The value INFPSZ, defined in ⟨sys/stream.h⟩, indicates that there is no limit.

The high and low water marks are used to implement flow control, described in Section 6.5, and represent the total amount of space, measured in bytes, consumed by all of the messages in a message queue.

The module stat structure

The module_stat structure is optional, and is not used at present by the SCO UNIX kernel. In the future, it will be used to gather Stream statistics about the module, possibly including message service time.

6.4.3 The streamtab structure

A module's two qinit structures are described by the module's struct streamtab:

```
/*
 * Streamtab (used in cdevsw and fmodsw to point to module
 * or driver)
 */
struct streamtab {
    struct qinit   *st_rdinit;      /* read QUEUE */
    struct qinit   *st_wrinit;      /* write QUEUE */
    struct qinit   *st_muxrinit;    /* mux read QUEUE */
    struct qinit   *st_muxwinit;    /* mux write QUEUE */
};
```

The elements describe the upstream and downstream QUEUEs of a module, as described in Section 6.4.1 above. The structure should be declared in the Stream module or Stream driver as follows:

```
static struct qinit XXrinit = { ... };
static struct qinit XXwinit = { ... };
struct streamtab XXinfo = {
        &XXrinit,
        &XXwinit,
        NULL,
        NULL
};
```

Depending on whether the streamtab structure is describing a Stream driver or a module, it will be pointed to by either the d_str field of the cdevsw table or the f_str field of the fmodsw table (see ⟨sys/conf.h⟩). These tables are set up from information provided to the configure(ADM) command when the module or Stream driver is added to the kernel (see Section 6.9), and are used to access the module. For example, if a user process opens a character device that has an entry in the d_str field of cdevsw, the kernel recognizes the device as a Stream driver and calls the XXopen routine specified in the upstream qinit structure. It does not call the XXopen routine from the cdevsw. The operation of the open(S) system call is described in more detail in Section 6.6.1.

The st_muxrinit and st_muxwinit fields are described in Section 6.7.

6.5   Flow control and STREAMS scheduling

When an XXput routine decides to defer the processing of messages to an XXservice routine, a mechanism is required to ensure that the XXservice routine is called at an appropriate point in the future. It is also necessary to ensure that an XXput routine cannot overwhelm an XXservice routine with too many messages to process. In this section, we shall describe the STREAMS mechanisms that satisfy these two requirements.

6.5.1 Flow control

Flow control is necessary in STREAMS to ensure that the pool of message blocks managed by allocb and freeb does not empty, and also to ensure that XXservice routines do not become overwhelmed with too many messages to process and therefore consume too much CPU resource. It should be noted that flow control is applied only to ordinary messages, as described in Section 6.3.1 above. Flow control does not apply to priority messages.

We have already seen that allocb allocates message blocks according to a priority BPRI_LO, BPRI_MED and BPRI_HI, and under certain circumstances may fail. In addition, a Stream head always asks for BPRI_LO message blocks in response to write(S) system calls, so that when resources are low it will be one of the first modules to block, waiting for a message block to become available (see Section 6.7.3 below). A desirable side-effect of this is that output on a Stream happens at a lower priority than input.

An additional advisory flow control mechanism limits the amount of processing that XXservice routines are allowed to do when they are invoked by the STREAMS scheduler. Advisory flow control should be applied only to ordinary messages, as described in Section 6.3.1. Priority messages, identified by the following test, are not subject to flow control:

```
if (mp->b_datap->db_type > QPCTL) {
```

An XXservice routine should use the canput routine to determine if there is sufficient space in the next message queue to contain another message. The parameter passed to canput should identify the QUEUE to be examined (for example, q->q_next):

```
canput(q)
    queue_t *q;
```

If the total amount of space being consumed by the next message queue is greater than the high water mark defined for that module, canput returns 0. If there is sufficient space to receive another message, canput returns 1.

Whenever canput returns 0, XXservice should use the putbq routine to put the message back onto its own message queue, and return. In addition, the STREAMS scheduler blocks the XXservice routine from further execution, and will not reschedule it again until the next message queue drops beneath its low water mark. As soon as the next message queue does drop beneath its low water mark, the STREAMS scheduler will automatically reschedule the blocked QUEUE. This automatic rescheduling is called back-enabling.

An XXservice routine should process all of its messages whenever it is invoked by the STREAMS scheduler, unless it is blocked by flow control:

```
while ((mp = getq(q)) != NULL) {
    if (mp is a priority message || canput(q->q_next)) {
        process message;
        putnext(q, message);
    } else {
        putbq(q, message);
    }
}
```

6.5.2 STREAMS scheduling

STREAMS scheduling ensures that CPU resource is allocated to QUEUEs whose XXput routines have deferred message processing to the corresponding XXservice routine. This happens either when an XXput routine or an XXservice routine cannot putnext a message onto the adjacent QUEUE because of constraints imposed by flow control (see above). The provision of an XXservice routine is at the module developer's discretion, and there are no definite rules about when to use them. However, an XXservice routine should be used when there are other, more time-sensitive activities elsewhere in the system, such as lower priority interrupt handling. Without XXservice routines, messages would flow downstream all the way from the Stream head to the Stream driver at task-time (not necessarily a great inconvenience), but more importantly, all the way upstream from the Stream driver to the Stream head at interrupt-time (potentially very inconvenient). The use of XXservice routines also permits full use of STREAMS flow control including automatic back-enabling of QUEUEs.

An XXput routine can defer processing to the appropriate XXservice routine by using the putq routine to add the current message to the QUEUE's message queue:

```
putq(q, mp)
    queue_t *q;
    mblk_t *mp;
```

The call to putq causes the appropriate XXservice routine to be scheduled for execution by the STREAMS scheduler at the next convenient opportunity.

The implementation of STREAMS scheduling varies between different versions of UNIX. On SCO UNIX, the QUEUE is added to the end of a linked list of other QUEUEs requiring CPU resource, using the q_link field of the QUEUE structure, and the STREAMS scheduling flag, extern int qrunflag, is set.

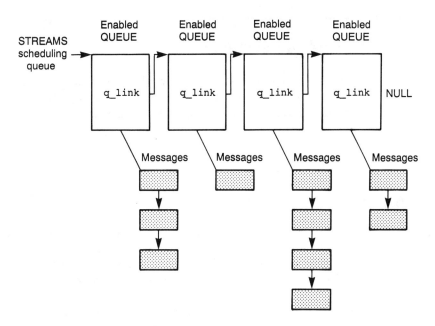

Figure 6.12   The STREAMS scheduling queue.

This flag is examined at least once during every STREAMS-related system call, at interrupt-time whenever a QUEUE is enabled, and also each time the kernel enters the idle loop. If it is set, the kernel calls runqueues to execute the XXservice routine of each of the scheduled QUEUEs:

- The QUEUE is unlinked from q_link.
- The QENAB bit is cleared from q_flag.
- The XXservice routine is called at spl1(K).

Finally, qrunflag is cleared. Figure 6.12 shows a typical state of the scheduling queue.

Remember that STREAMS can automatically back-enable a QUEUE, which causes the QUEUE to be added to the end of the scheduling queue in a similar way to how putq operates.

If you are planning to write XXput and XXservice routines, it is worth including a final reminder about the potential pitfalls (repeated from Section 6.4.2):

- Never access any context-related data, such as the U-area, or any part of the user's address space.
- Never go to sleep(K) inside an XXput or an XXservice routine.
- Always return to the caller.

6.6   STREAMS system calls

In this section, we shall explain the operation of the open(S), close(S), read(S), write(S), getmsg(S), putmsg(S), poll(S) and ioctl(S) system calls with respect to STREAMS.

6.6.1   Open(S), close(S)

When a Stream is opened with the open(S) system call, the kernel recognizes that it should open a Stream because the d_str field in the appropriate cdevsw entry will have a non-NULL value, and will be pointing to a streamtab structure, described in Section 6.4.3 above.

On the first open(S) of the Stream, the kernel calls stropen to allocate a struct stdata[5] for the Stream head (see ⟨sys/stream.h⟩), and then to attach and initialize two QUEUEs. The downstream QUEUE does not have a XXwput routine, but does have an XXservice routine called strwsrv. The upstream QUEUE has an XXrput routine called strrput, but does not have an XXservice routine.

The kernel then calls qattach to attach the Stream driver to the Stream head, passing the pointer to the streamtab structure obtained from the cdevsw entry. The qattach routine allocates a pair of QUEUEs from the NQUEUE resource, attaches each queue to its respective upstream QUEUE in the Stream head (via the q_next pointers), initializes each QUEUE from the streamtab, and finally calls the Stream driver's XXopen routine, as specified in the upstream qinit structure. Figure 6.13 shows the result of an open(S) system call on a device called exst.

If this is not the first open(S) on the Stream, the kernel only calls the XXopen routines of each of the Stream modules and the Stream driver.

On the last close(S) of a Stream, the kernel calls strclose to dismantle the Stream. The strclose routine works downstream towards the Stream driver, closing each module. If the file's O_NDELAY bit is not set, strclose waits for 15 seconds to allow the module's messages to drain, before calling qdetach for the module. The qdetach routine calls the module's XXclose routine, frees each of the module's messages, pops the module from the Stream, and then frees the QUEUEs.

Finally, strclose frees the QUEUEs from the Stream head, and then returns the Stream head itself to the NSTREAM resource.

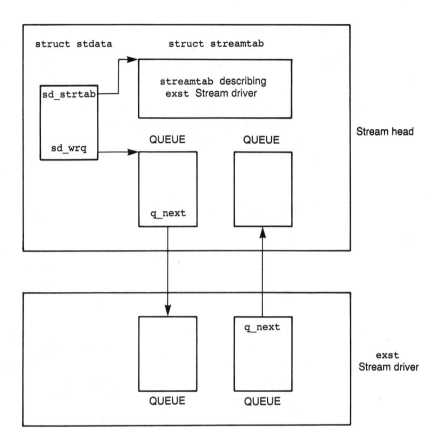

Figure 6.13   The open(S) system call attaches the Stream driver to the Stream head.

6.6.2 Read(S), write(S)

The read(S), write(S), getmsg(S) and putmsg(S) system calls should be used to receive or send messages between a user process and the Stream head. The read(S) and write(S) system calls are byte-stream oriented, so they can transfer only M_DATA messages, and have no regard for message boundaries (the separation between one message and the next).

The read(S) system call moves data from the Stream head into user space. The kernel calls the routine strread which attempts to satisfy the u.u_count request by reading one or more messages from the Stream head's upstream QUEUE message queue, attached to q_first. Messages arrive from downstream via the Stream head's strrput routine.

For M_DATA messages, strread moves data from the buffer starting at address b_rptr, as shown in Figure 6.8, and calls freeb to free up any message blocks that become available. Strread then examines the remaining messages on the message queue, looking for M_SIG messages. If a SIGPOLL is found (that is, *b_rptr == SIGPOLL), the kernel calls strsendsig to send a SIGPOLL to the user process (see Section 6.6.4 below). All other signals are posted to the process group. Any M_SIG messages are freed by freeb.

Message types other than M_DATA are not readable by the read(S) system call, and are returned to the message queue with putbq. They cause EBADMSG to be returned.

Note that the read(S) system call does not invoke any routines in the Stream driver, unlike a read(S) system call on an ordinary character device.

The write(S) system call copies data from user space into the kernel, builds a message and sends the message downstream. The kernel calls the routine strwrite, which first calls canput to ensure that there is sufficient space downstream for the new message. If canput indicates that space isn't available, strwrite will sleep(K). When the Stream head is next back-enabled, strwsrv will wakeup(K) the sleeping strwrite,[6] which can then continue to process the write(S) system call.

Strwrite calls strmakemsg to allocate a message buffer of type M_DATA, and to copy the data from user space into the buffer.

Finally, strwrite uses putnext to send the message downstream, and then returns.

6.6.3 Getmsg(S), putmsg(S)

We have already explained that the read(S) and write(S) system calls are byte-stream oriented, and have no regard for message boundaries. If an implementation wants to define and use its own control messages and preserve message boundaries, it should use getmsg(S) and putmsg(S), which recognize non-M_DATA message types. A non-M_DATA message type can be M_PROTO, M_PCPROTO or user-defined.

The getmsg(S) system call retrieves the next message from the Stream head:

```
getmsg(fd, ctlptr, dataptr, flags)
     int fd, *flags;
     struct strbuf *ctlptr;
     struct strbuf *dataptr;
```

The ctlptr and dataptr parameters each describe a strbuf structure, which will contain the control and data parts of the received message respectively:

```
struct strbuf {
        int   maxlen;        /* maximum buf length */
        int   len;           /* actual number of bytes */
        char  *buf;          /* buffer */
}
```

The kernel calls the strgetmsg routine in response to the getmsg(S) system call. Strgetmsg copies the non-M_DATA part of the message from the Stream head into the buffer described by ctlptr, and copies the M_DATA part into dataptr. Note that a message need contain only one of these components, so the user process should check the contents of both strbuf structures to determine what has been received. Figure 6.14 shows an M_PROTO message being returned to a user process.

The putmsg(S) system call works in a similar way:

```
putmsg(fd, ctlptr, dataptr, flags)
        int fd, *flags;
        struct strbuf *ctlptr;
        struct strbuf *dataptr;
```

The kernel routine strputmsg calls strmakemsg to construct a control message from the data described by ctlptr and dataptr, then uses putnext to send the message downstream.

For further details of these two system calls, please refer to the *SCO UNIX Programmer's Reference Manual*, Volume 2.

6.6.4 Poll(S)

The poll(S) system call provides the user with a mechanism to monitor activity on a number of STREAMs simultaneously. For each Stream (file descriptor) of interest, the user can specify that he wants to be notified of a variety of different events, described in ⟨sys/poll.h⟩:

- If the user specifies POLLIN, poll(S) will return as soon as data arrives on the appropriate file descriptor (or immediately, if data is already available).

- If the user specifies POLLPRI, poll(S) will return as soon as a priority message arrives on the appropriate file descriptor (or immediately, if a priority message is already present).

- If the user specifies POLLOUT, poll(S) will return as soon as the STREAMs flow control mechanism back-enables the first down-stream QUEUE (or immediately, if the QUEUE is already enabled).

These events can be OR'd together.

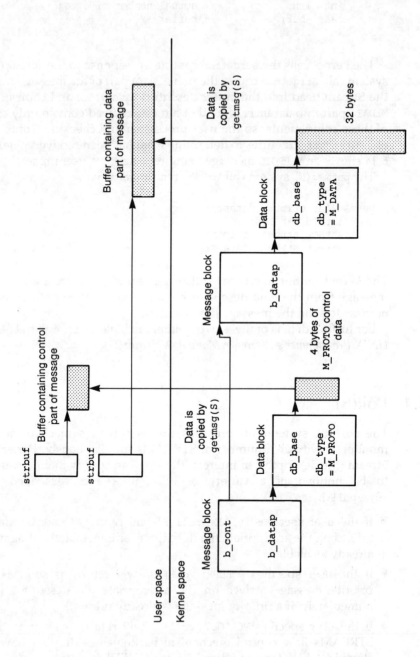

Figure 6.14   An M_PROTO message being received by getmsg(S).

The poll(S) system call takes three arguments:

```
poll(fds, nfds, timeout)
    struct pollfd fds[];
    unsigned long nfds;
    int timeout;
```

The file descriptors and the events of interest (POLLIN, POLLOUT and POLLPRI) are specified in an array of pollfd structures:

```
struct pollfd {
    int fd;              /* fd of Stream */
    short events;        /* events requested */
    short revents;       /* events returned */
}
```

The revents field contains a description of what actually happened on the corresponding file descriptor. As well as containing the events described above, it can also contain the following:

- POLLERR indicates that a priority M_ERROR message has arrived at the Stream head.

- POLLHUP indicates that a priority M_HANGUP message has arrived at the Stream head.

- POLLNVAL indicates that the corresponding file descriptor does not describe an open Stream.

The timeout argument specifies how long the poll(S) system call should wait, in milliseconds,[7] before returning if none of the requested events occurs. The caller should specify −1 to make poll(S) block indefinitely, until one of the requested events occurs.

The poll(S) system call as described allows for synchronous I/O over a Stream. If the user process prefers (or needs) to do asynchronous I/O, the poll(S) system call should be used in conjunction with the SIGPOLL signal. The process should use the I_SETSIG ioctl(S) system call (see Section 6.6.5 below) to indicate that a SIGPOLL should be sent when one of the following events occurs on a Stream. Inside the signal handler, the process must make a poll(S) system call to determine what to do next:

- If the user process requests S_INPUT, it will receive a SIGPOLL as soon as a message arrives at the Stream head, providing that a message was not already present.

- If the user process specifies S_HIPRI, it will receive a SIGPOLL as soon as a priority message arrives at the Stream head.

- If the user process specifies S_OUTPUT, it will receive a SIGPOLL as soon as the first downstream QUEUE is back-enabled.

- If the user process specifies S_MSG, it will receive a SIGPOLL as soon as either an M_SIG or an M_PCSIG message containing a SIGPOLL signal arrives at the Stream head.

If you are planning to implement asynchronous I/O, remember that System V signals are inherently unreliable. Under certain circumstances, your process is liable to be killed by the kernel if it receives another SIGPOLL signal before it has restored the signal handler. We recommend that you use reliable POSIX signals, as described by the sigaction(S), sigprocmask(S) and sigsuspend(S) manual pages in the *SCO UNIX Programmer's Reference Manual*, Volume 2.

6.6.5   Ioctl(S)

The user's ioctl(S) interface follows the same mechanism as all other ioctl(S) system calls:

```
ioctl(fd, command, arg)
    int fd, command;
    char *arg;
```

The full list of STREAMS ioctl(S) requests, giving the possible values for the command parameter, is described in the STREAMIO(M) manual page.

In order to send an ordinary ioctl(S) request downstream to either a module or the Stream driver, the user should make an I_STR ioctl(S) request, using the arg parameter to pass any data. There are some examples in Section 6.10. In response to an I_STR request, the Stream head constructs an M_IOCTL message, consisting of an iocblk structure describing the ioctl(S) request and zero or more M_DATA message blocks containing any ioctl(S) data:

```
#include ⟨sys/stream.h⟩
struct iocblk {
        int     ioc_cmd;      /* ioctl(S) request */
        ushort  ioc_uid;      /* effective user ID */
        ushort  ioc_gid;      /* effective group ID */
        uint    ioc_id;       /* ioctl ID, generated by
                                 Stream head */
        uint    ioc_count;    /* number of bytes in
                                 M_DATA buffer */
        int     ioc_error;    /* error code from
                                 downstream */
        int     ioc_rval;     /* return value from
                                 downstream */
}
```

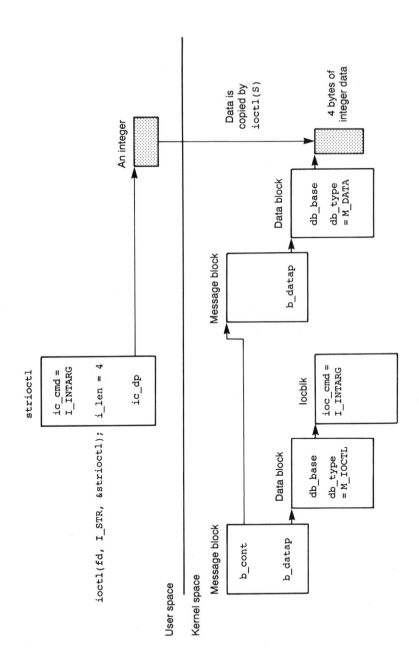

Figure 6.15   A user-defined I_INTARG ioctl(S) request at the Stream head.

Figure 6.15 shows a user-defined I_INTARG ioctl(S) request and the corresponding M_IOCTL message (see Section 6.10). The Stream head then sends the M_IOCTL message downstream. Modules which don't recognize ioc_cmd should putnext the message to the adjacent module. Eventually, an XXwput routine in one of the modules (or the Stream driver) will recognize ioc_cmd, and either deal with it locally or dispatch it to a private XXioctl routine, thus preserving the familiar structure of character device drivers.

If the M_IOCTL message is processed successfully, the Stream driver should respond with an M_IOCACK message, by changing the original message type to M_IOCACK and then calling qreply to send the message back upstream to the Stream head:

```
qreply(q, mp)
     queue_t *q;
     mblk_t *mp;
```

Any data that either a module or a Stream driver wants to return to the user process in response to the ioctl(S) request should be stored in M_DATA message blocks and then attached to the original iocblk message block. The module should set ioc_count to be the number of bytes being returned.

The Stream head waits for the M_IOCACK response, and compares the ioc_id received from downstream with the ioc_id from the original ioctl(S) request. If the two values don't match, the response is discarded.

A Stream driver should respond to unrecognized M_IOCTL messages by calling qreply to send an M_IOCNAK message to the Stream head.

Finally, if a response is not received within the interval specified by the original ioctl(S) request (see STREAMIO(M)), the Stream head will time out and the ioctl(S) will fail with ETIME.

6.7   Advanced topics

6.7.1   Cloning

STREAMS includes a special pseudo-driver, called clone. The clone driver provides a convenient way for a user process to open a Stream device without having to specify the minor device number. This mechanism can be useful for network applications which must establish their own Stream connection to a Stream driver (for example, /dev/e3A0 is the Stream driver for the 3COM 3C501 Etherlink card) and do not need to be concerned about which minor devices are actually available.

A clone device is associated with the target Stream driver as follows:

- The major device number corresponds to the clone driver. This is major device 40 in SCO UNIX 3.2v4.

- The minor device number corresponds to the target Stream driver.

For example, if the major device number of the 3COM 3C501 device is 36, and the device driver supports cloning (see below), the following two entries in /dev are equivalent:

```
crw-rw-rw- 1 root other 36, 0  Dec 27 1992 /dev/e3A0
crw-rw-rw- 1 root other 40, 36 Dec 27 1992 /dev/e3A0
```

The first entry specifies minor device 0. This may already have been open(S)ed by somebody else, which means that the user should then try to open(S) the next minor device, and so on, until the open(S) completes successfully.

The second entry open(S)s the clone device, which examines the minor device number, establishes the corresponding entry in cdevsw, and then calls that driver's XXopen routine with sflag set to CLONEOPEN (see Section 6.4.2). The driver should respond by examining an internal table of available minor device numbers, pick one that isn't already allocated, and then return that minor device number to the clone driver.

The clone driver completes the open(S) call by allocating a new inode to record the final major and minor device numbers. Note that this inode has no name associated with it in the filesystem.

Therefore, the user's first open(S) system call always completes successfully, whether or not any minor devices are already open.[8]

There are some additional points to note:

- It is up to the driver designer to decide whether to implement cloning. The example Stream driver provided in Section 6.10 illustrates how an XXopen should respond to CLONEOPEN in sflag.

- The driver designer should document his decision so that application developers know how to implement their open(S) system calls.

- The driver designer should ensure that the installation procedure for his Stream driver creates the appropriate entry (entries) in /dev.

6.7.2 Multiplexing

Until now, we have limited our discussions to linear STREAMS connections, where each Stream module is linked to only one upstream
module (or the Stream head) and only one downstream module (or
the Stream driver).

STREAMS also allows for multiplexed connections between modules, so that there can be a many-to-many relationship between the
connections above and below a module. A Stream module configured
in such a way is called a STREAMS multiplexor. The two fundamental
multiplexor types are called **1-to-M** (or **lower**) and **N-to-1** (or **upper**)
multiplexors, and are illustrated in Figure 6.16. Figure 6.2 showed a
high-level representation of an implementation of TCP/IP, with a
choice of either Ethernet or Token Ring network drivers. In this
scenario, the IP module is an example of a lower STREAMS multiplexor.

In the next two sections, we shall explain how a process should
construct and subsequently dismantle such a configuration.

Constructing a multiplexor

The connection of each of the modules is done by a reasonably
complex combination of open(S) and I_LINK ioctl(S) system calls. In
order that the actual users of the implementation (for example,
ftp(TC), rlogin(TC)) should not have to concern themselves with the
mechanisms required to connect the components together, this
responsibility is offloaded to a daemon process. This daemon process
constructs the multiplexor and then keeps the Stream open for other
processes to use.

STREAMS does not allow ioctl(S) requests to pass through a
multiplexed module – they must be sent directly to the required
module or driver. For this reason, any multi-level multiplexing configuration, such as those illustrated in Figure 6.16, must be built from
the bottom up. The basic algorithm for the daemon process is therefore:

```
open(S) the Ethernet driver;
open(S) the IP module;
I_LINK the Ethernet driver to the bottom of IP;
open(S) the Token Ring driver;
I_LINK the Token Ring driver to the bottom of IP;
open(S) the TCP module;
I_LINK the IP module to the bottom of TCP;
close(S) the Ethernet driver, Token Ring driver, and
  IP module;
pause(S), to hold multiplexor open forever.
```

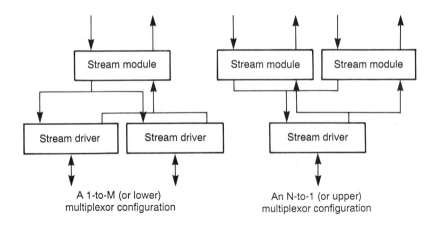

A 1-to-M (or lower)
multiplexor configuration

An N-to-1 (or upper)
multiplexor configuration

Figure 6.16   1-to-M and N-to-1 Stream multiplexors.

Note that the controlling Stream head is connected to the TCP module, so we can close the Ethernet driver, Token Ring driver and IP modules without breaking the multiplexor.

The basic source code for the daemon is as follows:

```
#include ⟨fcntl.h⟩
#include ⟨sys/stropts.h⟩
main()
{
    int efd, tfd, ipfd, tcpfd;
    /*
     * Make this process a daemon, and disconnect it
     * from its process group.
     */
    switch (fork()) {
        case 0:       /* child - continue */
                      break;

        case -1:      perror("fork failed");
                      exit(1);

        default:      /* parent - exit */
                      exit(0);
    }
    /*
     * Set a new process group so that pause(S) will
     * not receive any signals sent to our old process
     * group.
     */
    setpgrp();
```

```
        if ((efd = open("/dev/ethernet", O_RDWR)) == -1) {
            perror("couldn't open /dev/ethernet");
            exit(1);
        }
        if ((ipfd = open("/dev/ip", O_RDWR)) == -1) {
            perror("couldn't open /dev/ip");
            exit(1);
        }
        /*
         * Now link Ethernet to bottom of IP
         */
        if (ioctl(ipfd, I_LINK, efd) == -1) {
            perror("couldn't I_LINK Ethernet to IP");
            exit(1);
        }
        if ((tfd = open("/dev/token", O_RDWR)) == -1) {
            perror("couldn't open /dev/token");
            exit(1);
        }
        if (ioctl(ipfd, I_LINK, tfd) == -1) {
            perror("couldn't I_LINK Token Ring to IP");
            exit(1);
        }
        if ((tcpfd = open("/dev/tcp", O_RDWR)) == -1) {
            perror("couldn't open /dev/tcp");
            exit(1);
        }
        if (ioctl(tcpfd, I_LINK, ipfd) == -1) {
            perror("couldn't I_LINK IP to TCP");
            exit(1);
        }
        close(efd);
        close(tfd);
        close(ipfd);
        pause();                    /* wait forever */
    }
```

Now that the multiplexor has been built by the daemon, all other applications can establish their own connections to TCP by making an open(S) system call on /dev/tcp.

In SCO's TCP/IP, the daemon that builds a TCP/IP multiplexor similar to the one described here is called slink(ADMN), which is started up at run level 2. The slink(ADMN) daemon parses the file /etc/strcf to find a list of Stream modules to I_LINK together.

Dismantling a multiplexor

The kernel will automatically dismantle the multiplexor when the last close(S) is received on the controlling Stream head, which is owned by our daemon process. Thus, when the daemon process receives a signal and exits, the multiplexor will automatically be dismantled.

A multiplexor can be explicitly dismantled by I_UNLINK ioctl(S) calls, which pass the multiplexor ID returned by the corresponding I_LINK call. If our daemon process wanted to dismantle the multiplexor for itself, it would have to save the multiplexor IDs from the I_LINK calls, and then install a signal handler to pass them to the appropriate I_UNLINK calls:

```
if ((iemuxid = ioctl(ipfd, I_LINK, efd)) == -1) {
    perror("couldn't I_LINK Ethernet to IP");
    exit(1);
}
```

And then inside the daemon's signal handler:

```
if (ioctl(ipfd, I_UNLINK, iemuxid) == -1) {
    perror("couldn't I_UNLINK Ethernet from IP");
    exit(1);
}
```

Configuring a multiplexor

In order that the system calls being made by the daemon process described above have the desired effect, additional functionality must be added to the multiplexor. In particular, the I_LINK calls to link each of the Stream drivers to the IP module require that the multiplexor fields of the struct streamtab described in Section 6.4.3 be properly filled out:

```
struct streamtab {
    struct qinit   *st_rdinit;      /* read QUEUE */
    struct qinit   *st_wrinit;      /* write QUEUE */
    struct qinit   *st_muxrinit;    /* mux read QUEUE */
    struct qinit   *st_muxwinit;    /* mux write QUEUE */
};
```

An I_LINK call to the target multiplexor causes STREAMS to replace the initial contents of the Stream head describing the lower module with the contents of the multiplexor's st_muxrinit and st_muxwinit respectively. For example, the call

```
ioctl(ipfd, I_LINK, efd)
```

replaces the contents of st_rdinit and st_wrinit from the Ethernet driver's struct streamtab with the contents of the st_muxrinit and st_muxwinit fields of the IP module's own struct streamtab. The effect of this is that all messages subsequently sent upstream by the Ethernet driver will pass through the multiplexor, and eventually arrive at the multiplexor's Stream head, rather than at the Ethernet driver's Stream head.

Finally, the Stream head sends an M_IOCTL message to the multiplexor's XXwput routine with ioc_cmd set to I_LINK (see Section 6.6.5). The attached M_DATA message block contains a struct linkblk, defined in ⟨sys/stream.h⟩:

```
struct linkblk {
    queue_t    *l_qtop;    /* lowest level write
                              queue of upper Stream */
    queue_t    *l_qbot;    /* highest level write
                              queue of lower Stream */
    int        l_index;    /* file[] index for lower
                              Stream */
};
```

The multiplexor should record the information from the linkblk in private storage, and return an M_IOCACK to the Stream head. The Stream head returns the value of l_index to the process requesting the I_LINK (this is the value iemuxid in our example above). The two QUEUEs identify the upper write QUEUE from where the M_IOCTL came (l_qtop), and the new lower write QUEUE where the multiplexor should putq its data (l_qbot) in the future. The l_qtop QUEUE is always the same as the original upper write QUEUE, but l_qbot identifies the former QUEUE from the Stream driver's Stream head.

Thus the logical connection between the multiplexor and the Stream driver is established.

6.7.3 Recovering from no message blocks

Calls to allocb are liable to fail if there are no message blocks left to allocate (see Section 6.3.3). If allocb does fail, a module can register an asynchronous call to a recovery routine with bufcall:

```
bufcall(size, pri, func, arg)
    int size, pri, (*func)();
    long arg;
```

The bufcall routine calls (*func)(arg) when a message block of size bytes at pri priority is available. It returns 1 on success, indicating that the request has been registered successfully, and 0 on failure.

When func is called, it has no user context so it must complete without referencing the U-area or calling routines such as sleep(K). Although a message block is available when bufcall initially dispatches func, the message block may already have been used by an interrupt routine before control arrives in func. This means that if func calls allocb to get a message block, allocb will fail again, and there could be a potential deadlock situation.

A more sensible strategy in the event of an allocb failure is to return the current message to the module's QUEUE, and to use bufcall to re-enable the QUEUE when a buffer becomes available. The STREAMS support routine qenable can be used to do this. Here is some sample code to illustrate this technique:

```
XXservice(q)
    queue_t *q;
{
    int qenable();
    mblk_t *mp, *bp:

    while ((mp = getq(q)) != NULL) {

        /*
         * Check for priority messages and canput() ...
         */

        ...
        ...

        /*
         * Allocate a message block to contain some header
         * information, then prepend this to mp
         */

        if ((bp = allocb(HDRSZ, BPRI_MED)) == NULL) {

            /*
             * No message blocks left, so use bufcall()
             * to reschedule this XXsrv() routine when
             * space is available.
             */

            if (bufcall(HDRSZ, BPRI_MED, qenable, q) ==
                0) {

                /*
                 * Give up completely - discard the
                 * current message and continue around
                 * the while() loop
                 */

                freemsg(mp);
                continue;
            }
```

```
                              /*
                               * bufcall() has succeeded, so return mp to
                               * our queue and wait to be re-enabled
                               * later on
                               */
                              putbq(q, mp);
                              return;
                      }
                      /*
                       * allocb() succeeded, so we can continue and
                       * process the message
                       */
                      ...
                      ...
              } /* end while () */
      }
```

6.8   Error logging

STREAMS includes error logging and event tracing mechanisms, to
provide STREAMS diagnostics for the Systems Administrator and to
provide a debugging facility for the STREAMS developer.

Log messages and trace messages can be generated by a module or
a Stream driver by using the strlog(STR) support routine:

```
strlog(mid, sid, level, flags, fmt, arg, ...)
      short mid, sid;
      char level;
      ushort flags;
      char *fmt;
```

The mid is the module ID of either the module or Stream driver, as
defined by the mi_idnum field of the module_info structure described in
Section 6.4.2. The sid is a sub-ID, usually used to identify the particular minor device. The level is an arbitrary value that is intended to
denote an indication of the priority or severity of the trace message
(see strace(ADM)). The flags are any combination of SL_ERROR (the
message is for the error logger), SL_TRACE (the message is for the
tracer), SL_FATAL (the reported condition is considered to be fatal) and
SL_NOTIFY (a copy of the message should be mailed to the System
Administrator).

The fmt and arg parameters follow the conventions of the kernel's
printf(K) routine. The maximum number of arguments allowed is
fixed by the value of NLOGARGS, which is currently defined to be 3 in
⟨sys/strlog.h⟩.

The user interfaces to the error logger and the tracer are via strace(ADM) and strerr(ADM), which read the special STREAMS driver /dev/log. The strerr(ADM) process writes error log messages to files in the directory /usr/adm/streams, which should be cleaned out periodically by strclean(ADM).

6.9   Configuring Stream modules and drivers

As might be expected, the configuration of a module or a Stream driver is somewhat more complex than the equivalent process for a regular character or block device driver.

For each Stream module or Stream driver to be configured, the developer must provide the following:

- A struct streamtab XXinfo, containing pointers to qinit structures describing the module QUEUEs. See Section 6.4.3.

- A qinit structure for each of the module's QUEUEs, containing the names of the QUEUE functions and pointers to module_info and optional module_stat structures. See Section 6.4.2.

- A module_info structure, shared by each of the QUEUEs, containing module identification information. See Section 6.4.2.

- An optional module_stat structure (not used by SCO at present).

Finally, the developer must provide the module routines described by the qinit structures. An example Stream driver is presented in Section 6.10 below.

A Stream driver should be added to the kernel using the configure(ADM) command, specifying -s with -m and -c to indicate that you are configuring a Stream driver. A Stream module should be specified by -s with -h (-m and -c are not required).

The SCO UNIX Link Kit does not have STREAMS configured by default, so before relinking the kernel for the first time you must do one of the following:

- If you are working with $ROOT set to / (see Appendix A), run the command mkdev streams and follow the prompts to add STREAMS to your Link Kit.

- If you are working with $ROOT identifying a private Link Kit hierarchy, use vi(C) to change the configure field in sdevice.d/str from an N to a Y, and then run the configure(ADM) command to add the clone driver (major device 40) to your Link Kit.

Table 6.1 STREAMS resources. Default values are for SCO UNIX release 3.2 version 4.

Resource name	Resource description	Default
NQUEUE	Total number of QUEUEs available	96
NSTREAM	Total number of STREAMS that can be opened	32
NMUXLINK	Total number of STREAMS that can be linked beneath a multiplexor	87
NSTREVENT	Total number of events available to support bufcall() and poll()	256
MAXSEPGCNT	Total number of additional memory pages that can be allocated for events	1
NSTRPUSH	Maximum number of modules that can be pushed onto a Stream	9
STRMSGSZ	Maximum size (in bytes) of a write(S) or putmsg(S) M_DATA message	4096
STRCTLSZ	Maximum size (in bytes) of a putmsg(S) M_PROTO or M_PCPROTO message	1024
STRLOFRAC	Percentage of data blocks available from a class for BPRI_LO requests	80
STRMEDFRAC	Percentage of data blocks available from a class for BPRI_MED requests	90
NLOG	Total number of minor devices to be configured for the log(STR) driver	3
NUMSP	Total number of Stream pipe devices supported	64
NUMTIM	Total number of Stream modules that can be pushed by the TLI	16

When the kernel is relinked, the -s will cause references to your streamtab to be included in cf.d/conf.c (see Appendix A). If you have configured a Stream driver, the streamtab will be referenced from cdevsw, and if you have configured a module, the streamtab will be referenced from fmodsw.

Here are some additional points to note:

- You should not specify the names of the QUEUE routines, as these are defined indirectly via the streamtab.
- You should not specify the names of any XXread, XXwrite or XXioctl routines to be included in cdevsw.

Table 6.2 STREAMS resources. Default values are for SCO UNIX release 3.2 version 4.

Resource name	Resource description	Default
NBLK4096	Total number of 4096-byte data blocks	0
NBLK2048	Total number of 2048-byte data blocks	20
NBLK1024	Total number of 1024-byte data blocks	20
NBLK512	Total number of 512-byte data blocks	8
NBLK256	Total number of 256-byte data blocks	8
NBLK128	Total number of 128-byte data blocks	8
NBLK64	Total number of 64-byte data blocks	40
NBLK16	Total number of 16-byte data blocks	40
NBLK4	Total number of 4-byte data blocks	40

- All other routines, including XXpoll and XXintr, should be specified as required.

The following configure(ADM) command shows you how to configure the example Stream driver from Section 6.10 into the kernel. We assume that major device number 17 is available:

```
$ ./configure -a exstopen exstclose -c -s -m 17
```

Tables 6.1 and 6.2 summarize the tunable parameters applicable to STREAMS.

6.10   An example STREAMS driver

The STREAMS loopback driver shown here and the accompanying test harness are adapted from original versions published in the *SCO UNIX Device Driver Writer's Guide*.

6.10.1 A STREAMS loopback driver

```
/*
 * src/exst.c
 *
 * A STREAMS loopback driver.
 *
 * Copyright (c) The Santa Cruz Operation, 1986, 1987.
 * This Module contains Proprietary Information of
 * The Santa Cruz Operation, Microsoft Corporation
 * and AT&T, and should be treated as Confidential.
 *
 * This is a pseudo-driver designed to loop data from one
 * open Stream to another open Stream. The user processes
 * view the associated files as a full duplex pipe. This
 * driver is a simple multiplexor which passes messages from
 * one Stream's write queue to the other Stream's read queue.
 * The driver also illustrates a Stream's ioctl() function.
 *
 * Note from the authors:
 *
 * We have added additional comments and calls to cmn_err(K)
 * to help you to see what is happening when this driver is
 * invoked by strtest.c. Compile with -DDEBUG to see all of
 * the diagnostics.
 *
 * ./configure -a exstopen exstclose -m MAJOR -c -s
 */
/*
 * necessary include files
 */
#include <sys/types.h>
#include <sys/param.h>
#include <sys/sysmacros.h>
#include <sys/stream.h>
#include <sys/stropts.h>
#include <sys/dir.h>
#include <sys/signal.h>
#include <sys/page.h>
#include <sys/seg.h>
#include <sys/user.h>
#include <sys/errno.h>
#include <sys/strlog.h>
#include <sys/log.h>
#include <sys/cmn_err.h>
*/
 * function declarations
 */
int nodev(), exstopen(), exstclose(), exstsrv();
/*
 * streams structure declarations
 */
```

```
static struct module_info exstm_info = {
     40,              /* module ID number */
     "exst",          /* module name */
     0,               /* min packet */
     256,             /* max packet */
     512,             /* hi-water mark */
     256              /* lo-water mark */
};

/*
 * Initialization for the read QUEUE.
 *
 * There is no need for an XXrput(), as messages
 * are queued on the write side and sent upstream
 * by the shared XXservice().
 */

static struct qinit exstrinit = {
     NULL,            /* put procedure */
     exstsrv,         /* service procedure */
     exstopen,        /* called on each open or push */
     exstclose,       /* called on last close */
     NULL,            /* reserved for future use */
     &exstm_info,     /* information structure */
     NULL             /* statistics structure */
};

/*
 * Initialization for the write QUEUE.
 *
 * XXwput() (i.e. putq()) is called by the Stream head
 * to accept messages.
 */

static struct qinit exstwinit = {
     putq,            /* put procedure */
     exstsrv,         /* service procedure */
     exstopen,        /* called on each open or push */
     exstclose,       /* called on last close */
     NULL,            /* reserved for future use */
     &exstm_info,     /* information structure */
     NULL             /* statistics structure */
};

struct streamtab exstinfo = {
     &exstrinit,      /* defines read queue */
     &exstwinit,      /* defines write queue */
     NULL,            /* no multiplexing */
     NULL             /* no multiplexing */
};

/*
 * The private exst structure is used to create
 * an array of clonable devices.
 */
```

```
struct exst {
    unsigned exst_state;        /* driver state flag,
                                   see below */
    queue_t *exst_rdq;          /* queue pointer */
};
/*
 * Driver state values
 */
#define    EXSTOPEN    01    /* device is opened */
#define    EXSTFAIL    02    /* open failed */
#define    NEXST       4     /* number of clonable devices */
*/
 * Allocate streams blocks
 */
struct exst exst_lo[NEXST];
int exstcnt = NEXST;

/*
 * User-defined ioctl(S) requests
 */
#define    I_NOARG      20
#define    I_INTARG     21
#define    I_ERRNAK     23
#define    I_ERROR      25
#define    EXSTSLPTEST  32
#define    I_SETHANG    42
#define    I_SETERR     43

exstopen(q, dev, flag, sflag)
    queue_t *q;
    dev_t dev;
    int flag, sflag;
{
    struct exst *lp;
#ifdef DEBUG
    cmn_err(CE_CONT, "DEBUG: in exstopen()\n");
#endif

    dev = minor(dev);
    /*
     * If CLONEOPEN, pick a minor device
     * number to use.
     */
    if (sflag == CLONEOPEN) {
        for (dev = 0; dev < exstcnt; dev++) {
            if (!( exst_lo[dev].exst_state & EXSTOPEN)) {
                break;
            }
        }
    }
```

```
        /*
         * Check to see if we have a
         * good device number
         */
        if ((dev < 0) || (dev >= exstcnt)) {
            return(OPENFAIL);   /* default = ENXIO */
        }
        lp = &exst_lo[dev];
        if (lp->exst_state & EXSTFAIL) {
            /*
             * Clear the fail flag so it can be
             * reopened later
             */
            lp->exst_state &= ~EXSTFAIL;
            return(OPENFAIL);
        }
        /*
         * Set up data structures
         */
        if (!(lp->exst_state & EXSTOPEN)) {
            lp->exst_rdq = q;
            q->q_ptr = (caddr_t)lp;
            WR(q)->q_ptr = (caddr_t)lp;
            return(dev);
        } else {
            /*
             * Check that we are not opening the same Stream
             * twice - this might happen if the user is not
             * opening the clone device.
             */
            if (q != lp->exst_rdq) {
                return(OPENFAIL);
            }
        }
    }
exstclose(q, flag)
    queue_t *q;
    int flag;
{
#ifdef DEBUG
    cmn_err(CE_CONT, "DEBUG: in exstclose()\n");
#endif
    /*
     * Remove all the messages from the write
     * message queue.
     */
    ((struct exst *)(q->q_ptr))->exst_state &= ~EXSTOPEN;
    ((struct exst *)(q->q_ptr))->exst_rdq = NULL;
    flushq(WR(q), FLUSHALL);
    q->q_ptr = NULL;
}
```

```
/*
 * The XXservice() routine takes messages off write
 * queue and sends them back up the read queue,
 * processing them along the way.
 *
 * Messages arrive on the queue from putq(), which is
 * called via putnext() from strwrite() in the Stream
 * head.
 */
exstsrv(q)
    queue_t *q;
{
    mblk_t *bp;
    /*
     * If exstsrv has been called from the
     *  read side, set q to write side
     */
    q = ((q)->q_flag & QREADR ? WR(q) : q);
#ifdef DEBUG
    cmn_err(CE_CONT, "DEBUG: in exstsrv(): ");
#endif
    /*
     * If the upstream queue is full,
     * only process priority messages
     */
    while ((bp = getq(q)) != NULL) {
        if (((bp->b_datap->db_type) <= QPCTL)
            && !canput(RD(q)->q_next)) {
            cmn_err(CE_NOTE,
                "exstsrv(): upstream queue is full");
            putbq(q, bp);
            return;
        }
        switch (bp->b_datap->db_type) {
            case M_IOCTL:
#ifdef DEBUG
                cmn_err(CE_CONT,
                    "message type is
                    M_IOCTL\n");
#endif
                exstioctl(q, bp);
                if (((struct exst *)
                    (q->q_ptr))->exst_state &
                    EXSTSLPTEST) {
                    return;
                }
                break;
            /*
             * If testing offset, calculate and place at
             * start of data message.
             */
```

```
                     case M_DATA:
                     /* flow through */
                     case M_PROTO:
                     case M_PCPROTO:
#ifdef DEBUG
                             cmn_err(CE_CONT,
                                     "message type is
                                     M_DATA, M_PROTO,
                                     or M_PCPROTO\n");
#endif
                             qreply(q, bp);
                             break;
                     case M_CTL:
#ifdef DEBUG
                             cmn_err(CE_CONT,
                                     "message type is M_CTL\n");
#endif
                             freemsg(bp);
                             break;
                     case M_FLUSH:
#ifdef DEBUG
                             printf(CE_CONT,
                                     "message type is M_FLUSH\n");
#endif
                             if (*bp->b_rptr & FLUSHW) {
                                 flushq(q, FLUSHALL);
                                 *bp->b_rptr &= ~FLUSHW;
                             }
                             if (*bp->b_rptr & FLUSHR) {
                                 qreply(q,bp);
                             } else {
                                 freemsg(bp);
                             }
                             break;
                 default:
                             freemsg(bp);
                             break;
             }
         }
}
/*
 * XXioctl() tests the User-defined
 * ioctl commands, passed to us from the
 * test harness.
 */
exstioctl(q, bp)
     queue_t *q;
     mblk_t *bp;
{
     register s;
     int i, n;
```

```
        mblk_t *tmp;
        struct iocblk *iocbp;
        struct stroptions *so;
#ifdef DEBUG
        cmn_err(CE_CONT, "DEBUG: in exstioctl(): ");
#endif
        /*
         * Each particular ioctl has a special function for
         * testing the streams error mechanism.
         */
        iocbp = (struct iocblk *)bp->b_rptr;
        switch (iocbp->ioc_cmd) {
            case I_NOARG:
#ifdef DEBUG
                cmn_err(CE_CONT, "ioctl type is I_NOARG\n");
#endif
                bp->b_datap->db_type = M_IOCACK;
                qreply(q, bp);
                return;
            case I_INTARG:
#ifdef DEBUG
                cmn_err(CE_NOTE, "ioctl type is I_INTARG\n");
#endif
                /*
                 * Send integer argument back as return
                 * value
                 */
                if (bp->b_cont == NULL) {
                    freemsg(bp);
                    return;
                }
                iocbp->ioc_rval = *((int *)
                                    bp->b_cont->b_rptr);
                tmp = unlinkb(bp);
                freeb(tmp);
                iocbp->ioc_count = 0;
                bp->b_datap->db_type = M_IOCACK;
                qreply(q, bp);
                return;
            case I_ERROR:
#ifdef DEBUG
                cmn_err(CE_CONT, "ioctl type is I_ERROR\n");
#endif
                /*
                 * Verify that error return works.
                 */
                iocbp->ioc_error = EPERM;
                bp->b_datap->db_type = M_IOCACK;
                qreply(q, bp);
                return;
```

```
            case I_ERRNAK:
#ifdef DEBUG
                cmn_err(CE_CONT, "ioctl type is I_ERRNAK\n");
#endif

                /*
                 * Send a NAK back with an error value.
                 */
                iocbp->ioc_error = EPERM;
                bp->b_datap->db_type = M_IOCNAK;
                qreply(q, bp);
                return;
            case I_SETHANG:
#ifdef DEBUG
                cmn_err(CE_CONT, "ioctl type is I_SETHANG\n");
#endif

                /*
                 * Send ACK followed by M_HANGUP upstream.
                 */
                bp->b_datap->db_type = M_IOCACK;
                qreply(q, bp);
                putctl(RD(q)->q_next, M_HANGUP);
                return;
            case I_SETERR:
#ifdef DEBUG
                cmn_err(CE_CONT, "ioctl type is I_SETERR\n");
#endif

                /*
                 * Send ACK followed by M_ERROR upstream -
                 * value is sent in second message block.
                 */
                tmp = unlinkb(bp);
                bp->b_datap->db_type = M_IOCACK;
                ((struct iocblk *)bp->b_rptr)->ioc_count = 0;
                qreply(q, bp);
                tmp->b_datap->db_type = M_ERROR;
                qreply(q, tmp);
                return;

        default:
#ifdef DEBUG
                cmn_err(CE_CONT, "\n");
#endif

                /*
                 * NAK anything else.
                 */
                bp->b_datap->db_type = M_IOCNAK;
                qreply(q, bp);
                return;
    }
}
```

6.10.2 A STREAMS test harness

```
/*
 * src/strtest.c
 *
 * A test harness for the STREAMS loopback driver exst.c
 *
 * Copyright (c) The Santa Cruz Operation, 1986, 1987.
 * This Module contains Proprietary Information of
 * The Santa Cruz Operation, Microsoft Corporation
 * and AT&T, and should be treated as Confidential.
 *
 * Note from the authors:
 *
 * We have added additional comments and calls to printf(S)
 * to help you to see what is happening as this test harness
 * invokes exst.c. We have also corrected the use of the
 * I_INTARG call so that the driver correctly returns the
 * integer argument.
 */
#include <errno.h>
#include <fcntl.h>
#include <stdio.h>
#include <sys/stropts.h>

/* Loopback driver ioctl() commands */

#define I_NOARG     20
#define I_INTARG    21
#define I_ERRNAK    23
#define I_ERROR     25
#define I_SETHANG   42

struct strioctl ioc;

main(argc, argv)
     int argc;
     char *argv[];
{
     int fd, i, foo = 55;
     char buf[BUFSIZ];
     /*
      * Open the loopback device.
      */
     if ((fd = open("/dev/exst", O_RDWR)) == -1) {
          perror("main(): Cannot open() /dev/exst");
          exit(1);
     }
     /*
      * Try writing to the loopback device,
      * and reading data from it.
      */
     printf("Please enter a string to write to stream's
          loopback device\n");
```

```
        if ((fgets(buf, BUFSIZ, stdin)) == NULL) {
            perror("main(): fgets() failed");
            exit(1);
        }
        /*
         * strwrite() writes, strread() reads
         */
        strwrite(fd, buf);
        strread(fd);
        /*
         * Test the ioctl calls
         */
        strioctl(fd, I_NOARG, 0, 0, NULL);
        strwrite(fd, buf);
        strread(fd);
        strioctl(fd, I_INTARG, 0, sizeof(foo), &foo);
        strwrite(fd, buf);
        strread(fd);
        strioctl(fd, I_ERRNAK, 0, 0, NULL);
        strwrite(fd, buf);
        strread(fd);
        strioctl(fd, I_ERROR, 0, 0, NULL);
        strwrite(fd, buf);
        strread(fd);
        strioctl(fd, I_SETHANG, 0, 0, NULL);
        strwrite(fd, buf);
        strread(fd);
        close(fd);
        exit(0);
}
strwrite(fd, s)
int fd;
char *s;
{
        printf("\nWriting to loopback device ...\n");
        if (write(fd, s, BUFSIZ) == -1) {
            perror("strwrite(): write() failed");
            exit(2);
        }
}
strread(fd)
int fd;
{
        char buf[BUFSIZ];
        printf("\nReading from loopback device ...\n");
        if (read(fd, buf, BUFSIZ) == -1) {
            perror("strread(): read() failed");
            exit(3);
        }
```

```
        /* print the results of the read */
        printf("String = %s\n",buf);
}
strioctl(fd, arg, time, len, s)
        int fd, arg, time, len;
        char *s;
{
        int i;
        char *p, *e;

        ioc.ic_cmd = arg;
        ioc.ic_timout = time;
        ioc.ic_len = len;
        ioc.ic_dp = s;

        switch (arg) {
                case I_NOARG:
                        p = "i_noarg";
                        e = "Will complete successfully.";
                        break;
                case I_ERRNAK:
                        p = "i_errnak";
                        e = "Will fail with EPERM.";
                        break;
                case I_ERROR:
                        p = "i_error";
                        e = "Will fail with EPERM.";
                        break;
                case I_SETHANG:
                        p = "i_sethang";
                        e = "Subsequent read()'s and write()'s
                            will fail.";
                        break;
                case I_INTARG:
                        p = "i_intarg";
                        e = "Will complete successfully (55).";
                        break;
                default:
                        p = "unknown ioctl";
                        e = "Will fail with ETIME.";
                        break;
        }
        printf("\nTrying ioctl() call '%s': %s\n", p, e);
        if ((i = ioctl(fd, I_STR, &ioc)) == -1) {

                perror("strioctl(): ioctl failed");
                printf("ioctl() return code = %d\n", i);
        } else {

                printf("ioctl() return code = %d\n", i);
        }
        sleep(5);
}
```

6.11 Summary

STREAMS provides a convenient mechanism to construct protocol stacks from functionally distinct layers of software. Any character-based I/O subsystem that does intermediate processing of data as it moves between the user and a device can be implemented as a Stream module, thus imposing a layered, structured approach to the software design. Some obvious examples are a TCP/IP stack, and line disciplines for serial device drivers.

This chapter has described how STREAMS works in the SCO UNIX kernel, and we have presented a simple STREAMS loopback driver to illustrate the important principles.

In the exercise at the end of this chapter, you will have an opportunity to write your own Stream driver for the mouse, and reinforce the theory that we have presented.

QUIZ

To test your understanding of this chapter, try to answer the following questions.

6.1 Do modules and Stream drivers have entries for XXread, XXwrite and XXioctl routines in cdevsw?

6.2 What are the two main characteristics of priority messages, when compared with ordinary messages?

6.3 If an XXput routine defers processing to the XXservice routine, how is that XXservice ultimately invoked?

6.4 When is the XXopen routine of a module or Stream driver called?

6.5 What is the purpose of the routine called strwsrv in the Stream head?

6.6 Which option of the crash(ADM) utility should you use to determine whether allocb has failed to allocate a data buffer from a particular class?

6.7 What are the three message types that can be handled by read(S), write(S), getmsg(S) and putmsg(S) at the Stream head?

6.8 What software priority level does the STREAMS support software in the kernel run at?

EXERCISE

Convert the mouse driver from Chapter 4 to a Stream driver.
   Here are some hints:

- As the mouse is an input-only device, you should declare a qinit only for the upstream QUEUE. Use NULL as a placeholder for the downstream QUEUE in the streamtab.

- Modify your XXintr routine to allocb a message block to contain the data from the mouse. Use bcopy(K) to copy the data into the message block, then call putq to add the message to the read QUEUE.

- Provide an XXservice routine which uses getq to get messages from the read QUEUE, and then calls putnext to send the message to the Stream head.

- Put some cmn_err(K) calls into your driver so that you can see the routines being called. In particular, check that the STREAMS scheduler is calling your XXservice procedure.

- Configure your driver to run at spl5(K).

   The mouse and mousey test programs will work without any modification.

   Advanced sessions:

- Add support for CLONEOPEN in your XXopen routine.

- Add support for M_FLUSH messages in your XXservice routine.

   A suggested answer is given in 'Answers to Exercises'.

NOTES

1. A Stream driver should not be configured to run at sp16(K) or higher, unless the Stream driver is implemented in a similar way to the example serial driver in Chapter 5.

2. The default value for STRLOFRAC is 80% on SCO UNIX 3.2v4.

3. The default value for STRMEDFRAC is 90% on SCO UNIX 3.2v4.

4. The maximum number of QUEUEs available is determined by NQUEUE. The default value is 96 on SCO UNIX 3.2v4.

5. The maximum number of STREAMS that can be active is dependent on how many stdata structures are configured. The configurable resource is NSTREAM. The default value is 32 on SCO UNIX 3.2v4.

6. The only purpose of the Stream head's strwsrv routine is to wakeup(K) anyone who is asleep, whenever the Stream head is back-enabled.

7. The length of time the poll(S) system call should wait is rounded to the nearest clock tick by the kernel.

8. The statement that the user's first open(S) system call always completes assumes that there is a minor device available.

7

Block device drivers

7.1   Overview

The previous chapters in this book have all described different types
of character device drivers. In this chapter, we shall examine device
drivers which conform to the block device model, first described in
Chapter 1.

Block device drivers transfer data between the machine's memory
and devices which structure and manage their data in fixed-size
blocks, such as disks and tapes. For example, a disk drive might
organize data in sectors of 512 bytes, and a tape might organize data
in blocks of 1024 bytes.

In practice, block devices are used almost exclusively to support
UNIX filesystems and swapping, and so the terms block device driver
and disk device driver are normally used interchangeably.[1] In this
chapter, we shall discuss the operation of an SCO UNIX disk device
driver for a disk controller with an ST506 register interface, emulated
in software.

In the exercise at the end of this chapter, we shall test the extended
RAM disk driver presented in Section 7.10.

A disk driver's job is to manage the data on the device so that it can
be presented to the kernel as a logically contiguous single-dimensional
array of filesystem blocks. To do this, it must translate the operating
system's logical interpretation of the filesystem blocks into divisions
and partitions (see Section 7.7), and reconcile this with the physical
attributes of the device (cylinders, tracks, sectors and bad blocks).

Users' requests to read files in the filesystem are translated by the
kernel's filesystem support routines into requests to transfer one or
more blocks between the kernel's buffer cache and the device. When
the transfer is complete, the kernel copies the data which the process
actually wants from the buffer cache into the process' address space.

A similar sequence of events happens in response to requests to write to files in the filesystem.

For example, a request to read 16 bytes from /etc/passwd is translated by the kernel to read the first block of /etc/passwd from the filesystem (this might be block number 2654) into the buffer cache. The disk driver receives a request from the kernel to read block 2654, and is told whereabouts to put it in memory. When the disk driver indicates that the data has been read from the device, the kernel copies the first 16 bytes out to the user process and control returns through the read(S) system call.

The buffer cache serves two purposes for block devices:

- It is an intermediate buffer between the user process at task-time and the device driver's XXintr routine at interrupt-time. In this sense, it is comparable to the clists used by character device drivers.

- It contains copies of the kernel buffers used during previous transfers, so that user requests to read commonly-accessed files can, in the majority of cases, be satisfied directly from the contents of the buffer cache, rather than a new request being sent to the device.

The operation of the buffer cache is described in more detail in Section 7.3.

Figure 7.1 shows the layers of software between the system call code and the device driver.

7.2   Block device characteristics

The principal kernel interface to a block device driver is through the routine called XXstrategy. The kernel calls XXstrategy whenever a user's read(S) request cannot be satisfied from the buffer cache, or whenever it wants to synchronize the filesystems with the buffer cache contents, by flushing out to the disk any buffers that have been changed by write(S) system calls. The kernel fills out a struct buf to describe the request (see Section 7.4), and passes the address of this structure to XXstrategy. The struct buf includes:

- The block number that is required, and which device (filesystem) contains it.

- How many bytes should be transferred (this number is the same as the kernel's internal block size, 1024 bytes on SCO UNIX).

- The address of a 1 Kb entry in the buffer cache.

- A flag indicating whether to read or write.

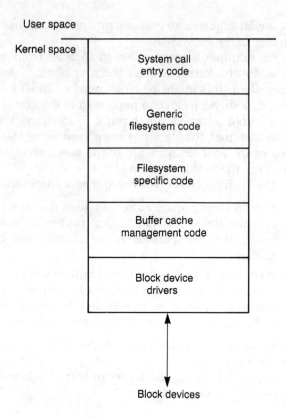

Figure 7.1   Block device drivers.

Since the device can only deal with one request at a time, the device driver must maintain a queue of requests that it receives from the kernel. As soon as the device finishes with one request, the driver sends it the next request from the queue.

The filesystem code and the buffer cache management code take care of everything else, including blocking and unblocking of data, read-ahead and management of the buffer cache.

7.2.1 Blocking and unblocking of data

The filesystem code blocks and unblocks data to ensure that variable-sized read(S) and write(S) requests from the user are translated to fixed-size requests before passing them on to the buffer cache management code. An example of how this is done for a read(S) system call was described in Section 7.1 above.

For a write(S) system call, the sequence of events can be more complex. Consider a request to write into only the first 15 bytes of /etc/termcap. In order to preserve the fixed-size block interface, the kernel must first of all read the first block of /etc/termcap from the filesystem into the buffer cache. When the block has been read into the buffer cache, the kernel can copy the 15 bytes from the user process into the buffer cache, leaving the remaining 1009 bytes intact. Finally, the modified buffer is passed to the device driver for writing back out to the filesystem.

Blocking and unblocking are completely transparent to the device driver.

7.2.2   Read-ahead

Empirical evidence demonstrates that user processes tend to access files sequentially. That is, they open a file, read and process each of the file's data blocks, and after they have read and processed the last data block, the file is closed. For example, consider the behaviour of grep(C), more(C), cc(CP), and so on.

Because sequential access of files is such a common occurrence, the filesystem support code contains checks to determine if sequential I/O is happening, and if so, to start making read-ahead requests on behalf of the process. Each time a block is read, the block address is recorded in the file's inode entry in the inode table. If the next block requested by the process is the one following the block that has just been read, the kernel assumes that the file is being accessed sequentially.

The kernel now issues two requests to the device driver instead of one. The first request is to read the block that is required, and the second request is to read the following block. Thus, when the user process has finished processing the first block, the next block will already be in the buffer cache, and the next read(S) system call can be satisfied without accessing the device. The kernel sees that the process is still accessing the file sequentially, and sends another request to the device to read the next block, so that the process' next read(S) system call can also be satisfied from the buffer cache, and so on.

Although the number of requests arriving at the device is the same,[2] the read-ahead ensures that the process' hit-rate on the buffer cache is maximized, therefore improving the process' throughput.

Read-ahead is implemented transparently by the filesystem support code, and is therefore transparent to the device driver.

The Acer Filesystem (AFS) supported by SCO UNIX extends the idea of read-ahead a step further, and sends requests to the device to read clusters of blocks in advance, rather than just single blocks. A cluster is a logically contiguous sequence of disk blocks,[3] and the AFS attempts to allocate clusters of blocks to files when they are created. For most of the time, logically contiguous means physically contiguous on the disk surface (the exception is if there are bad blocks in a cluster), so it is an advantage to be able to read-ahead entire clusters. As well as improving the hit-rate on the buffer cache, clustering helps to minimize disk head movement as all files can be read with significantly fewer disk accesses.

Support for clustering read-ahead and the associated scatter–gather I/O operations requires modifications to the device driver which are beyond the scope of this book.

7.3   The buffer cache

The buffer cache is a key mechanism which contributes significantly to the overall effectiveness of the block I/O subsystem. As illustrated in Figure 7.1, the buffer cache system is a layer of software positioned between the filesystem code and the block device drivers. It has the following responsibilities:

- To decouple the task-time and interrupt-time components of an I/O request. All buffer cache manipulation is protected at spl6(K).

- To maintain copies of the buffers that have been recently used for I/O.

- To provide an efficient mechanism for searching the cache contents so that read(S) requests can be satisfied directly from the cache, without needing to call the device driver to access the disk.

- To provide a mechanism for asynchronous write(S) requests. This allows user processes to write data into the cache and return from the write(S) system call, without having to wait for the data to be written to the disk.

In SCO UNIX, the size of the buffer cache is dependent on the total amount of memory available, and is determined by the kernel as it starts up. A typical size on a machine with 4 Mb of RAM would be 600 1K blocks. The upper limit of the size of the buffer cache is the resource MAXBUF which can be modified with configure(ADM).[4] Depending on the actual mix of processes that are being run on the machine, the overall performance of the I/O subsystem can sometimes be improved by configuring the buffer cache to be as large as possible. However, note that a larger cache implies that less memory will be available for user processes, which in turn may increase the overall amount of paging and swapping activity. This may have exactly the opposite effect on overall performance to that which is desired!

7.3.1   The buffer header structure

Each buffer in the buffer cache is described by a struct buf buffer header, and the buffer headers are linked onto one or more doubly-linked lists. It is important to note that the buffer header *is not* the actual buffer, merely a description of it.

The doubly-linked lists are called the free list and the cache, and there is a busy list for each device. The XXstrategy routine is passed the address of one of these structures whenever it is called to initiate an I/O request. The structure is defined in ⟨sys/buf.h⟩:

```
typedef struct buf
{
        int     b_flags;            /* status of buffer */
        struct  buf *b_forw;        /* headed by driver's
                                       XXtab */

        struct  buf *b_back;
        struct  buf *av_forw;       /* position on free list
                                       if not B_BUSY */

        struct  buf *av_back;
        dev_t   b_dev;              /* major+minor device
                                       name */

        struct  lockb b_cilock;     /* MPX buf struct
                                       synchronization */

        unsigned b_bcount;          /* how many bytes to
                                       transfer */

        union {
                caddr_t b_addr;     /* virtual address of
                                       buffer */

                int   *b_words;     /* words for clearing */
                daddr_t *b_daddr;   /* disk blocks */
#ifdef FFS
                struct filsys *b_filsys; /* superblocks */
#endif
        } b_un;

#define paddr(X)     (paddr_t)(X->b_un.b_addr)
        daddr_t  b_blkno;           /* block # on device,
                                       in 512 byte blocks */

        char b_error;               /* returned after I/O */
        char b_res;                 /* XENIX Compatibility */
        ushort b_cylin;             /* XENIX Compatibility */
        unsigned int b_resid;       /* bytes not transferred
                                       after error */

        daddr_t b_sector;           /* physical sector of
                                       disk request */

        time_t   b_start;           /* request start time */
        struct   proc *b_proc;      /* process doing physical
                                       or swap I/O */

        unsigned long  b_reltime;   /* previous release
                                       time */
```

```
#ifdef FFS
    int  b_s2;                      /* temporary space */
    int  b_s3;                      /* temporary space */
#define b_umd  b_s2
#define b_fbit b_s2
#define b_pt   b_s3
#endif
    int  b_want;                    /* Stores B_WANTED to
                                       avoid race */
} buf_t;
```

Most of these fields are used only by the filesystem and buffer cache management code, and do not need to be examined or modified by the device driver. The most relevant fields are presented here.

b_flags

Contains a mask of bits OR'd together describing the status of the buffer. The possible bits are defined in ⟨sys/buf.h⟩. The only two bits of interest to the device driver are the B_READ or B_WRITE bit, which indicates whether the request received in XXstrategy is a read or a write, and B_ERROR, which the device driver should set to indicate an error.

b_forw, b_back

Used to link the buffer header into the cache (see Section 7.3.3 below).

av_forw, av_back

Used to link the buffer header into the free list (see Section 7.3.2 below), or onto the device's busy list if an I/O request is outstanding (see Section 7.3.4 below).

b_dev

The major and minor device number of the device where the block resides (for example, the root filesystem).

b_bcount

The number of bytes to be transferred in this request. This is always 1024 bytes when the device is being accessed through the block interface.

b_un.b_addr

The virtual address of the buffer in the kernel's buffer cache.[5] The device driver should transfer data between here and the device.

b_blkno

The offset within the device (specified by b_dev) of the start of the transfer, measured in 512-byte blocks.

b_error

Used to return error codes from the device driver to the user process. A list of valid error codes is given in ⟨sys/errno.h⟩. Whenever B_ERROR is set in b_flags, the kernel will return EIO through the system call, unless an alternative error code is put here by the device driver.

b_resid

This value should be set by XXstrategy to indicate the number of bytes that cannot be transferred due to an error in the request. For example, a request to read beyond the end of a device.

b_sector

Set by XXstrategy to be the absolute physical offset into the drive of the start of the transfer. It is used as a sort key to insert the request into the device's busy list (see Section 7.3.4 below).

7.3.2 The free list

When the system starts up, all of the buffer headers are linked onto the free list anchored at bfreelist, using the av_forw and av_back pointers. They are not linked onto either of the other two lists.

Buffer headers are removed from the free list whenever an I/O request is sent to the device, and put back onto the free list when the I/O request completes.

7.3.3 The cache

When the buffer cache management code wants to send a request to the device, it unlinks a buffer header from the free list and links it into the cache, using the b_forw and b_back pointers. The cache is the set of buffers which contain useful data (data that has either been read from the device, or written by the kernel or a user process). Access to the cache is via a hash key, generated by the bhash macro in ⟨sys/buf.h⟩:

```
#define bhash(dev,blkno) \
    ((struct buf *)&hbuf[((int)dev + (int)(blkno >> 1)) &
        v.v_hmask])
struct hbuf
{
    int  b_flags;
    struct    buf  *b_forw;
    struct    buf  *b_back;
    int  b_pad;                    /* round size to 2^n */
};
extern struct hbuf hbuf[];
```

The hash key is used to index the array hbuf,[6] which is a list of entry points (called **hash buckets**) into the cache. When adding a buffer to a hash bucket, the kernel searches along b_forw, comparing the b_dev and b_blkno fields with those in the request, and inserts the new buffer header into the appropriate position. The b_flags field is marked B_BUSY.

A similar sequence of operations is used to establish a cache hit or a miss.

Figure 7.2 shows some buffer headers in the cache.

7.3.4 The busy list

After the buffer header has been linked into the cache, the kernel calls XXstrategy to deal with the request. If there are many processes making I/O requests, XXstrategy will be called at a rate higher than the device can deal with the requests, so XXstrategy must maintain a queue of requests that it receives from the kernel, and issue these one by one to the device.

This final queue is called the busy list. Typically, a device driver will maintain one busy list for each drive attached to the controller, assuming that the controller is able to operate the drives independently of each other. The kernel provides a support routine called disksort(K) which sorts a request onto the appropriate busy list, using the av_forw and av_back pointers in the buffer header. Note that these pointers are the same as those used when the buffer header was on the free list.

Each busy list is anchored by a struct iobuf XXtab (see ⟨sys/iobuf.h⟩), and is sorted in ascending b_sector order. The

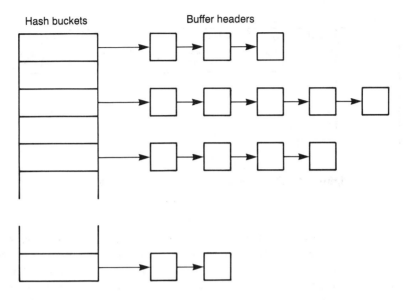

Figure 7.2 The buffer cache.

XXstrategy routine sets b_sector to be the physical sector number of the start of the request before calling disksort(K).

Each time the device completes a request and the device becomes free, the device driver issues the next request from the head of the busy list.

A higher physical sector corresponds to a higher offset into the drive, which means that the disk heads will typically move from the outermost cylinders towards the innermost cylinders as the device driver issues each of the requests from the busy list. Figure 7.3 shows

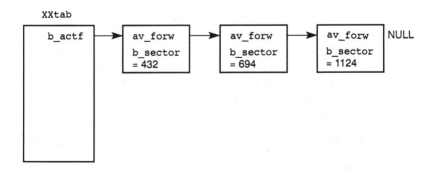

Figure 7.3 Buffer headers on a busy list.

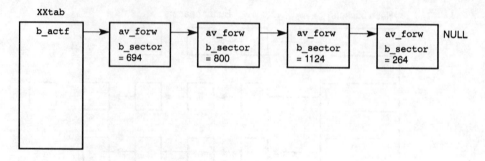

Figure 7.4   The same busy list a short while later.

a typical busy list. Figure 7.4 shows the same list after some more requests have been received from the kernel. Note that the request to read/write starting at sector 432 has been completed. The two new requests are sectors 800 and 264. The request to read/write starting at sector 264 is appended to the end of the busy list, as the disk heads are already beyond this position, dealing with the current request at sector 694.

When an I/O request completes, the device driver's XXintr routine calls iodone(K) to set B_DONE in b_flags, unlink the buffer header from the busy list, and return it to the free list.[7] Note that the buffer header is still in the cache when iodone(K) is called. The exact behaviour of iodone(K) depends on whether B_ASYNC is set in b_flags:

- Buffer headers that have been used for asynchronous I/O, such as those written by the system process bdflush, and those written by a write(S) system call where O_SYNC was not specified in the open(S) request, will have B_ASYNC set. These buffer headers will be returned to the free list directly by iodone(K), and a wakeup(K) will be issued to wake up any processes which may be waiting for a free buffer.

- Buffer headers that have been used for synchronous I/O (all read(S) requests are synchronous) will not have B_ASYNC set, and will require further task-time processing by the filesystem management code after it has been woken up by iodone(K).

  At task-time, the filesystem copies the data from the buffer cache out to the user's address space, and then returns the buffer header to the free list.

Figure 7.5 shows how a buffer header moves between the lists during a read(S) request.

Buffer activity can be monitored with the -b option of the sar(ADM) utility. Figure 7.6 shows a typical report from sar(ADM). The bread and

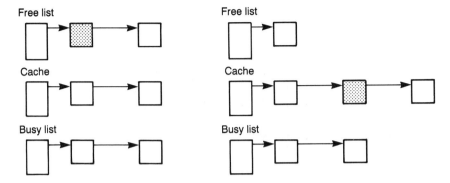

(a) A buffer header is removed from the free list.   (b) The buffer header is linked into the cache.

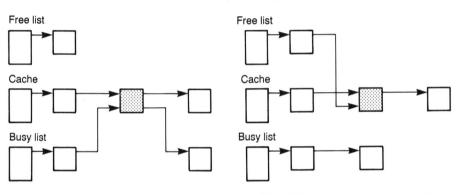

(c) The buffer header is linked onto a busy list.   (d) The buffer header is returned to the free list

Figure 7.5   Buffer header activity.

bwrit figures report the number of transfers between the cache and the device. The lread and lwrit figures report on the number of transfers between either the kernel or user processes and the cache (a cache hit). On a typical system, the cache hit rate for reads should be approximately 85%, and approximately 65% for writes.

7.4   The kernel interface

As we have seen, the principal interface between the kernel and a block device driver is through the XXstrategy routine, which is called when the kernel wants to transfer data between the buffer cache and the device:

	bread/s	lread/s	%rcache	bwrit/s	lwrit/s	%wcache	pread/s	pwrit/s
12:57:44	0	2	100	14	15	10	0	0
12:57:49	14	100	86	3	32	89	0	0
12:57:54	37	401	91	2	136	99	0	0
12:57:59	55	290	81	5	46	89	0	0
12:58:04	8	259	97	20	155	87	0	0
12:58:09	2	299	99	29	186	84	0	0
12:58:14	16	179	91	19	104	82	0	0
12:58:19	8	253	97	20	152	87	0	0
12:58:24	2	259	99	19	144	86	0	0
12:58:29	8	220	96	30	138	78	0	0
Average	15	230	93	16	113	86	0	0

Figure 7.6   Buffer activity measured with sar -b.

```
void
XXstrategy(bp)
    struct buf *bp;
```

The bp parameter describes the kernel's request, as discussed in Section 7.3.1 above. The XXstrategy routine should do the following:

(1)   Validate the request described by bp.

(2)   Calculate the physical offset, b_sector.

(3)   Call spl6(K) to interlock other buffer activity.

(4)   Call disksort(K) to add the request to the device's busy list.

(5)   Call XXstart to start up the device.

(6)   Call splx(K) to re-enable interrupts.

(7)   Return to the caller.

The XXstart routine is private to the device driver, and is responsible for issuing requests from the busy list to the device. A description of the XXstart routine is given in Section 7.10.4.

The device driver must also provide an XXprint routine which the kernel can call to display error messages on the console. All the XXprint routine has to do is call cmn_err(K) to display the message:

```
void
XXprint(dev, message)
    dev_t dev;
    char *message;
```

There is an example XXprint routine in the RAM disk driver below.

The remainder of the kernel interface (XXinit, XXopen, XXclose, XXintr and XXhalt) is described in Section 7.10. XXstrategy and XXprint routines are all that we require to write a simple RAM disk driver.

7.5   A RAM disk driver

The following RAM disk device driver illustrates the principles that we have discussed so far. It manages an area of kernel virtual memory of RAMD_SIZE kilobytes, set up by a call to memget(K) in XXinit. Since there is no actual hardware to be controlled, all of the kernel's requests can be satisfied at task-time, without the need for a busy list or an XXstart routine. The XXstrategy routine is responsible for copying data between the RAM disk and the buffer cache, using the copyio(K) routine:

```
copyio(paddr, caddr, nbytes, mapping)
    paddr_t paddr;
    caddr_t caddr;
    int nbytes, mapping;
```

Note that the paddr parameter must be a physical address. The ktop(K) macro is used to convert b_un.b_addr from a kernel virtual address to a physical address.

Here is the device driver:

```
/*
 * src/ramd.c
 *
 * A sample block device driver.
 *
 * ./configure -a ramdinit open close strategy -b -m MAJOR
 */

#include ⟨sys/types.h⟩
#include ⟨sys/param.h⟩
#include ⟨sys/sysmacros.h⟩
#include ⟨sys/errno.h⟩
#include ⟨sys/cmn_err.h⟩
#include ⟨sys/dir.h⟩
#include ⟨sys/signal.h⟩
#include ⟨sys/page.h⟩
#include ⟨sys/seg.h⟩
#include ⟨sys/user.h⟩
#include ⟨sys/mmu.h⟩
#include ⟨sys/map.h⟩
#include ⟨sys/iobuf.h⟩
#include ⟨sys/buf.h⟩
#include ⟨sys/immu.h⟩
#include ⟨sys/region.h⟩
#include ⟨sys/proc.h⟩

/*
 * The following XXtab is the anchor for the device's busy
 * list. We must declare it to keep configure(ADM) content,
 * even though this device driver doesn't use it.
 */

struct iobuf ramdtab;

#define RAMD_SIZE   400                     /* Kilobytes */

char *ramdbase;

/*
 * ramdinit()
 *
 * Allocate RAMD_SIZE kilobytes of memory with memget(K)
 */
```

```
ramdinit()
{
     ramdbase = (char *)ctob(memget(btoc(RAMD_SIZE * BSIZE)));
     printcfg("ramd", 0, 0, -1, -1, "%dK allocated",
             RAMD_SIZE);
}
ramdopen()
{}
ramdclose()
{}
void
ramdprint(dev, str)
     dev_t dev;
     char *str;
{
     cmn_err(CE_NOTE, "%s on RAM disk major %d, minor %d",
         str, major(dev), minor(dev));
}
/*
 * XXstrategy() is called when the kernel wants us
 * to do I/O. The I/O request is described by bp.
 */
void
ramdstrategy(bp)
     register struct buf *bp;
{
     int flag;
     char *base;
     if (bp->b_blkno < 0) {
          bp->b_flags |= B_ERROR;
          iodone(bp);
          return;
     }
     if (bp->b_blkno >= (RAMD_SIZE * 2)) {
          /*
           * The request starts at the end of, or beyond
           * the end of, the device.
           */
          if (bp->b_blkno == (RAMD_SIZE * 2)
              && (bp->b_flags & B_READ)) {
               /*
                * If we're reading, that's OK. Indicate
                * end-of-file by setting b_resid, then
                * return. DO NOT set B_ERROR.
                */
               bp->b_resid = bp->b_bcount;
          } else {
               /*
                * If we're writing, that's an error.
                */
```

```
                        bp->b_flags |= B_ERROR;
                        bp->b_error = ENXIO;
                }
                iodone(bp);
                return;
        }
        /*
         * The request is valid. Compute the starting offset
         * into the RAM disk, and copyio(K) data from this
         * point.
         */
        base = ramdbase + (bp->b_blkno * 512);
        flag = bp->b_flags & B_READ? U_WKD: U_RKD;
        if (copyio(ktop(paddr(bp)), base, bp->b_bcount, flag)
            == -1) {
                cmn_err(CE_WARN, "bad copyio(K) on RAM disk");
        }
        iodone(bp);
}
```

7.6   The geometry of a hard disk

A hard disk typically contains a number of platters mounted onto a spindle. Each platter has two surfaces, and there is a separate read/write head for each surface. Each surface is organized into a number of concentric tracks, and the tracks are divided into sectors. Each track contains the same number of sectors,[8] and the sectors contain the data that is read or written by the kernel.

7.6.1   Cylinders, heads and sectors

From the device driver's point of view, a disk is a set of cylinders, heads and sectors. A cylinder is the vertical set of tracks which are at the same offset within each of the surfaces. The track to be accessed is specified by a cylinder and head number, and the sector is specified within the track. Figure 7.7 illustrates these components.

As previously described, the device driver's job is to present the data on the device as a logically contiguous single-dimensional array of fixed-size blocks. The kernel might issue a request to the disk driver to 'read block 167 from the root filesystem', which must be translated by the device driver's XXstart routine to a request such as

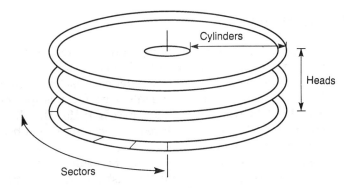

Figure 7.7   Cylinders, heads and sectors.

'read 2 sectors from the disk at {cylinder, head, starting sector}'. The XXstart routine translates the kernel's request, dealing with any bad track mapping, and then passes the request out to the hardware.

7.6.2 Low-level formatting

Before the hard disk firmware is able to recognize tracks and sectors, the disk must be formatted. Formatting is a low-level operation that is done before the Operating System is first installed, and it varies between one type of disk controller and another.

For example, to format drives attached to an Adaptec ACB-2322 ESDI disk controller, you must boot from DOS, and then run DEBUG. At the − prompt, type G=C800:5 to run the formatting software on the disk controller:

```
A> DEBUG
−G=C800:5
```

The disk controller writes track numbers and sector numbers (called sector IDs) onto the disk, and computes an Error Correction Code (ECC) value for each sector. The track numbers and sector IDs are used by the disk drive to locate individual sectors on the disk, in response to requests from the device driver and controller. The ECC is used to check that the sector was read correctly, and is recomputed and rewritten each time a sector is written. The ECC can also be used to repair corrupted parts of the sector if a bad block develops whilst the disk is in use.

7.6.3 Interleave

The physical gap between logically adjacent sectors is called the interleave factor. If the controller has no on-board caching facility, it is essential to specify the correct interleave factor in order to optimize I/O performance. If the wrong interleave factor is specified, the kernel may have to wait longer than necessary for the disk controller to interrupt at the end of each request, leading to a substantial drop in throughput of sequential I/O.

Figure 7.8 shows a disk formatted with an interleave of 1. An interleave of 1 implies that the disk drive, the controller and the device driver can together respond to an interrupt from one request and issue a request to read or write the next logical sector in less than the time it takes for the disk to spin from the end of one sector to the beginning of the next. That is, an entire track can be read sector-by-sector within one revolution of the disk. If the drive, controller or device driver is too slow, then the next logical sector may have already passed beneath the disk head, and in the worst possible case there will be a delay of almost an entire disk revolution before the sector comes underneath the disk head again and can be read. That is, for a disk that has 33 sectors per track, it will take 33 disk

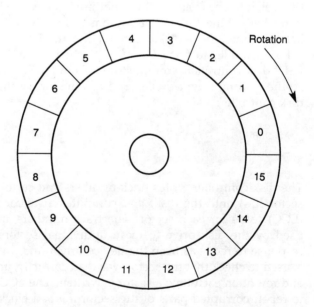

Figure 7.8   A disk interleave factor of 1.

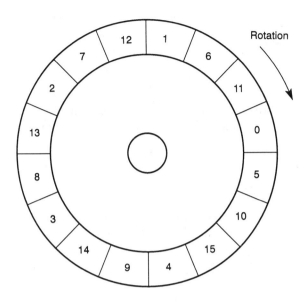

Figure 7.9   A disk interleave factor of 3.

revolutions to read the entire track, sector-by-sector! Controllers such
as the Adaptec ACB-2322 have an on-board cache which effectively
alleviates this problem. Whenever they receive a request to read a
sector, the entire track is read into the cache. Subsequent read
requests from that track can then be satisfied from the controller's
cache without making any further disk accesses.

Figure 7.9 shows a disk formatted with an interleave of 3, which
gives the drive, controller and device driver more time to respond to
an interrupt and issue the next request. The entire track can be read
within three disk revolutions.

Being aware of the disk controller's capabilities and being aware of
the overheads of the device driver and the kernel are important
factors when specifying the interleave for the disk format. The manufacturer of the disk controller usually advises which interleave factor
you should use, but it is often worth experimenting with different
values to see which gives you the best results.

The mkfs(ADM) command has two optional parameters called gap
and inblocks,[9] which allow you to specify different values for filesystem interleave (the gap parameter), without having to reformat the
disk.

7.7   Partitions and divisions

The translation of kernel requests to requests which the controller can understand is complicated by a further abstraction of the physical disk surface into partitions and divisions. Partitions and divisions have special meanings in SCO UNIX, and we shall explain them here.

7.7.1   Partitions

A hard disk has between one and four partitions,[10] which together span the entire surface of the disk. A partition contains a complete Operating System, such as DOS, SCO XENIX, or SCO UNIX. It is therefore possible to have many different Operating Systems installed on a single hard disk. Partitions are maintained by the fdisk(ADM) utility, and are set up during the installation procedure. The sizes, locations and types of each partition are maintained in a partition table at the end of the Masterboot block in sector 0 on the disk. See Figure 7.10. This partition table is read into memory when the disk is first opened and is used by the device driver to validate and translate I/O requests from the kernel.

One of the partitions is designated the active partition, and it is this partition the machine's BIOS will boot from. The active partition can be changed with fdisk(ADM).

A bootable partition contains a number of other structures, including primary and secondary bootstraps, a division table and possibly a table of bad tracks. Figure 7.11 summarizes these structures.

7.7.2   Divisions

Each partition can be further divided into between one and eight divisions.[11] A division can contain a filesystem, it may be empty, or it may have special functionality dependent on the Operating System installed on the partition. By convention, division 0 in the bootable UNIX partition on the primary drive contains the root filesystem, and division 1 is the swap area. The machine will normally boot from /boot and /unix in the root filesystem.

SCO UNIX uses division 6 to record diagnostics from fsck(ADM), and division 7 to map the entire partition. Divisions are maintained by the divvy(ADM) utility, and are set up during the installation procedure. Each partition has its own division table. See Figure 7.11.

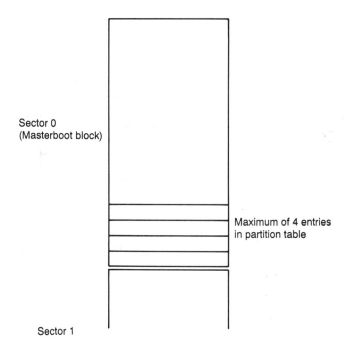

Figure 7.10 The Masterboot block contains the partition table.

The partition table should be modified only during installation. However, it is possible to change division information at any time, although you must be careful. For example, you could use divvy(ADM) to split an existing division, containing a filesystem called /u, into two new divisions containing filesystems /x and /y. Remember to take a backup of the /u filesystem before you start!

7.7.3 The minor device number

A disk driver identifies partitions and divisions by examining bits in the minor device number. Hard disk drivers for SCO UNIX should interpret the eight bits as follows:

- Bits 7 and 6 encode the physical drive number within the controller (physical drive 0, 1, 2 or 3).

- Bits 5, 4 and 3 encode the partition within the drive (partition 1, 2, 3 or 4).
  The active partition is a special case and is indicated by setting bits 5 and 3.

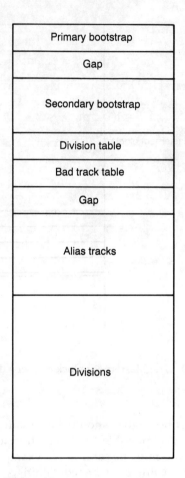

Figure 7.11   A bootable partition.

- Bits 2, 1 and 0 encode the division within the partition (division 0, 1, 2, 3, 4, 5, 6 or 7).

For example, minor device 40, represented as 00 101 000 in binary, selects division 0, on the active partition, on physical drive 0. Minor device 40 identifies /dev/root.

Note that in the XXstrategy routine, the device number is available in b_dev.

Section 7.9 will show how a hard disk driver should use the minor device number in cooperation with the kernel disk support routines to support partitions and divisions.

7.8 Bad blocks

All ST506 and ESDI disk controllers, and some SCSI disk controllers, require support from the device driver to deal with bad blocks. A bad block is a block that cannot be read or written without causing a checksum error, and which cannot be fixed by the controller's ECC firmware. When a bad block is detected, the controller sets an error bit in the status register, so that the device driver's XXintr routine can decide whether to retry the same request again, or to report an error on the console.

A typical 300 Mb ESDI drive may have between 20 and 50 bad blocks when it is shipped from the manufacturer, and of course more bad blocks may develop during the drive's lifetime.

SCO UNIX provides kernel support routines for use by the badtrk(ADM) utility and the device driver, which maintain a bad track table on each non-DOS partition on the drive. The bad track table is located at a fixed location within the partition, and is read into memory when the disk is first opened. It is followed by an area reserved for the alias tracks. The table is created and initialized by badtrk(ADM) during the installation procedure,[12] and can be modified later if any new bad tracks develop. See Figure 7.12.

The device driver's XXstart routine examines the in-core bad track table each time it translates an I/O request. If the request spans a bad track, it is remapped by XXstart into smaller sub-requests before being issued to the device.

Of course, mapping a bad track to an alias track can undo all of the good work of disksort(K), as the disk heads have to move to the alias track to access the data, and then back again for the next request. But this is a relatively small price to pay to ensure the integrity of the disk.

The next section will explain how a hard disk driver can use the kernel support routines to manage bad tracks.

Figure 7.13 shows a complete physical disk with partitions, divisions, bootstraps and a bad track table.

7.9 Kernel support for disk drivers

SCO UNIX provides a number of kernel support routines for hard disk device drivers to use. These routines allow the device driver to support partitions, divisions and bad tracks. You should use these routines if you want your device driver to be able to respond correctly

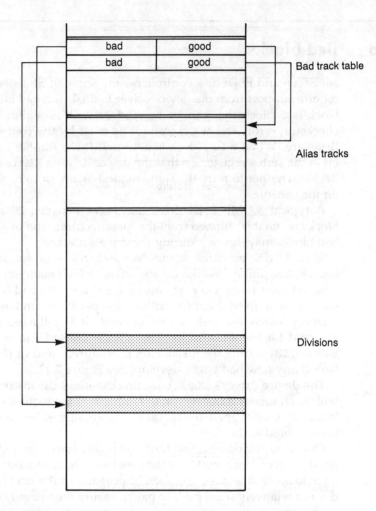

Figure 7.12 Bad tracks.

to the standard SCO UNIX commands badtrk(ADM), divvy(ADM), dparam(ADM) and fdisk(ADM).[13]

The next section shows these routines being used in the RAM disk driver from Section 7.5.

7.9.1 Data structures

The principal data structure used by each of the routines is a struct diskinfo, defined in ⟨sys/disk.h⟩. A dip_t is a pointer to one of these structures. Secondary data structures are in ⟨sys/dio.h⟩:

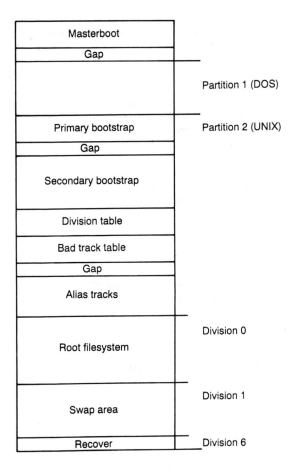

Figure 7.13   A disk with two partitions, DOS and UNIX.

```
/*
 * Disk geometry (from <sys/dio.h>). Included
 * in the struct diskinfo, below.
 */
struct dparam {
     unsigned short d_cylin;      /* cylinders per drive */
     unsigned short d_heads;      /* heads per drive */
     unsigned short d_sectors;    /* sectors per cylinder */
     unsigned short d_bytes;      /* bytes per sector */
     unsigned short d_reserved;   /* sectors reserved for
                                     system use at
                                     beginning of disk */
};
```

```
/*
 * Drive parameters. Included in the
 * struct diskinfo, below.
 */
struct dkparms {
    unsigned short prcmp;          /* Write precompensation */
    unsigned short lzone;          /* Landing zone */
    unsigned short wrt_reduce;     /* Write reduce cylinder */
    unsigned char  ecc;            /* Ecc level */
    unsigned char  ctrl;           /* Control surface */
};
/*
 * The diskinfo structure. Only the parts
 * directly relevant to the device driver
 * are shown.
 */
struct diskinfo {
    int    dkflags;
    int    (*dkstrat)();           /* XXstrategy() */
    struct    dparam    dkparam;   /* drive params */
    struct    dkparms   dkparms;   /* more drive params */
    int    spcyl;                  /* sectors per cylinder */
    int    dkcinit;                /* re-initialize
                                      controller when set */
/*
 * Device drivers should not set or examine
 * anything past this point.
 */
    ...
    ...
}
```

A diskinfo structure is allocated by the dkalloc(K) support routine:

```
dip_t
dkalloc()
```

This routine should be called from XXopen on the first open of each
physical drive. It allocates an empty struct diskinfo for use by the
device driver. There should be one of these structures for each physical drive.

The device driver's XXopen should fill out dkstrat with the address
of XXstrategy, and fill out dkparam and dkparms with disk geometry
information obtained from the ROM BIOS, see ⟨sys/rom.h⟩.

When the physical drive is closed, the struct diskinfo should be
freed. In practice, most disk drivers do not call dkfree(K), as the last
close of a physical drive implies that the kernel is shutting down:

```
dkfree(dip)
    dip_t dip;
```

Once the struct diskinfo has been allocated and filled out, the device driver's XXopen routine should call dksetup(K) to read the Masterboot block, partition table, division table and bad track table from the drive. The dksetup(K) routine makes calls to the device driver's XXstrategy routine to read the appropriate blocks from the device. If all is well, dksetup(K) calls printcfg(K) to display the information from the struct dkcntlrtab (see ⟨sys/disk.h⟩):

```
dksetup(dip, dev, dkcntlr)
    dip_t dip;
    dev_t dev;
    struct dkcntlrtab *dkcntlr;
```

The badtrk(ADM), divvy(ADM), dparam(ADM) and fdisk(ADM) commands all send ioctl(S) requests to the device driver's XXioctl routine. The XXioctl routine should validate the ioctl(S) request against those listed in ⟨sys/dio.h⟩, and then just call dkiocomm(K). The dkiocomm(K) routine uses information from the struct diskinfo, and the tables obtained from the drive by dksetup(K). It will arrange for all relevant changes (for example, a new division table from divvy(ADM)) to be written out to the disk:

```
dkiocomm(dip, dev, cmd, addr, mode)
    dip_t dip;
    dev_t dev;
    caddr_t addr;
    int cmd, mode;
```

7.9.2 Partitions and divisions

The information set up and managed by dksetup(K) and dkiocomm(K) is available for use by other routines in the device driver. In particular, XXstrategy and XXstart can both call dksecstart(K) to determine the physical offset (in 512-byte sectors) of the start of the minor device described by b_dev:

```
dksecstart(dip, dev)
    dip_t dip;
    dev_t dev;
```

The size (in 512-byte sectors) of the minor device described by b_dev can be obtained from dksecsize(K):

```
dksecsize(dip, dev)
    dip_t dip;
    dev_t dev;
```

7.9.3 Bad blocks

The bad track table described in Section 7.8 is set up and managed by the badtrk(ADM) command. It is read from the disk during dksetup(K), called by XXopen.

The table must be examined by XXstart before each I/O request is sent to the disk controller. If the I/O request spans a bad track, it must be divided into two separate sub-requests:

(1) If the I/O request is already on a bad track (which has been mapped to an alias track), the first sub-request will be to transfer the sectors up to the end of the alias track.

   If the I/O request is starting on a good track but extends onto a bad track, the first sub-request will be to transfer the sectors up to the beginning of the bad track.

(2) The second sub-request will be to transfer the remaining sectors.

Note that the second sub-request may span further bad tracks. The XXstart and XXintr routines must cooperate to ensure that both sub-requests are sent to the device before the buffer header is released with iodone(K).

The kernel support routine dktrkcnt(K) examines the bad track table for the partition described by the struct diskinfo:

```
dktrkcnt(dip, dev, tp)
     dip_t dip;
     dev_t dev;
     unsigned *tp;
```

The starting track of the current I/O request is *tp. If *tp is a bad track, dktrkcnt(K) replaces it with its alias track and returns 0.

If there are no bad tracks between *tp and the end of the partition, dktrkcnt(K) returns −1.

If there is a bad track between *tp and the end of the partition, dktrkcnt(K) returns the number of good tracks between *tp and the next bad track.

Figure 7.14 shows a typical bad track situation.

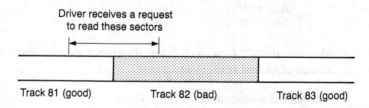

Figure 7.14 A typical bad track situation.

7.10 An extended RAM disk driver

We have extended the RAM disk driver from Section 7.5 to illustrate all the principles that we have been discussing in this chapter, including the use of the kernel support routines described in Section 7.9 to support partitions, divisions and bad tracks.

We have simulated disk latency by setting a timeout(K) after data has been transferred between the buffer cache and the device. When the timeout(K) expires, XXintr is called.

The XXstrategy routine must now maintain a queue of outstanding I/O requests, which is ordered with disksort(K), and the XXstart routine becomes responsible for sending requests to the device. In our example device driver, XXstart calls copyio(K) and then sets the timeout(K).

We have added an XXioctl routine, via the character device interface,[14] so that the driver can respond to divvy(ADM), fdisk(ADM) and badtrk(ADM) commands.[15] A simple disk geometry is defined by RAMD_SECTORS, RAMD_TRACKS and RAMD_CYLINDERS.

We will describe the remaining block device driver routines before presenting the complete device driver.

7.10.1 XXinit

```
void
XXinit()
```

The XXinit routine is not used in SCO UNIX disk device drivers. Instead, initialization of the hardware and the disk management data structures (partition table, division tables, and so on) is deferred until XXopen. The reason for this is that many of the data structures are initialized by actually reading them from the disk. This is done by making calls to XXstrategy, and that of course implies that interrupts must be enabled. Recall from Chapter 3 that interrupts are *not* enabled during XXinit.

We use XXinit in our RAM disk driver to allocate some virtual memory for the device.

7.10.2 XXopen

```
XXopen(dev, flag, id)
    dev_t dev;
    int flag, id;
```

The XXopen routine is called on each open of a device (typically a partition or division).

The flag parameter is a bitwise OR of the following values from ⟨sys/file.h⟩:

- FAPPEND to open the device for appended writes.
- FEXCL to open the device for exclusive access.
- FNDELAY to open the device immediately and return without sleeping, even if there is a problem.
- FREAD to open the device for reading.
- FSTOPIO to prevent further I/O.
- FSYNC to open the device for synchronous writes.
- FWRITE to open the device for writing.

The id parameter is a bitwise OR of the following values from ⟨sys/open.h⟩:

- OTYP_BLK to open the device for block I/O.
- OTYP_CHR to open the device for raw I/O.
- OTYP_MNT to open the device to mount a filesystem.
- OTYP_SWP to open the device as a swap device.

On the first open, XXopen should use the kernel support routines dkalloc(K) and dksetup(K) described in Section 7.9 to initialize a struct diskinfo for the drive.

7.10.3 XXclose

```
XXclose(dev, flag)
     dev_t dev;
     int flag;
```

This routine is called on the last close of a device. The flag parameter corresponds to the flag parameter of XXopen.

In some disk drivers, XXclose calls dkfree(K) to release the struct diskinfo allocated in XXopen, although this is not actually necessary.

7.10.4 XXstart

```
void
XXstart()
```

The XXstart routine is called at task-time from XXstrategy, and at interrupt-time from XXintr, to send the next I/O request from the busy list to the device. The buffer header describing the request is at XXtab.b_actf.

XXstart can use dksecstart(K) to obtain the physical offset of the start of the device specified by b_dev, and add b_blkno to obtain the physical offset of the start of the transfer, in sectors.

After mapping the request to a disk coordinate (a starting sector within a track and cylinder), XXstart can check for any bad blocks by calling dktrkcnt(K), and remap the request accordingly.

The request can then be sent to the controller. Recall that ST506 and ESDI disk controllers do not have any DMA capability, so additional support is required from the XXstart and XXintr routines:

- If the request is a B_READ, XXstart sends the disk coordinates to the controller, followed by a command to initiate the read.

  Soon afterwards, the controller will raise an interrupt to indicate that the data has been read from the device, and is now available via the controller's data register. The XXintr routine must then transfer the data from the controller into the buffer cache.

- If the request is a B_WRITE, XXstart sends the disk coordinates to the controller, followed by the data from the buffer cache, followed by a command to initiate the write.

  Soon afterwards, the controller will raise an interrupt to indicate that the data has been written to the device.

The extended RAM disk driver uses copyio(K) to simulate DMA activity.

7.10.5 XXintr

```
void
XXintr(irq)
     int irq;
```

The XXintr routine is responsible for dealing with interrupts from the controller. The majority of these interrupts will be to indicate that read and write requests issued by XXstart have completed, but the controller may interrupt for a number of other reasons:

- The device driver has issued a head recalibration request to seek the disk heads back to cylinder 0, before retrying a read or write request that previously returned an error.

- There has been a hardware failure on the controller or on one of the drives attached to it.

- The hardware has generated a spurious interrupt, which must be ignored.

If the device driver is expecting an interrupt, XXtab.b_active and/or XXtab.b_actf will be set, so it is straightforward for XXintr to distinguish real and spurious interrupts.

Transfer errors are usually indicated by an error bit in the status register – the actual error can then be obtained by reading the error register. The total number of errors for the current request is maintained in XXtab.b_errcnt. If this count exceeds a predetermined value (for example, 4), an error is returned to the user via b_flags, and the request is aborted.[16] However, if the error count has not exceeded the limit, the request is retried from where it failed. This is done by issuing a call to XXstart from inside XXintr, which will retry the same request from XXtab.b_actf.

Some disk device drivers issue a request to recalibrate the disk heads before re-attempting the request, and if the request continues to fail (a bad block may have developed), you are sometimes able to hear the disk heads seeking backwards and forwards before the error is finally reported on the console.

If there are no errors, the next action of XXintr depends on whether the interrupt is the result of a read or write request, as described in XXstart, above:

- A read interrupt indicates that the data has been read from the device into the controller, and should now be transferred into the buffer cache.

- A write interrupt indicates that the data has been written from the controller to the device.

If the request spanned any bad tracks, XXintr must now reprogram the controller to transfer the remaining sectors,[17] and then return to wait for the next interrupt to arrive.

When the complete request has been transferred, XXintr should clear XXtab.b_active and XXtab.b_errcnt, and move XXtab.b_actf along the busy list:

```
XXtab.b_actf = bp->av_forw;
```

Finally, XXintr should call iodone(K) to wakeup(K) anyone who is waiting for the transfer to complete, and then call XXstart to send the next request from the busy list to the device.

7.10.6 XXhalt

```
void
XXhalt()
```

XXhalt is called when the Operating System is shutting down. It should do device-specific tasks as required, such as seeking the disk heads to the landing zone.

Here is the extended RAM disk driver. At the exercise at the end of this chapter, you will have an opportunity to test it with badtrk(ADM), divvy(ADM) and fdisk(ADM):

```
/*
 * src/ramd.c
 *
 * A sample block device driver which uses the dk*() kernel
 * support routines.
 *
 * We have added a simulated interrupt routine, called by a
 * timeout(K) primed from XXstart().
 *
 * We have also added an XXioctl() routine in the raw
 * interface for use by fdisk(ADM), divvy(ADM), etc.
 *
 * The XXread() and XXwrite() routines of the raw interface
 * will not be functional until Chapter 8.
 *
 * To configure this driver, you must specify -b and -c
 * together, so that the block and character switches are
 * correctly filled out.
 *
 * ./configure -a ramdinit open close strategy read write
 * ioctl -b -c -m MAJOR
 */
#include <sys/types.h>
#include <sys/param.h>
#include <sys/sysmacros.h>
#include <sys/errno.h>
#include <sys/cmn_err.h>
#include <sys/dir.h>
#include <sys/signal.h>
#include <sys/page.h>
#include <sys/seg.h>
#include <sys/user.h>
#include <sys/mmu.h>
#include <sys/map.h>
#include <sys/iobuf.h>
#include <sys/buf.h>
```

```
#include ⟨sys/immu.h⟩
#include ⟨sys/dio.h⟩
#include ⟨sys/disk.h⟩
#include ⟨sys/region.h⟩
#include ⟨sys/proc.h⟩

/*
 * The following XXtab is the anchor for the device's busy
 * list. This driver uses it.
 */

struct iobuf ramdtab;

/*
 * The following is the disk geometry:
 *
 *     RAMD_SECTORS    sectors per track
 *     RAMD_TRACKS     tracks/heads
 *     RAMD_CYLINDERS  cylinders
 *
 *     RAMD_SIZE size of disk, kilobytes
 */

#define RAMD_SECTORS    16
#define RAMD_TRACKS     4
#define RAMD_CYLINDERS  32
#define RAMD_SIZE(RAMD_SECTORS * RAMD_TRACKS *
                  RAMD_CYLINDERS / 2)

/*
 * The following structure manages requests
 * split across bad tracks.
 */

struct ramdreq {
    int blkno;          /* copy of b_blkno */
    int rsectors;       /* requested sectors */
    int nsectors;       /* sectors available before
                           bad track */
    int tsectors;       /* actual number to be transferred */
} ramdreq;

char *ramdbase;
void ramdintr(), ramdstart(), ramdstrategy();

struct diskinfo *ramddip;
int ramdflags;

/*
 * ramdinit()
 *
 * Allocate RAMD_SIZE kilobytes of memory with memget(K).
 */

ramdinit()
{
    ramdbase = (char *)ctob(memget(btoc(RAMD_SIZE *
                                        BSIZE)));
}
```

```
/*
 * ramdopen()
 *
 * On the first XXopen(), dkalloc() a struct diskinfo
 * and then fill it out with the details of the RAM
 * disk geometry.
 *
 * Call dksetup() on every XXopen().
 */
ramdopen(dev, flag, id)
     dev_t dev;
     int flag, id;
{
     static int firsttime = 1;
     struct dkcntlrtab ramdctlr;
     struct dparam *dp;
     struct dkparms *dkp;
     if (ramddip == NULL) {
          /*
           * The first XXopen() will allocate a
           * struct diskinfo
           */
          if ((ramddip = dkalloc()) == NULL) {
               return;
          }
          ramddip->dkstrat = ramdstrategy;
     }
     if ((ramdflags & DK_PARAM) == 0) {
          /*
           * At this point a real driver would load the
           * disk parameters from the ROM BIOS, which
           * contains a struct hdpblk, see ⟨sys/rom.h⟩.
           *
           * Our example RAM driver fakes it.
           */
          dp = &ramddip->dkparam;
          dp->d_cylin = RAMD_CYLINDERS;
          dp->d_sectors = RAMD_SECTORS;
          dp->d_heads = RAMD_TRACKS;
          dp->d_bytes = DKSECTOR;        /* bytes per sector */

          ramddip->spcyl = dp->d_heads * dp->d_sectors;

          dkp = &ramddip->dkparms;
          dkp->prcmp = -1;               /* write precomp */
          dkp->ctrl = 0;                 /* control surface */
          dkp->lzone = RAMD_CYLINDERS;   /* landing zone */
          dkp->wrt_reduce = 0;           /* write reduce */
          dkp->ecc = 0;                  /* ecc */

          ramdflags |= DK_PARAM;
     }
```

```
            if (firsttime) {

                /*
                 * Set up ramdctlr.  These parameters will be
                 * printcfg(K)'d inside dksetup().
                 *
                 * Our example RAM driver fakes it.  The numbers
                 * are from an Adaptec ESDI controller.
                 */

                ramdctlr.base = 0x1f0;
                ramdctlr.offset = 7;
                ramdctlr.vec = 16;
            } else {

                ramdctlr.base = 0;
                ramdctlr.offset = 0;
                ramdctlr.vec = -1;
            }

            ramdctlr.dma = -1;
            ramdctlr.type = "RAM";

            /*
             * Now call dksetup() to read the Masterboot,
             * and printcfg(K) the RAM disk description.
             */

            dksetup(ramddip, dev, &ramdctlr);
            if (u.u_error) {

                return;
            }

            firsttime = 0;
    }

ramdclose()
{}

ramdread()
{}

ramdwrite()
{}

ramdprint(dev, str)
    dev_t dev;
    char *str;
{
    cmn_err(CE_NOTE, "%s on RAM disk major %d, minor %d",
        str, major(dev), minor(dev));
}

/*
 * XXstrategy() is called when the kernel wants us
 * to do I/O.  The I/O request is described by bp.
 */
```

```
void
ramdstrategy(bp)
     register struct buf *bp;
{
     int s;
     if (bp->b_blkno < 0) {
          bp->b_flags |= B_ERROR;
          iodone(bp);
          return;
     }
     if (bp->b_blkno >= (RAMD_SIZE * 2)) {
          /*
           * The request starts at the end of, or beyond
           * the end of, the device.
           */
          if (bp->b_blkno == (RAMD_SIZE * 2)
              && (bp->b_flags & B_READ)) {
               /*
                * Indicate End-Of-File by setting b_resid,
                * then return.  DO NOT set B_ERROR.
                */
               bp->b_resid = bp->b_bcount;
          } else {
               /*
                * Error
                */
               bp->b_flags |= B_ERROR;
               bp->b_error = ENXIO;
          }
          iodone(bp);
          return;
     }
     bp->b_sector = dksecstart(ramddip, bp->b_dev) +
                              bp->b_blkno;
     s = spl6();
     disksort(&ramdtab, bp);
     ramdstart();
     splx(s);
}
/*
 * ramdstart()
 *
 * Take the next request from the busy list and
 * send it to the device.
 *
 * The hard work is done for us by ramdxfer().
 */
```

```
      void
      ramdstart()
      {
            register struct buf *bp;
            /*
             * Nothing to do if we're already busy, or our
             * busy list is empty
             */
            if (ramdtab.b_active
                || ((bp = ramdtab.b_actf) == NULL)) {
                  return;
            }
            ramdtab.b_active++;

            /*
             * Set up a description of the request in ramdreq.
             *
             * This request may be updated by XXintr() if the
             * transfer has to be split by ramdxfer(), due to
             * bad tracks.
             */
            ramdreq.blkno = bp->b_blkno;
            ramdreq.rsectors = bp->b_bcount >> DKSSHIFT;

            ramdxfer(bp);
      }
      /*
       * ramdxfer()
       *
       * Called by XXstart() and by XXintr() to transfer
       * data between the buffer cache and the device.
       *
       * If the request spans a bad track, we will transfer
       * as much as we can until the next track, and arrange
       * for XXintr() to call us to transfer the remainder.
       */
      ramdxfer(bp)
            struct buf *bp;
      {
            daddr_t offset;
            int sector, tc, track, head, cylinder;
            /*
             * Determine the physical offset into the device,
             * then translate this to a disk coordinate:
             *
             * - starting sector
             * - starting track (0 thru RAMD_TRACKS *
             *   RAMD_CYLINDERS)
             * - starting head (not used by this RAM disk driver)
             * - starting cylinder (not used by this RAM disk
             *   driver)
             */
```

```
        offset = ramdreq.blkno + dksecstart(ramddip,
                                            bp->b_dev);
        sector = offset % RAMD_SECTORS;
        track = offset / RAMD_SECTORS;
        /*
         * dktrkcnt will tell us about any
         * bad tracks ahead
         */
        tc = dktrkcnt(ramddip, bp->b_dev, &track);

        head = track % RAMD_TRACKS;
        cylinder = track / RAMD_TRACKS;

        if (tc == -1) {
            /*
             * The request doesn't span any bad tracks,
             * so it's OK to transfer the number of sectors
             * required.
             */
            ramdreq.nsectors = ramdreq.rsectors;
            ramdio(bp);
            return;

        } else {
            /*
             * This track is bad and has already been replaced
             * by dktrkcnt() (tc == 0), or there is a bad
             * track somewhere ahead (tc >= 1).
             */
            if ((tc == 0) || (tc == 1)) {
                /*
                 * nsectors is the space available until
                 * the end of this track.
                 */
                ramdreq.nsectors = RAMD_SECTORS - sector;
                ramdio(bp);
                return;

            } else {
                /*
                 * nsectors is the space available until
                 * the next bad track.
                 */
                ramdreq.nsectors = RAMD_SECTORS - sector;
                ramdreq.nsectors += tc * RAMD_SECTORS;
                ramdio(bp);
                return;
            }
        }
}
```

```
/*
 * ramdio()
 *
 * Determine how much data we can xfer before
 * hitting a bad track, and then transfer it.
 *
 * Note that:
 *
 * ramdreq.rsectors is how many we want
 * ramdreq.nsectors is how many available
 * ramdreq.tsectors is how many we'll actually xfer
 */
ramdio(bp)
    struct buf *bp;
{
    char *base;
    int flag;
    if (ramdreq.rsectors > ramdreq.nsectors) {
        ramdreq.tsectors = ramdreq.nsectors;
        ramdreq.rsectors -= ramdreq.tsectors;
    } else {
        ramdreq.tsectors = ramdreq.rsectors;
        ramdreq.rsectors = 0;
    }
    base = ramdbase + ( ramdreq.blkno * 512 );
    flag = bp->b_flags & B_READ? U_WKD: U_RKD;
    if (copyio(ktop(paddr(bp)), base, ramdreq.tsectors <<
        DKSSHIFT, flag) == -1) {
        cmn_err(CE_WARN, "bad copyio(K) on RAM disk");
    };
    /*
     * Call XXintr() after approx 3 clock ticks
     */
    timeout(ramdintr, 0, 3);
}
/*
 * ramdintr() is called via a timeout(K) primed
 * in XXstart().
 *
 * Check for spurious interrupts (shouldn't be
 * any of these), and then wakeup everyone with
 * iodone(K).
 */
void
ramdintr()
{
    register struct buf *bp;
    if ((ramdtab.b_active == 0)
        || ((bp = ramdtab.b_actf) == NULL)) {
        return;
    }
```

```
        /*
         * Determine whether all of the request has
         * completed.  If not, call ramdxfer() to
         * do the remainder
         */
        if (ramdreq.rsectors != 0) {
            ramdreq.blkno += ramdreq.tsectors;
            ramdxfer(bp);
        }
        ramdtab.b_active = 0;
        /*
         * Move to the next request
         */
        ramdtab.b_actf = bp->av_forw;
        iodone(bp);
        ramdstart();
}
/*
 * ramdioctl() responds to ioctl(S) requests
 * from fdisk(ADM), divvy(ADM), etc.  We just
 * have to validate the request and pass it
 * to dkiocomm().
 */
ramdioctl(dev, cmd, addr, mode)
        dev_t dev;
        int cmd, mode;
        char *addr;
{
        switch (cmd) {
            case DIOGETP:
            case DIORPART:
            case DIOWPART:
            case DIORBTRK:
            case DIOWBTRK:
            case DIORBTRK22:
            case DIOWBTRK22:
            case DIORVDT:
            case DIOWVDT:
            case DIOBITP:
            case DIOSDISK:
            case DIORDISK:
            case DIOWDISK:
            case DIOSBTRK:
            case DIODKTYPE:
            case DIOFORCE22:
                    dkiocomm(ramddip, dev, cmd, addr, mode);
                    break;
            default:
                    u.u_error = EINVAL;
                    break;
        }
}
```

7.11   Direct memory access (DMA)

We have confined our discussions so far to ST506 and ESDI disk controllers, which do not have any DMA capability. We have seen that all data transfers between the kernel and the disk are managed by the kernel, either in XXstart for a B_WRITE or in XXintr for a B_READ.

Devices that do have DMA capability (including tapes, SCSI disks, CD-ROM drives) can relieve the kernel and the CPU of the overhead of transferring data, and leave them free to attend to more useful tasks such as executing processes! DMA controllers transfer data directly between the device and memory, without any intervention from the kernel or the CPU. See Figure 7.15.

7.11.1 Hardware support for DMA

ISA, EISA and MCA machines have two i8237 DMA controllers, which provide four 8-bit DMA channels and three 16-bit DMA channels, each capable of transferring up to 65535 bytes (words) between a device and memory.

The 8-bit channels are numbered from 0 through 3, and the 16-bit channels are numbered from 5 through 7. The channels are managed by a set of kernel support routines which provide for the allocation, configuration and release of each channel. Some controllers, such as the floppy disk controller, are hard-wired to use a specific channel (the floppy disk controller uses channel 2). Others (such as tape controllers) have a jumper on the card to configure the channel to be used. Once the channel number has been set, it can be read by the device driver's XXinit routine and used for all subsequent transfers.

7.11.2 Programming the DMA controllers

The kernel support routines for DMA provide two different methods for using the DMA controllers, called managed DMA and queued DMA.

Managed DMA

To use managed DMA, the device driver should allocate a channel with dma_alloc(K), program the details of the transfer with dma_param(K) and then enable the transfer with dma_enable(K). The device and the DMA controller then cooperate to manage the transfer.

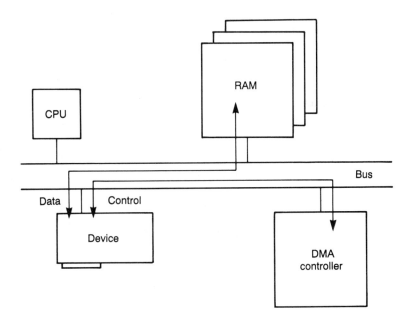

Figure 7.15 Direct memory access.

When the transfer is complete, the device raises an interrupt.

Block device drivers, including SCO's floppy disk driver, typically use managed DMA.

Queued DMA

To use queued DMA, the device driver should set up a struct dmareq (see ⟨sys/dma.h⟩) to describe the transfer, and then call dma_start(K) to add the structure to a queue of outstanding DMA requests.

When the required DMA channel becomes free, the routine specified in the d_proc field of the DMA request is called to program the details of the transfer with dma_param(K), and then enable the transfer with dma_enable(K), as with managed DMA.

When the transfer is complete, the device raises an interrupt.

Transfer errors

If the device indicates an error during the transfer, the device driver's XXintr routine can use dma_resid(K) to establish how much data was not transferred.

If the DMA channel is not being used exclusively by a particular device, the device driver should release it when it is not being used, using dma_relse(K).

7.11.3 An example of managed DMA

The following code extracts show you how SCO's floppy device driver uses managed DMA:

```
XXstrategy(bp)
    struct buf *bp
{
    ...
    ...
    disksort(&XXtab, bp);
    /*
     * Allocate DMA channel 2. We block (DMA_BLOCK)
     * until the channel is released by XXstart(), so
     * we may be put to sleep(K) inside dma_alloc(K).
     *
     * Hence MUST NOT call dma_alloc from XXstart()!
     */
    dma_alloc(DMA_CH2, DMA_BLOCK);
    XXstart();
}
XXstart()
{
    ...
    ...
    if ((XXtab.b_active == 0)
        || ((bp = XXtab.b_actf) == NULL)) {
        /*
         * Nothing to do. Release the DMA channel.
         */
        dma_relse(DMA_CH2);
    }
    /*
     * Issue SEEK request to position the head.
     * The device will call XXintr() when this has
     * been done.
     */
    ...
    ...
}
XXintr()
{
    ...
    ...
    /*
     * The SEEK command issued from XXstart() has
     * completed. Program the DMA transfer, and then
     * enable it.
     *
```

```
                    * Note that we specify the number of bytes to
                    * transfer, less 1. A transfer size of 0
                    * indicates 64K.
                    */
                  dma_param(DMA_CH2,
                        bp->b_flags & B_READ? DMA_Rdmode: DMA_Wrmode,
                        vtop(paddr(bp), bp->b_proc),
                        bp->b_bcount - 1);
                  dma_enable(DMA_CH2);

                  ...
                  ...
            }
```

Note the use of vtop(K) rather than ktop(K) in XXintr. This driver must use vtop(K) as it can do block and raw I/O, which means that paddr(bp) can be a kernel virtual address or a user virtual address. Raw I/O is discussed in the next chapter.

7.12 Summary

In this chapter, we have described the structure and operation of block device drivers. A block device driver is used to transfer fixed-size blocks of data between the buffer cache and a device such as a disk or tape. UNIX filesystems reside on divisions within a partition on a hard disk, and are accessed through a block device driver interface. The SCO UNIX kernel provides a number of support routines for disk drivers, which simplify the implementation of partitions, divisions and bad blocks. These routines were demonstrated in the extended RAM disk driver in Section 7.10.

In Chapter 8, we shall complete our description of block devices by adding a raw interface to the RAM disk driver.

QUIZ

To test your understanding of this chapter, try to answer the following questions.

7.1 What are the names of the three different lists of buffer headers maintained by the buffer cache system?

7.2 Is it possible for user processes to read(S) less than one block of data at a time from a regular file?

7.3 Can a read(S) system call complete before data is transferred from the device into the buffer cache? What about a write(S) system call?

7.4 Which kernel support routine is responsible for freeing buffer headers that have been used for write requests? What about read requests?

7.5 Assuming the disk controller is not capable of doing any DMA, which device driver routine is responsible for moving data between the buffer cache and the controller during a write request? Which routine is responsible during a read request?

7.6 Why isn't the XXinit routine responsible for initializing the data structures which the kernel uses to manage the drive?

7.7 What is one of the first things that the XXintr routine should do when it is called?

7.8 Why are I/O requests sorted onto the device's busy list?

EXERCISE

Compile, install and test the extended RAM disk driver from Section 7.10. Use fdisk(ADM) and badtrk(ADM) to set up the disk, and create a filesystem with divvy(ADM).

Here are some hints:

- Specify the -b and -c options together in the same configure(ADM) command to add details of the block and character interfaces.
- Refer to Section 7.7.3 to determine the minor device numbers to set up.

    You will need entries in /dev for the entire physical drive and the entire partition (both of these are special character device files).

- Use the -f rawdevice option of fdisk(ADM) to specify the entire physical drive:

    ```
    fdisk -f /dev/rawdevice
    ```

- Use the -e and -f options of badtrk(ADM) to specify the entire partition:

    ```
    badtrk -e -f /dev/rawdevice
    ```

- Use the -m option of divvy(ADM) to create one or more mountable filesystems:

    ```
    divvy -m /dev/rawdevice
    ```

    Advanced sessions:

- Follow the same steps again, but this time do not use badtrk(ADM). You will find that divvy(ADM) is able to allocate more space for your filesystem.
- Use divvy(ADM) to divide the single filesystem into two new filesystems.
- Experiment with different disk geometries.

NOTES

1. Tape devices are usually accessed through the raw device interface, described in Chapter 8.

2. Note that some read-ahead blocks may already be in the buffer cache from previous requests.

3. The maximum cluster size is 32 blocks, specified with the -c option of mkfs(ADM).

4. The default value is 600 on SCO UNIX 3.2v4.

5. b_un.b_addr is a user virtual address when the process is doing raw I/O rather than block I/O. Raw I/O is described in Chapter 8.

6. The size of the array hbuf is the tunable parameter NHBUF, which should be approximately one quarter of the total size of the buffer cache, rounded to the nearest power of 2. The v.v_hmask component of the bhash macro is NHBUF - 1.

7. iodone(K) must be called at the end of every I/O request, whether or not the request completed successfully.

8.   Hard disk technology is evolving so that the outermost tracks will in future contain more sectors than the innermost tracks.

9.   Although mkfs(ADM) requires gap and inblocks to be specified together, the value for inblocks is always ignored.

10. In other versions of UNIX, partitions may be referred to as virtual drives.

11. In other versions of UNIX, divisions may be referred to as partitions.

12. Disks that do not require kernel support for bad track mapping do not have space reserved for a bad track table nor any alias tracks. The division table is followed immediately by division 0.

13. The badtrack(ADM), divvy(ADM), dparam(ADM) and fdisk(ADM) commands work by issuing ioctl(S) requests to the character (raw) interface of the device driver.

14. The remaining parts of the character interface, XXread and XXwrite, will be described in Chapter 8.

15. The dkinit(ADM) command is not supported by this device driver.

16. The XXintr routine can report errors by calling deverr(K).

17. Note that XXintr cannot call XXstart to transfer the remaining sectors, because XXstart will issue the next request from the busy list!

8

Raw device drivers

8.1   Overview

In Chapter 7, we explained that block device drivers work by transferring fixed-size blocks of data between the kernel and the device, via
the buffer cache. The kernel interface to a block device driver is
through the XXstrategy routine, which is passed requests to read or
write 1 Kb blocks of data. The buffer cache and the block interface
offer many benefits with respect to ordinary file I/O.

However, there are times when the characteristics of a block device
driver interface prove to be more of a drawback than a benefit. For
example, when a filesystem is being archived onto a backup medium
with either the tar(C) or cpio(C) utilities, there is no advantage in
writing the archive via the buffer cache in 1 Kb blocks, as the backup
medium is not being accessed as a filesystem. The same argument
applies when an archive is being extracted into a filesystem – the
archive will be read sequentially. Indeed, if it were possible to completely bypass the buffer cache and to read and write the data in blocks
larger than 1 Kb, we could achieve a much faster transfer of data:

- Data would be transferred directly between user address space and
  the device, bypassing the buffer cache. That means that data is
  copied only once, not twice as is the case for block devices.
- The block size would not be limited to 1 Kb.
  On devices that have a DMA capability (for example, tapes), the
  block size is limited by the capabilities of the DMA controllers,
  which is 64 Kb on ISA, EISA and MCA machines.
  On devices that do not have a DMA capability, the block size is
  limited by the size of a segment, which is 4 Gb on i386 and i486
  based machines.

The ability to transfer larger blocks of data means that the hardware is
accessed less often, and the result is a much higher throughput.

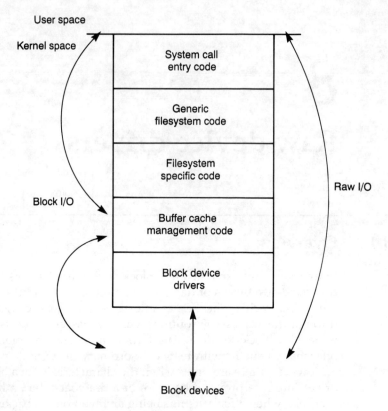

Figure 8.1 Block I/O and raw I/O.

This method of data transfer which bypasses the buffer cache is called raw I/O. Figure 8.1 summarizes the differences between block and raw I/O.

In this chapter, we shall explain how raw I/O is implemented via the character device kernel interface for disk and tape devices. In the exercise at the end of the chapter, we shall add a raw I/O capability to the disk device driver from Chapter 7.

8.2 Raw I/O on paged architectures

Devices that have a DMA capability require additional support from the device driver when doing raw I/O on machines that have a paged memory management architecture, such as the i386 and i486 CPUs.

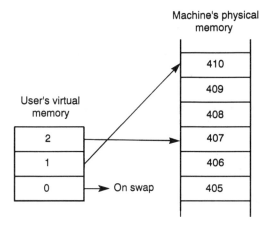

Figure 8.2   User's virtual memory in the machine's physical memory.

This is because the DMA controllers have no knowledge of the underlying architecture of the machine, and deal with physical addresses only. The user's virtual address space is *not* physically contiguous, and the pages spanning a user's buffer may be scattered throughout physical memory, possibly even paged or swapped out to the swap device. Figure 8.2 illustrates a typical situation.

Therefore, before a raw I/O operation can start, the driver must ensure that all of the appropriate pages are resident in the user's address space, and that DMA activity will not cross page boundaries which are not physically contiguous.

By contrast, neither of these issues arises for a block device driver, as the blocks are always resident in the buffer cache (they are part of the kernel), and they never cross page boundaries.

Disk drivers and tape drivers which do raw I/O deal with these problems in different ways.

8.3   Conventions for raw device drivers

Adding a raw interface to a device driver is relatively straightforward, once the underlying block device driver is working. The following conventions apply:

- The additional kernel interface routines which are required for the character device share the same source file as the block device.

- The same major and minor device numbers are used as for the block device.
- The special file names in /dev are prefixed with the letter r. For example, /dev/fd096ds15 is the block device for the floppy disk, and the raw device is /dev/rfd096ds15.

The kernel accesses raw device drivers through the character device switch table cdevsw.

8.4   Disks and raw I/O

As described above, raw transfers to a disk pass directly between user address space and the device, and offer an improved throughput when compared with block I/O. In this section, we shall show how easy it is to add a raw interface to a disk driver.

8.4.1   Kernel support for raw disks

The SCO UNIX kernel provides three support routines for use by raw disk drivers, called physck(K), physio(K) and dma_breakup(K).

physck(K)

```
physck(nblocks, rw)
    int nblocks, rw;
```

The physck(K) routine should be called from XXread and XXwrite (see below) to check that the user's I/O request described in the U-area can be satisfied within the size of the device (that is, the partition or division) which the user has specified. The nblocks parameter describes the size of the device in 512-byte blocks, and is typically the result of a call to dksecsize(K):

```
if (physck(dksecsize(XXdip, dev), B_READ)) {
    /*
     * User's request is valid
     */
    ...
    ...
}
```

The physck(K) routine returns non-zero if the request is valid. If the request is invalid, physck(K) returns 0, and sets u.u_error to ENXIO.

physio(K)

```
physio(breakup, bp, dev, rw)
    int (*breakup)(), rw;
    struct buf *bp;
    dev_t dev;
```

The physio(K) routine is central to the operation of disk and tape raw I/O. Its main job is to set up a buffer header with details of the user's request, described in the U-area fields u.u_base, u.u_offset and u.u_count, and then to initiate I/O by calling the driver's XXbreakup routine, as specified by the breakup parameter. The XXbreakup routine is described in the next section. Physio(K) is called from the driver's XXread or XXwrite routines, after they have validated the request with physck(K):

```
XXread(dev)
    dev_t dev;
{
    if (physck(dksecsize(XXdip, dev), B_READ)) {
        physio(XXbreakup, (struct buf *)0, dev, B_READ)
    }
}
```

Physio(K) first of all probes the user's data pages by reading a byte from each of them. Pages that are not present in memory will either be faulted in from the disk, or allocated Demand-Fill-With-Zeros by the kernel. Each of the pages is then locked into memory so that they cannot be swapped or paged out whilst the raw I/O is happening. See Figure 8.3, and compare this with Figure 8.2. Note that page 0 has been faulted in from swap, and that page 2 has been paged out and faulted back in again to a *different* physical page whilst the user process has been running.

If the caller has not passed a struct buf parameter, physio(K) allocates one from the NPBUF resource, and fills out the details of the transfer as described in the U-area. Before the request is dispatched to XXbreakup, physio(K) checks that each of the user's pages can be accessed by the DMA controller. On ISA and MCA architectures, only the first 16 Mb of memory can be DMA'd – if any of the user's data pages are above this threshold, the entire request is remapped into kernel address space using pages from the DMAABLEBUF resource.[1]

Finally, physio(K) calls XXbreakup to initiate the transfer, and then sleep(K)s waiting for B_DONE.

When the transfer is complete, XXbreakup returns, physio(K) unlocks the user's data pages, returns the buffer header to the NPBUF resource, and then returns to XXread or XXwrite.

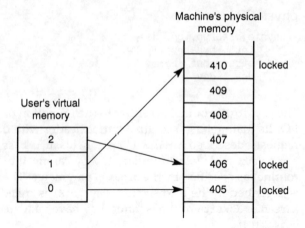

Figure 8.3   Physio(K) locks each page into memory.

The driver's XXbreakup routine is called by physio(K), and is responsible for dividing the complete raw I/O request into separate pages, arranging for I/O to happen to each page, and stopping and restarting DMA at the page boundaries. Fortunately, this isn't as difficult as it sounds, as the kernel support routine dma_breakup(K) does all of the difficult work, calling XXstrategy when necessary.

dma_breakup(K)

```
dma_breakup(strat, bp)
    int (*strat)();
    struct buf *bp;
```

The dma_breakup(K) routine examines the U-area request, and divides the transfer into page-sized blocks (4Kb on an i386 or an i486 CPU), and calls XXstrategy for each page. It adjusts u.u_base, u.u_offset and u.u_count after each transfer, and uses these to set new values for bp->b_bcount and bp->b_un.b_addr before each new call to XXstrategy.

Recall from Chapter 7 that the final conversion of bp->b_un.b_addr to a physical address is done by a call to ktop(K) from the driver's XXstart routine. In a raw device driver, bp->b_un.b_addr can be a kernel virtual address *or* a user virtual address, so XXstart must use vtop(K) instead:

```
vtop(paddr(bp), bp->b_proc);
```

The implementation of XXbreakup is described in the next section.

8.4.2 The kernel interface

The character device switch table contains entry points for XXopen, XXclose, XXread, XXwrite and XXioctl. Of these, the XXopen and XXclose routines from the block device driver can be used without any modification, so only the XXread, XXwrite and XXioctl routines need to be written.

The implementation of XXread and XXwrite should be clear from the description of the kernel support routines, above, and an XXioctl routine for a disk driver was provided in Chapter 7. However, for completeness, we shall provide examples of each of the routines here:

```
XXread(dev)
     dev_t dev;
{
     int XXbreakup();
     if (physck(dksecsize(XXdip, dev), B_READ)) {
          physio(XXbreakup, (struct buf *)0, dev, B_READ)
     }
}
XXwrite(dev)
     dev_t dev;
{
     int XXbreakup();
     if (physck(dksecsize(XXdip, dev), B_WRITE)) {
          physio(XXbreakup, (struct buf *)0, dev, B_WRITE)
     }
}
XXbreakup(bp)
     struct buf *bp;
{
     dma_breakup(XXstrategy, bp);
}
XXioctl(dev, cmd, addr, mode)
     dev_t dev;
     int cmd, mode;
     char *addr;
{
     switch (cmd) {
          case DIOGETP:
          case DIORPART:
          case DIOWPART:
          case DIORBTRK:
          case DIOWBTRK:
          case DIORBTRK22:
          case DIOWBTRK22:
          case DIORVDT:
          case DIOWVDT:
```

```
                   case DIOBITP:
                   case DIOSDISK:
                   case DIORDISK:
                   case DIOWDISK:
                   case DIOSBTRK:
                   case DIODKTYPE:
                   case DIOFORCE22:
                           dkiocomm(XXdip, dev, cmd, addr, mode);
                           break;

                   default:
                           u.u_error = EINVAL;
                           break;
             }
        }
```

The actual I/O request received by XXbreakup is described by an
ordinary buffer header structure, identical to those used to describe
block I/O requests. Unless the device driver has special reasons why it
must provide its own buffer header for raw I/O, the XXread and
XXwrite routines should pass a null pointer (struct buf *)0 to
physio(K), as illustrated above. The buffer header is used by
XXstrategy and disksort(K) in the same way as for block devices,
except that when I/O is complete, it is released back to the raw buffer
header pool rather than being linked back onto the ordinary buffer
free list.

8.5   Tapes and raw I/O

Raw I/O is important for tape devices because of the way that data is
organized on the media. Tape drives write a fixed-size gap between
each data block (or record), so it is desirable to make the records as
large as possible, and therefore reduce the proportion of wasted inter-
record space.

In addition, raw I/O to and from streamer devices, such as the
Archive Scorpion 5945, requires support from the device driver to
ensure that the device is able to stream properly and isn't constantly
stopping and starting whilst it waits for the user process to be scheduled to write or read more data.

Tape drivers, generally implemented only as raw devices, solve
these problems by allocating a large, physically contiguous buffer[2] at
XXinit time, containing only pages that are guaranteed to be accessible by the DMA controllers.

8.5.1 The kernel interface

The tape driver's XXread and XXwrite routines are implemented in exactly the same way as for raw disk drivers (see above), using physio(K) and dma_breakup(K) to call XXstrategy.[3]

For read requests, the XXstrategy routine copies data from the contiguous buffer out to the user process. When the buffer empties, XXstrategy calls XXstart to initiate further activity on the device to refill the buffer. Note that the size of DMA transfers between the device and the buffer is limited only by the size of the buffer,[4] and the large buffer allows the device to stream properly.

For write requests, the XXstrategy routine copies data from the user process into the contiguous buffer. When the buffer fills up, XXstrategy calls XXstart to empty the buffer. The same benefits for DMA transfers and streaming ability apply as for read requests. Figure 8.4 summarizes the I/O mechanisms of a streaming tape driver.

The SCO UNIX kernel does not provide any support for tape XXioctl routines. A list of standard tape ioctl(S) requests, such as those issued by the tape(C) command, is provided in ⟨sys/tape.h⟩.

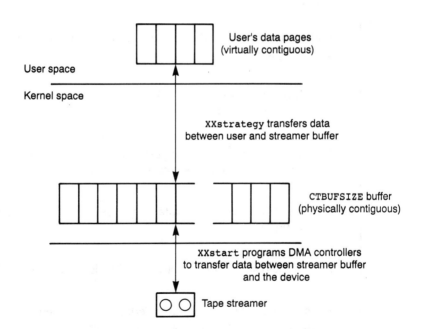

Figure 8.4 I/O to a tape streamer.

8.6   Summary

Raw I/O offers major performance benefits over block I/O, and should be used whenever the buffering facility of the block I/O system is not required, for example, when archiving files onto a tape or floppy disk with the tar(C) or cpio(C) commands. On tapes, raw I/O allows a larger blocking factor to be specified, which reduces the proportion of wasted inter-record space as well as improving throughput. In addition, the raw I/O interface provides an ioctl(S) mechanism through cdevsw, which can be used by utilities such as badtrk(ADM), divvy(ADM) and fdisk(ADM).

We have seen that the addition of a raw I/O interface to a disk driver is trivial – simply add XXread, XXwrite, XXbreakup and XXioctl routines to the block device driver.

QUIZ

To test your understanding of this chapter, try to answer the following questions.

8.1   In raw I/O, does data pass between the user and the device via the buffer cache?

8.2   What is the size of the largest raw transfer that can happen *directly* between user space and a device on an i386 CPU?

8.3   Why must the user's data pages be locked into memory during raw I/O?

8.4   Are filesystems implemented on block or raw devices?

8.5   Is it necessary for the intermediate buffer used in streaming tape drivers to be physically contiguous?

EXERCISE

Add a raw I/O interface to the disk device driver from Chapter 7.
Here are some hints:

- Add XXread, XXwrite and XXbreakup routines to the device driver, as described in Section 8.4.2.
- Replace ktop(K) with vtop(K) in XXstart.

Test your device driver with tar(C). Put a text file onto the disk through the block interface, and extract it through the raw interface. Compare the two files with diff(C).

Choose a fairly large file (for example, /etc/termcap), and use the time(C) utility to compare the throughput of the block and raw devices. You should see a significant improvement when using the raw interface with a large block size.

A suggested set of modifications is given in 'Answers to Exercises'.

NOTES

1. If the entire request is remapped into kernel address space, an additional overhead is incurred as the data can no longer move directly between the user process and the device. It has to be copied into and out of the kernel's DMA buffers, in much the same way that data in a block I/O request moves via the buffer cache.

    The default value for DMAABLEBUF is 16 on SCO UNIX release 3.2v4.

2. The configurable parameter CTBUFSIZE fixes the size of the buffer. The default value is 128 Kb on SCO UNIX release 3.2v4.

3. The XXstrategy routine is local to the device driver if only the character interface is implemented.

4. Streamers have a block size of only 512 bytes.

9

Where to now?

9.1 Overview

Congratulations! If you have followed and understood each of the chapters in this book, attempted the quizzes and completed the exercises, you will have arrived at this final chapter with a much improved knowledge of UNIX device drivers and the UNIX operating system.

We shall conclude with some final words of advice about the next actions that you should pursue, if you are planning to write production device drivers.

9.2 More device drivers

This book has demonstrated the following device drivers:

- A polled parallel printer driver.
- An interrupt-driven parallel printer driver.
- A mouse driver.
- A serial driver.
- A line discipline.
- A Stream driver.
- A RAM disk driver.
- An emulated ST506 disk driver.

- A raw device driver.

We have not described video drivers, network drivers, SCSI device drivers, or drivers for more exotic devices such as CD-ROMs, disk arrays and document scanners. However, the principles that you have learned can be applied to any type of device driver, as they will all conform to either the basic character (including STREAMS) or block device models that we have presented.

Two things that will change as UNIX evolves over the coming years will be the interface between the kernel and the device driver (the device driver entry points), and the kernel support routines available for device drivers to use. Until recently, these interfaces have been very much vendor-specific (this is particularly true of the kernel support routines), which can cause portability problems when moving a device driver from one UNIX implementation to another. AT&T has addressed both of these issues in UNIX System V Release 4.0 (more popularly known as System V/4). They have revised the kernel interface to device drivers (called the Device Driver Interface, or DDI), defined a list of kernel support routines (called the Driver–Kernel Interface, or DKI), and have made changes to some I/O-related data structures. AT&T has published all of this in a book called the *UNIX System V Release 4.0 Device Driver Interface/Driver–Kernel Interface (DDI/DKI) Reference Manual*. The book is in effect a list of manual pages which describe the DDI (for example, XXopen and XXclose), the DKI (for example, allocb, bzero and vtop), and data structures (for example, the STREAMS QUEUE structure), and represents a major step forward for UNIX device driver writers.

At the present time, SCO's kernel is based on UNIX System V Release 3.2 which, although there are many common areas, does not fully comply with the DDI/DKI. There are some new routines in the DDI, including XXsize, which returns the logical size of a device, and XXstart,[1] which is called during the kernel startup procedures, after XXinit but before the first XXopen. Many familiar routines are still present in the DKI, although some have had subtle name changes (for example, iodone(K) is called biodone), and some have disappeared altogether (including all of the line discipline support routines such as ttin(K), ttwrite(K), and so on[2]). Appendix B of the DDI/DKI provides some advice about migrating device drivers from Release 3.2 to Release 4.0.

Providing that you adhere to the current SCO equivalent of the DDI/DKI, using only the kernel support routines described in the *Device Driver Writer's Guide*, and try to write well-structured, thoroughly commented code, you will have relatively little difficulty migrating your device drivers to future releases of SCO UNIX, whichever technology they decide to pursue.

9.3   Further reading

The following is a suggested reading list. It includes all of the books that we have referenced in our text:

- The Santa Cruz Operation Inc. *SCO UNIX Device Driver Writer's Guide*. Available from SCO.

- The Santa Cruz Operation Inc. *SCO UNIX Version 4.0 Device Driver Writer's Guide Supplement*. Available from SCO.

- The Santa Cruz Operation Inc. *SCO UNIX System Administrator's Guide*. Available from SCO.

- The Santa Cruz Operation Inc. *SCO UNIX System Administrator's Reference*. Available from SCO.

- The Santa Cruz Operation Inc. *SCO UNIX User's Guide*. Available from SCO.

- The Santa Cruz Operation Inc. *SCO UNIX User's Reference*. Available from SCO.

- The Santa Cruz Operation Inc. *SCO UNIX Programmer's Reference Manual*, Volumes 1 and 2. Available from SCO.

- Intel (1986) *80386 Programmer's Reference Manual*. Intel Corporation. ISBN 1-55512-022-9.

- Intel (1990) *i486 Programmer's Reference Manual*. Intel Corporation. ISBN 1-55512-101-2.

- Bach M.J. (1986) *The Design of the UNIX Operating System*. Prentice-Hall, Englewood Cliffs, NJ. ISBN 0-13-201799-7.

- Pajari G. (1992) *Writing UNIX Device Drivers*. Addison-Wesley, Reading, MA. ISBN 0-201-52374-4.

- AT&T (1989) *The AT&T STREAMS Primer*. Prentice-Hall, Englewood Cliffs, NJ.

- AT&T (1989) *The AT&T STREAMS Programmer's Guide*. Prentice-Hall, Englewood Cliffs, NJ.

- AT&T (1990) *UNIX System V Release 4.0 DDI/DKI Reference Manual*. AT&T. ISBN 0-13-933680-X.

9.4   Summary

We hope that you have enjoyed this book, and that you have found it informative, interesting and a worthwhile investment.

Good luck!

NOTES

1.   XXstart is a private device driver routine in Release 3.2.
2.   Serial drivers are implemented as Stream drivers in Release 4.0, using a Stream module called *ldterm* which implements the equivalent of line discipline 0.

Answers to quizzes

Chapter 1

1.1 No. The hardware protection levels of the CPU prevent the peripheral control registers from being read from and written to directly.

1.2 No, /etc/init runs in user mode.

1.3 The kernel code is held in the file /unix.

1.4 Yes. Most disks have a block and a raw character interface.

1.5 No. Functions such as device driver routines, that are within the kernel, cannot make system calls. System calls are made by user processes requesting kernel services.

1.6 No. This facility is provided by other routines within the kernel.

Chapter 2

2.1 Yes, character device drivers can transfer blocks of data. However, they do not make use of the kernel support routines used by block device drivers that perform buffering, sorting of requests and read-ahead.

2.2 They are used to hold the major and minor device number.

2.3 The kernel needs to know whether the special device file is a character or block device file, the major device number and the operation that is required (for example, XXopen).

2.4 The major device number is used to index through the device switches cdevsw or bdevsw in order to select the device driver routines that correspond to the special device file being used.

2.5   The minor device number is passed to the device driver in order to vary its behaviour in some way. This could include directing data to a particular port on a device.

2.6   A context switch can occur whenever a process calls sleep(K), waiting for an event or a resource, or whenever the CPU returns from system mode to user mode.

Chapter 3

3.1   XXopen will be invoked ten times and XXclose will be invoked once, on the final close(S). This is assuming they have not been called from another device driver.

3.2   u.u_base should be incremented by 20 and u.u_count should be decremented by 20.

3.3   Spin loops will become shorter and hence may not work when CPU speeds increase. They also use valuable processing resource and prevent time-slicing.

3.4   When coding an XXread function, the copyout(K) routine can be used to copy data out from kernel to user space.

3.5   When coding an XXwrite function, the copyin(K) routine can be used to copy data from the user into kernel space.

Chapter 4

4.1   By calling sleep(K).

4.2   Yes, as wakeup(K) does not force a context switch – it sets runrun which causes a context switch to occur at the next opportunity.

4.3   Approximately 1000 clock cycles.

4.4   By calling spl(K).

4.5   By bitwise-ORing PCATCH into the priority parameter. If the sleep(K) is interrupted by a signal, sleep(K) will return 1, rather than 0.

4.6   By examining the CS segment selector saved on the system stack. If the TI bit is 1, the interrupt occurred in user mode. If the TI bit is 0, the interrupt occurred in system mode.

Chapter 5

5.1 There are three clists called t_rawq, t_canq and t_outq.

5.2 The canon(K) routine processes t_rawq at task-time.

5.3 The putc(K) routine adds characters to a clist, and the getc(K) routine removes characters from a clist.

5.4 The XXpoll routine calls l_input (ttin in line discipline 0) to transfer data from t_rbuf onto t_rawq.

5.5 Call XXproc with T_BLOCK to send an XOFF down the line.

5.6 The sequence of characters in t_outq would be carriage return, QESC, QESC bitwise-OR'd with 5.

5.7 Send an XON character down the line.

5.8 The input and output ccblocks are also accessed by the line discipline routines l_input and l_output, which indirectly make calls to putc(K) and getc(K). The putc(K) and getc(K) routines call spl5(K) to protect clist access, which allows the serial card to interrupt. Hence there must be a buffer between XXintr and the ccblocks.

5.9 Use idaddld(ADM) to add details of the line discipline to the kernel configuration files. Link the line discipline object module to the device driver object module, and name the file Driver.o.

5.10 The buffer between XXintr and the ccblocks can be made big enough to hold several full FIFOs of characters from the NS16550 chip, thus increasing overall serial I/O throughput as well as reducing the likelihood of data loss or overrun errors.

Chapter 6

6.1 No. These routines are not part of the kernel interface for a module or a Stream driver, and therefore do not appear in cdevsw. However, a module or a Stream driver can have private routines with these names.

6.2 Priority messages are not subject to flow control, and are always placed on a message queue before any ordinary messages.

6.3 The qrunflag is tested at each context switch. If it is set, the kernel calls queuerun to execute each of the XXservice routines on the linked list of scheduled QUEUES.

6.4 The XXopen routine is called on every open(S) system call on the Stream, and also on each push of a Stream module.

6.5 Its purpose is to wakeup(K) any writers who have been blocked by flow control downstream. The strwsrv routine will be called when the STREAMS scheduler back-enables the Stream head.

6.6 Examine the FAIL column displayed by the strstat option.

6.7 The three message types are M_DATA, M_PROTO and M_PCPROTO. The getmsg(S) and putmsg(S) system calls can also deal with user-defined message types.

6.8 STREAMS support software protects itself from interrupts by making calls to spl5(K).

Chapter 7

7.1 The lists are called free list, the cache and the busy list. There is one busy list for each device.

7.2 Yes. The kernel reads the entire block from the disk, but only copies the actual amount of data that the user requested from the buffer cache into the user's data segment.

7.3 A read(S) system call does not complete until the data has been transferred from the device into the user's data segment, via the buffer cache. A write(S) system call completes as soon as the data has been transferred from the user's data segment into the buffer cache.

7.4 The iodone(K) routine releases buffer headers that have been used for a write request. Buffer headers used for a read request are released by the filesystem code, a short while after iodone(K). The device driver only has to call iodone(K).

7.5 The XXstart routine transfers data on a write request. The XXintr routine transfers data on a read request.

7.6 The data structures (the Masterboot block, the partition table, the division table and the bad track table) are read from the disk by dksetup(K), which makes calls to XXstrategy. This means that interrupts must be enabled, but since the kernel doesn't enable interrupts until after all the XXinit routines have been called, dksetup(K) cannot be called until XXopen.

7.7 XXintr should read the controller's status register to see if there was an error during the transfer.

7.8 To minimize unnecessary movement of the disk heads between successive requests.

Chapter 8

8.1 No. Data passes directly between the user address space and the device.

8.2 4Kb. This limit is enforced by the paging mechanism of the i386. Larger transfers (for example, to tapes) pass via a large physically contiguous kernel buffer.

8.3 They must be locked so that they cannot be swapped or paged out from memory whilst the user process is waiting for the transfer to complete.

8.4 They are implemented on block devices.

8.5 No, because the actual DMA requests to the device transfer only 512 bytes.

Answers to exercises

This chapter contains sample answers and test programs (where appropriate) for all of the exercises set in this book.

The following sample Makefile shows you how to compile and build each of the device drivers in this chapter, and whereabouts to install them into your Link Kit directory tree:

```
#
# src/Makefile
#
# A sample Makefile with the appropriate C preprocessor
# flags to build device drivers for SCO UNIX 3.2v4.
#
# Modify this Makefile to suit your own requirements
#
CPPFLAGS=-DVPIX -DWEITEK -DSCO_VAL_ADDED -DSCO_ONLY \
        -DSecureWare -DFFS -DXNET -DMERGE386 -D_INKERNEL \
        -DM_S_UNIX -D_IBCS2

CFLAGS = -Olt -Gs $(CPPFLAGS) -c
LDFLAGS   = -r -o
PACKDIR = $(ROOT)/etc/conf/pack.d

mkdir:
        -mkdir $(PACKDIR)/dum
        -mkdir $(PACKDIR)/bm

dum.o:    dum.c
        $(CC) $(CFLAGS) dum.c
        cp dum.o $(PACKDIR)/dum/Driver.o

bm.o:     bm.c bm.h
        $(CC) $(CFLAGS) bm.c
        cp bm.o $(PACKDIR)/bm/Driver.o

bmintr.o: bmintr.c bm.h
        $(CC) $(CFLAGS) bmintr.c
        cp bmintr.o $(PACKDIR)/bm/Driver.o
```

```
bmevt.o:  bmev.c bmld.c bm.h
          $(CC) $(CFLAGS) bmev.c
          $(CC) $(CFLAGS) bmld.c
          ld $(LDFLAGS) bmevt.o bmev.o bmld.o
          cp bmevt.o $(PACKDIR)/bm/Driver.o
bmst.o:   bmst.c bm.h
          $(CC) $(CFLAGS) bmst.c
          cp bmst.o $(PACKDIR)/bm/Driver.o
mouse:    mouse.c
          $(CC) -o mouse mouse.c
mousey:   mousey.c
          cc -o mousey -DM_TERMCAP mousey.c -ltcap -ltermlib
```

The following shell script, called doconf, provides an easy-to-use front-end to the configure(ADM) command:

```
:
#
# src/doconf
#
# Copyright (c) Peter Kettle and Steve Statler, 1992
#
# Front-end to configure
#
# Adds and deletes configuration information from
# $ROOT/etc/conf
#
# This script assumes that bin/idaddld has been modified to
# interpret $ROOT correctly.
#
# This script assumes that major devices 75 and 76 are
# available.
#
dummajor=75
bmmajor=76
doadd() {
        cd $ROOT/etc/conf/cf.d
        case $1 in
            dum) ./configure -d -m $dummajor -c 2>&1 >
                    /dev/null
                 ./configure -a dumopen dumclose dumread
                    dumwrite dumioctl -m $bmmajor -c
                 return 0
                 ;;
            bm)  ./configure -d -m $bmmajor -c 2>&1 >
                    /dev/null
                 ./configure -a bminit bmopen bmclose bmpoll
                    bmread -m $bmmajor -c
                 return 0
                 ;;
```

```
                   bmintr) ./configure -d -m $bmmajor -c 2>&1 >
                           /dev/null
                           ./configure -a bminit bmopen bmclose bmintr
                           bmread -l 6 -v 5 -T 1 -m $bmmajor -c
                           return 0
                           ;;

                    bmevt) ./configure -d -m $bmmajor -c 2>&1 >
                           /dev/null
                           ./configure -a bminit bmopen bmclose bmintr
                           bmread -l 6 -v 5 -T 1 -m $bmmajor -c
                           ../bin/idaddld -d bmld
                           ../bin/idaddld -a bmld bmldopen bmldclose
                           bmldread nulldev nulldev bmldin nulldev
                           nulldev
                           return 0
                           ;;

                     bmst) ./configure -d -m $bmmajor -c -s 2>&1 >
                           /dev/null
                           ./configure -a bminit bmopen bmclose bmintr
                           -l 5 -v 5 -T 1 -m $bmmajor -c -s
                           return 0
                           ;;

                        *) echo "doconf: don't know how to add $1 yet"
                           return 1
                           ;;
         esac
}

dodel()
{
        cd $ROOT/etc/conf/cf.d

        case $1 in
                   dum) ./configure -d -m $dummajor -c 2>&1 >
                        /dev/null
                        return 0
                        ;;

                    bm) ./configure -d -m $bmmajor -c 2>&1 >
                        /dev/null
                        return 0
                        ;;

                bmintr) ./configure -d -m $bmmajor -c 2>&1 >
                        /dev/null
                        return 0
                        ;;

                 bmevt) ./configure -d -m $bmmajor -c 2>&1 >
                        /dev/null
                        ../bin/idaddld -d bmld
                        return 0
                        ;;
```

```
              bmst) ./configure -d -m $bmmajor -c -s 2>&1 >
                    /dev/null
                    return 0
                    ;;
              *) echo "doconf: don't know how to remove $1 yet"
                 return 1
                 ;;
      esac
}
#
# main starts here
#
case $# in
    2)   case $1 in
              -a)  doadd $2
                   exit 0
                   ;;
              -d)  dodel $2
                   exit 0
                   ;;
              *)   echo "Usage: $0 -a|-d device"
                   exit 1
                   ;;
         esac
         ;;
    *)   echo "Usage: $0 -a|-d device"
         exit 1
         ;;
esac
```

Chapter 1 – Fundamentals

Exercise 1
Type the command

```
# nm /unix | fgrep read | more
```

Exercise 2
Type in the following program called prog.c:

```
main()
{
    read();
}
```

Then compile it with the command:

```
$ make prog
```

Use adb(CP) to disassemble the read(S) system call code, which will have been linked into prog from the C library libc.a by the link editor. Use the following commands:

```
$ adb prog -
* read,4?ai
* Ctl-d
$
```

You should see the following output from adb(CP):

```
read:          mov  eax, 0x3
read+0x5:      call far 0x7:0x0
read+0xc:      jb   _cerror
read+0x12:     ret
```

The read(S) system call number, which is 3, is loaded into the general purpose 32-bit register called EAX, and is followed by a call to a call gate, which switches the CPU into system mode to run the kernel's system call handler.

The kernel system call handler examines the contents of EAX, and knows that the value 3 means that the user has made a read(S) system call, and calls the appropriate routines to deal with it.

When control returns through the call gate back into the user process, cerror is jumped to if the kernel has set the carry bit in the EFLAGS register, to indicate a failed system call.

Chapter 2 – A dummy device driver

```
/*
 * src/dummy.c
 *
 * Copyright (c) Peter Kettle and Steve Statler, 1992
 *
 * A simple dummy device driver
 *
 * This driver uses cmn_err(K) to print messages onto the
 * console when any of its routines are called.
 *
 *    ./configure -a dumopen dumclose dumread dumwrite
 *       dumioctl -c -m MAJOR
 */
#include <sys/types.h>
#include <sys/cmn_err.h>
```

```
dumopen(){
    cmn_err(CE_CONT, "dumopen()\n");
}
dumclose(){
    cmn_err(CE_CONT, "dumclose()\n");
}
dumread(){
    cmn_err(CE_CONT, "dumread()\n");
}
dumwrite(){
    cmn_err(CE_CONT, "dumwrite()\n");
}
dumioctl(){
    cmn_err(CE_CONT, "dumioctl()\n");
}
```

Chapter 3 - A Microsoft InPort Bus Mouse device driver

The sample answer is followed by the header file "bm.h" and the source for two user programs which will test the mouse device driver.

A Microsoft InPort Bus Mouse device driver

```
/*
 * src/bm.c
 *
 * Copyright (c) 1992 Peter Kettle and Steve Statler
 *
 * Simple device driver for Microsoft InPort Bus Mouse.
 * Polls the mouse controller updating a static structure
 * which is read and copied out to the user whenever a
 * read(S) is performed.
 *
 * ./configure -a bminit bmpoll bmread -c -m MAJOR
 */
#include <sys/errno.h>
#include <sys/types.h>
#include <sys/dir.h>
#include <sys/param.h>
#include <sys/user.h>
#include "bm.h"
#define  BM_BA      0x23c      /* Base Address for mouse
                                  registers */
#define  BM_CTL    (0+BM_BA)  /* Control Register */
#define  BM_DATA   (1+BM_BA)  /* Window to other mouse
                                  registers */
```

```
/*
 * Values written to BM_CTL
 */
#define  BM_REG_1   0          /* Select Internal Reg. 1:
                                  Buttons and Status */
#define  BM_REG_2   1          /* Select Internal Reg. 2:
                                  X Coordinate */
#define  BM_REG_3   2          /* Select Internal Reg. 3:
                                  Y Coordinate */
#define  BM_REG_4   7          /* Select Internal Reg. 4:
                                  Mode of operation */
#define  BM_RESET   0x80       /* Reset the mouse
                                  controller */
/*
 * Mask values used to read BM_DATA, when BM_REG_1
 * is selected
 */
#define  BM_BUTTONS    7       /* State of buttons
                                  1=Right Down, 4=Left Down*/
#define  BM_MOUSE_MVD 0x40     /* Set if the mouse
                                  is moved on the X/Y axis */
#define  BM_BTNS_MVD  0x38     /* Set if the buttons are
                                  pressed or released*/
/*
 * Values written to BM_DATA when BM_REG_4 is selected
 */
#define  BM_HOLD       0x20    /* Freeze counters so
                                  they can be read */
#define  BM_QUADMODE   0       /* Set mode for data
                                  to be read */
/*
 * Structure written to by bmpoll() and read from
 * by bmread() holding the current data from the mouse.
 */
struct bmouse bm;
/*
 * Flag indicating whether there is any data
 * ready to be read in the bm structure.
 */
char nodata = 1;
/*
 * bminit()
 *
 * Initialize the mouse hardware and print the
 * configuration message on the console.
 */
bminit()
{
    outb(BM_CTL, BM_RESET);
    outb(BM_CTL, BM_REG_4);
    outb(BM_DATA, BM_QUADMODE);
```

```
                     printcfg("bm", BM_BA, 3, -1, -1,
                              "InPort Mouse (Polling)");
    }

    /*
     * bmpoll()
     *
     * Called HZ times a second by kernel.  Checks to see if
     * mouse or buttons have moved, and if so it reads the new
     * data.
     */

    bmpoll(ps)
         int ps;
    {
         char bm_reg_1;

         outb(BM_CTL, BM_REG_4);
         outb(BM_DATA, BM_HOLD);

         outb(BM_CTL, BM_REG_1);
         bm_reg_1 = inb(BM_DATA);

         if (bm_reg_1 & (BM_MOUSE_MVD|BM_BTNS_MVD)) {
              bm.buttons = bm_reg_1 & BM_BUTTONS;

              outb(BM_CTL, BM_REG_2);
              bm.x = inb(BM_DATA);

              outb(BM_CTL, BM_REG_3);
              bm.y = inb(BM_DATA);

              nodata = 0;
              wakeup(&bm);
         }

         outb(BM_CTL, BM_REG_4);
         outb(BM_DATA, BM_QUADMODE);
    }

    /*
     * bmread()
     *
     * Copy data from bmouse into the user's memory.
     */

    bmread(dev)
         dev_t dev;
    {
         int nbytes;

         while (nodata)
              sleep(&bm, PZERO + 1);

         nbytes = min(sizeof(struct bmouse), u.u_count);
```

```
        if (copyout(&bm, u.u_base, nbytes) == -1 ) {
                seterror(EFAULT);
                return;
        }
        nodata = 1;
        u.u_count -= nbytes;
        u.u_base += nbytes;
        u.u_offset += nbytes;
}
```

The next file is the header file "bm.h":

```
/*
 * src/bm.h
 *
 * Copyright (c) Peter Kettle and Steve Statler, 1992
 *
 * Data structure passed to applications reading the mouse
 * device file
 */
struct bmouse {
        char buttons;
        char x, y;
};
```

User programs to test the mouse device driver

The following programs called mouse and mousey will test your mouse
device driver. We suggest that you use mouse to debug and test your
driver, and then use mousey when you are confident that all the bugs
are fixed.

```
/*
 * mouse.c
 *
 * Copyright (c) 1992, Peter Kettle and Steve Statler
 *
 * A basic interface to the mouse device driver
 *
 * Accepts as a parameter the device file which corresponds
 * to the mouse driver. Reads the mouse device printing the
 * status of the X/Y coordinates and the buttons. The
 * output scrolls up the screen.
 */
#include <stdio.h>
#include <sys/fcntl.h>
#include "bm.h"

struct bmouse mouse;
```

```
main(argc, argv)
    int argc;
    char *argv[];
{
    int cc, fd;
    char *file = "/dev/bm";
    char errmsg[32];
    if (argc > 1) {
        file = argv[1];
    }
    if ((fd = open(file, O_RDONLY)) == -1) {
        sprintf(errmsg, "couldn't open %s", file);
        perror(errmsg);
        exit(1);
    }
    while (1) {
        if ((cc = read(fd, &mouse, sizeof(mouse)))
              != sizeof(mouse)) {
            sprintf(errmsg, "couldn't read %s", file);
            perror(errmsg);
            exit(1);
        }
        printf("%s%4d  ", mouse.x < 0 ? "Left ":
            mouse.x == 0 ? "     ": "Right", mouse.x);
        printf("%s%4d  ", mouse.y < 0 ? "Up   ":
            mouse.y == 0 ? "     ": "Down ", mouse.y);
        printf("%c", mouse.buttons & 0x4 ? 'L': ' ');
        printf("%c", mouse.buttons & 0x2 ? 'M': ' ');
        printf("%c\n", mouse.buttons & 0x1 ? 'R': ' ');
    }
}
/*
 * mousey.c
 *
 * Copyright (c) 1989, Dave Tollow
 * Copyright (c) 1992, Peter Kettle and Steve Statler
 *
 * Displays current state of the mouse using curses.
 *
 * Sets up a curses screen and loops reading the mouse
 * device file and moving the '*' character around the
 * screen depending upon where the mouse is moved.
 *
 * The state of the mouse buttons is displayed at the base
 * of the screen. The delta values read from the mouse are
 * added to the record of the current mouse position. The
 * ratio of mouse to '*' movement is controlled by a scale
 * parameter that can be set as an argument.
 *
 * This program needs additional libraries:
 *
 *    cc -o mousey -DM_TERMCAP mousey.c -ltcap -ltermlib
 */
```

```
#include ⟨stdio.h⟩
#include ⟨curses.h⟩
#include ⟨fcntl.h⟩
#include ⟨signal.h⟩

#define   XLIMIT    79        /* Limit of screen size */
#define   YLIMIT    22        /* Limit of screen size */

#define   LBUTTON   0x04
#define   MBUTTON   0x02
#define   RBUTTON   0x01

#include "bm.h"

struct bmouse mouse;          /* Position delta, read from
                                 mouse */
/*
 * Scale of bus mouse coordinates relative to
 * position on the screen.
 *
 * A lower number yields a more sensitive mouse.
 */
int scale = 5;

WINDOW *curscr, *stdscr;

int x_limit, y_limit;         /* Maximum values for mouse
                                 coordinates */
int screen_x, screen_y;       /* Position on screen */
int cur_x, cur_y = 0;         /* Current position of mouse */
main(argc, argv)
    int argc;
    char *argv[];
{
    int fd, cc, restore();
    char errmsg[32];
    char *file = "/dev/bm";

    signal(SIGINT, restore);

    switch (argc) {
        case 1:
            break;

        case 2:
            file = argv[1];
            break;

        case 3:
            file = argv[1];
            scale = atoi(argv[2]);
            break;

        default:
            fprintf(stderr, "Usage: %s device scale\n",
                    argv[0]);
            exit(1);
    }
```

```
            if ((fd = open(file, O_RDONLY)) == -1) {
                sprintf(errmsg, "couldn't open %s", file);
                perror(errmsg);
                exit(1);
            }
            x_limit = XLIMIT * scale;
            y_limit = YLIMIT * scale;
            initscr();              /* initialize curses data
                                       structures */
            mvaddch(0, 0, '*');     /* display initial position */
            refresh();              /* and display it */
            while(1) {
                if ((cc = read(fd, &mouse, sizeof(mouse)))
                    != sizeof(mouse)) {
                    sprintf(errmsg, "couldn't read %s", file);
                    perror(errmsg);
                    endwin();
                    exit(1);
                }
                /*
                 * blank old position on screen
                 */
                mvaddch(screen_y, screen_x, ' ');
                cur_x += mouse.x;   /* accumulate the movement */
                cur_y += mouse.y;
                /*
                 * check screen bounds
                 */
                if (cur_x > x_limit)    cur_x = x_limit;
                if (cur_y > y_limit)    cur_y = y_limit;
                if (cur_x < 0)      cur_x = 0;
                if (cur_y < 0)      cur_y = 0;
                screen_y = cur_y/scale; /* scale coordinates to
                                           fit on screen */
                screen_x = cur_x/scale;
                /*
                 * update position of screen
                 */
                mvaddch(screen_y, screen_x, '*');
                if (mouse.buttons & LBUTTON)
                    mvaddstr(23, 10, "Left");
                else
                    mvaddstr(23, 10, "        ");
                if (mouse.buttons & MBUTTON)
                    mvaddstr(23, 35, "Middle");
                else
                    mvaddstr(23, 35, "        ");
                if (mouse.buttons & RBUTTON)
                    mvaddstr(23, 60, "Right");
```

```
                       else
                            mvaddstr(23, 60, "      ");
                       refresh();      /* update the virtual screen */
              }
    }
    /*
     * restore()
     *
     * restore sane tty settings
     */
    restore(sig)
           int sig;
    {
           endwin();
           exit(0);
    }
```

Chapter 4 – Adding interrupts to the mouse device driver

We present the complete device driver, although only small parts of it have changed from Chapter 3:

```
/*
 * src/bmintr.c
 *
 * Copyright (c) 1992 Peter Kettle and Steve Statler
 *
 * An interrupt-driven device driver for the Microsoft
 * Inport Bus Mouse.
 *
 * ./configure -d bmpoll -c -m MAJOR
 * ./configure -a bminit open close read intr -T 1 -v 5
 *    -l 6 -c -m MAJOR
 */
#include <sys/errno.h>
#include <sys/types.h>
#include <sys/dir.h>
#include <sys/param.h>
#include <sys/sysmacros.h>
#include <sys/user.h>
#include "bm.h"
#define    BM_BA         0x23c        /* Base Address for mouse
                                         registers */
#define    BM_CTL        (0+BM_BA)    /* Control Register */
#define    BM_DATA       (1+BM_BA)    /* Window to other mouse
                                         registers */
```

```
/*
 * Values written to BM_CTL
 */
#define    BM_REG_1      0          /* Select Internal Reg. 1:
                                        Buttons and Status */
#define    BM_REG_2      1          /* Select Internal Reg. 2:
                                        X Coordinate */
#define    BM_REG_3      2          /* Select Internal Reg. 3:
                                        Y Coordinate */
#define    BM_REG_4      7          /* Select Internal Reg. 4:
                                        Mode of operation */
#define    BM_RESET      0x80       /* Reset the mouse
                                        controller */
/*
 * Mask values used to read BM_DATA, when BM_REG_1
 * is selected
 */
#define    BM_BUTTONS    7          /* State of buttons
                                        1=Right Down,
                                        4=Left Down */
#define    BM_MOUSE_MVD  0x40       /* Set if the mouse
                                        is moved on the
                                        X/Y axis */
#define    BM_BTNS_MVD   0x38       /* Set if the buttons are
                                        pressed or released */
/*
 * Values written to BM_DATA when BM_REG_4 is selected
 */
#define    BM_HOLD       0x20       /* Freeze counters so they
                                        can be read */
#define    BM_INTR_ON    0x08       /* Enable interrupts */
#define    BM_INTR_30HZ  0x01       /* Interrupt at 30 Hz */
#define    BM_QUADMODE   0          /* Set mode for data to
                                        be read */
/*
 * Structure written to by bmpoll() and read from
 * by bmread() holding the current data from the mouse.
 */
struct bmouse bm;
/*
 * Flag indicating whether there is any data
 * ready to be read in the bm structure.
 */
char nodata = 1;
/*
 * Flag indicating whether we are using interrupts
 * or timeouts.
 */
char bmflags = 0;
#define BM_INTR 0x1
#define BM_OPEN 0x2
```

```
/*
 * bminit()
 *
 * Initialize the mouse hardware and print the
 * configuration message on the console.
 */
bminit()
{
    outb(BM_CTL, BM_RESET);
    outb(BM_CTL, BM_REG_4);
    outb(BM_DATA, BM_QUADMODE);
    printcfg("bm", BM_BA, 3, 5, -1,
            "InPort Mouse (Interrupts)");
}
/*
 * bmopen()
 *
 * Examine the minor device number:
 *    o If it is 0, turn on interrupts.
 *    o Otherwise, turn on polling via timeout(K).
 */
bmopen(dev, flag, id)
    dev_t dev;
    int flag, id;
{
    void bmintr();
    if (minor(dev) == 0) {
        outb(BM_CTL, BM_REG_4);
        outb(BM_DATA,
            BM_INTR_ON|BM_INTR_30HZ|BM_QUADMODE);
        bmflags |= BM_INTR;
    } else {
        outb(BM_CTL, BM_REG_4);
        outb(BM_DATA, BM_QUADMODE);
        timeout(bmintr, 0, 2);
    }
    bmflags |= BM_OPEN;
}
/*
 * bmclose()
 *
 * Turn off interrupts
 */
bmclose(dev, flag, id)
    dev_t dev;
    int flag, id;
{
    if (bmflags & BM_INTR) {
        outb(BM_CTL, BM_REG_4);
        outb(BM_DATA, BM_QUADMODE & ~BM_INTR_ON);
        bmflags &= ~BM_INTR;
    }
```

```
        bmflags &= ~BM_OPEN;
}
/*
 * bmintr(irq)
 *
 * Called whenever the mouse state changes or by a timeout.
 *
 * Read the mouse data and wake up any processes trying to
 * read from the device.
 */
void
bmintr(irq)
    int irq;
{
    char bm_reg_1, bm_reg_4;
    /*
     * Freeze the counters so that we can read them
     */
    outb(BM_CTL, BM_REG_4);
    bm_reg_4 = inb(BM_DATA);
    outb(BM_DATA, bm_reg_4|BM_HOLD);

    outb(BM_CTL, BM_REG_1);
    bm_reg_1 = inb(BM_DATA);

    if (bm_reg_1 & (BM_MOUSE_MVD|BM_BTNS_MVD)) {
        bm.buttons = bm_reg_1 & BM_BUTTONS;

        outb(BM_CTL, BM_REG_2);
        bm.x = inb(BM_DATA);

        outb(BM_CTL, BM_REG_3);
        bm.y = inb(BM_DATA);

        nodata=0;
        wakeup(&bm);
    }
    /*
     * Release the counters
     */
    outb(BM_CTL, BM_REG_4);
    bm_reg_4 = inb(BM_DATA);
    outb(BM_DATA, bm_reg_4 & ~BM_HOLD);
    /*
     * Reprime the timeout(K) if we are not
     * using interrupts
     */
    if (((bmflags & BM_INTR) == 0)
        && (bmflags & BM_OPEN)){
        timeout(bmintr, 0, 2);
    }
}
```

```
/*
 * bmread()
 *
 * Wait until bmintr() detects mouse movement and then
 * copy the data into the user's memory.
 */
bmread(dev)
     dev_t dev;
{
     int s, nbytes;
     s = spl6();
     while (nodata)
          sleep(&bm, PZERO+1);
     nbytes = min(sizeof(struct bmouse), u.u_count);
     if (copyout(&bm, u.u_base, nbytes) == -1) {
          seterror(EFAULT);
          splx(s);
          return;
     }
     nodata=1;
     splx(s);
     u.u_count -= nbytes;
     u.u_base += nbytes;
     u.u_offset += nbytes;
}
```

Chapter 5 – A simple line discipline

We present the line discipline routines first of all, followed by the device driver from Chapter 4, modified to use the line discipline.

```
/*
 * src/bmld.c
 *
 * Copyright (c) Peter Kettle and Steve Statler, 1992.
 *
 * Line discipline support for Microsoft Inport Bus Mouse.
 */
#include <sys/errno.h>
#include <sys/types.h>
#include <sys/dir.h>
#include <sys/param.h>
#include <sys/user.h>
#include <sys/cmn_err.h>
#include "bm.h"
#define NBMEVENT     16
struct bmevent {
     struct bmevent *next;
     struct bmouse bmouse;
} bmevent[NBMEVENT];
```

```
static int bmldflags;

#define BMLDOPEN     0x01

struct bmevent bmfree, bmqueue;
struct bmevent *bmget();

/*
 * bmldopen()
 *
 * Initialize the freelist
 */
bmldopen(dev)
    dev_t dev;
{
    int i;
    struct bmevent *ptr;

    if (bmldflags & BMLDOPEN) {
        return;
    }

    bmldflags |= BMLDOPEN;
    for (ptr = &bmfree, i = 0; i < NBMEVENT; ptr =
        ptr->next, i++) {
        ptr->next = &bmevent[i];
    }

    ptr->next = NULL;
}

/*
 * bmldclose()
 *
 * Clear the event queue (the freelist will be rebuilt at
 * the next open), and clear bmldflags.
 */
bmldclose(dev)
    dev_t dev;
{
    bmqueue.next = (struct bmevent *)NULL;
    bmldflags = 0;
}

/*
 * bmldread()
 *
 * Called from bmread() to return the next event structure
 * to the user.
 *
 * Get the next event structure from the event queue, copy
 * it out to the user, and then return it to the freelist.
 *
 * Sleep here if there is nothing to do.
 */
```

```
bmldread(dev)
     dev_t dev;
{
     int nbytes, s = spl6();
     struct bmevent *bmep;
     while ((bmep = bmget(&bmqueue)) == (struct bmevent *)
             NULL) {
          sleep(&bmqueue, PZERO + 1);
     }
     nbytes = min(u.u_count, sizeof(struct bmouse));
     if (copyout(&bmep->bmouse, u.u_base, nbytes) == -1) {
          seterror(EFAULT);
     } else {
          u.u_count -= nbytes;
          u.u_base += nbytes;
          u.u_offset += nbytes;
     }
     bmput(&bmfree, bmep);
     splx(s);
}
/*
 * bmldin()
 *
 * Called from bmintr() to copy a mouse movement or button
 * press into an event structure, and then link the event
 * structure onto the queue.
 */
bmldin(bmp)
     struct bmouse *bmp;
{
     struct bmevent *bmep;
     if ((bmep = bmget(&bmfree)) == (struct bmevent *)NULL) {
          /*
           * No free space left - just return
           */
          cmn_err(CE_WARN,
                  "No space left on event queue\n");
          return;
     }
     bmep->bmouse.x = bmp->x;
     bmep->bmouse.y = bmp->y;
     bmep->bmouse.buttons = bmp->buttons;
     bmput(&bmqueue, bmep);
     wakeup(&bmqueue);
}
/*
 * bmput()
 *
 * Put an event structure onto the front of either
 * the event queue or the freelist
 */
```

```
static
bmput(list, bmep)
     struct bmevent *list, *bmep;
{
     int s = spl6();

     bmep->next = list->next;
     list->next = bmep;

     splx(s);
}
/*
 * bmget(list)
 *
 * Unlink an event structure from either the
 * event queue or the freelist.
 *
 * Returns 0 if list is empty.
 */
static struct bmevent *
bmget(list)
     struct bmevent *list;
{
     struct bmevent *bmep;
     int s = spl6();

     if (list->next == (struct bmevent *)NULL) {
          splx(s);
          return( (struct bmevent *)NULL );
     }

     bmep = list->next;
     list->next = list->next->next;
     splx(s);

     return(bmep);
}
/*
 * src/bmev.c
 *
 * Copyright (c) 1992 Peter Kettle and Steve Statler
 *
 * An interrupt-driven device driver for the Microsoft
 * Inport Bus Mouse.
 *
 * This driver has been modified to call line discipline
 * routines from src/bmld.c.
 *
 * Assume line discipline 6 (BMLINE, below) is available.
 *
 * ./configure -d bmpoll -c -m MAJOR
 * ./configure -a bminit open close read intr -T 1 -v 5 -l
 *    6 -c -m MAJOR
 */
```

```
#include ⟨sys/errno.h⟩
#include ⟨sys/types.h⟩
#include ⟨sys/dir.h⟩
#include ⟨sys/param.h⟩
#include ⟨sys/user.h⟩
#include ⟨sys/conf.h⟩
#include "bm.h"

#define    BM_BA          0x23c        /* Base Address for mouse
                                           registers */
#define    BM_CTL         (0+BM_BA)    /* Control Register */
#define    BM_DATA        (1+BM_BA)    /* Window to other mouse
                                           registers */

/*
 * Values written to BM_CTL
 */

#define    BM_REG_1       0            /* Select Internal Reg. 1:
                                           Buttons and Status */
#define    BM_REG_2       1            /* Select Internal Reg. 2:
                                           X Coordinate */
#define    BM_REG_3       2            /* Select Internal Reg. 3:
                                           Y Coordinate */
#define    BM_REG_4       7            /* Select Internal Reg. 4:
                                           Mode of operation */
#define    BM_RESET       0x80         /* Reset the mouse
                                           controller */

/*
 * Mask values used to read BM_DATA, when BM_REG_1
 * is selected
 */

#define    BM_BUTTONS     7            /* State of buttons
                                           1=Right Down,
                                           4=Left Down */
#define    BM_MOUSE_MVD   0x40         /* Set if the mouse is
                                           moved on the
                                           X/Y axis */
#define    BM_BTNS_MVD    0x38         /* Set if the buttons are
                                           pressed or released */

/*
 * Values written to BM_DATA when BM_REG_4 is selected
 */

#define    BM_HOLD        0x20         /* Freeze counters so they
                                           can be read */
#define    BM_INTR_ON     0x08         /* Enable interrupts */
#define    BM_INTR_30HZ   0x01         /* Interrupt at 30 Hz */
#define    BM_QUADMODE    0            /* Set mode for data to
                                           be read */

#define    BMLINE         6            /* Use this line
                                           discipline */
```

```
/*
 * bminit()
 *
 * Initialize the mouse hardware and print the
 * configuration message on the console.
 */
bminit()
{
        outb(BM_CTL, BM_RESET);
        outb(BM_CTL, BM_REG_4);
        outb(BM_DATA, BM_QUADMODE);
        printcfg("bm", BM_BA, 3, 5, -1,
                "InPort Mouse (Event)");
}
/*
 * bmopen()
 *
 * Turn on interrupts
 */
bmopen(dev, flag, id)
        dev_t dev;
        int flag, id;
{
        outb(BM_CTL, BM_REG_4);
        outb(BM_DATA, BM_INTR_ON|BM_INTR_30HZ|BM_QUADMODE);
        (*linesw[BMLINE].l_open)(dev);
}
/*
 * bmclose()
 *
 * Turn off interrupts
 */
bmclose(dev)
        dev_t dev;
{
        outb(BM_CTL, BM_REG_4);
        outb(BM_DATA, BM_QUADMODE & ~BM_INTR_ON);
        (*linesw[BMLINE].l_close)(dev);
}
/*
 * bmintr(irq)
 *
 * Called whenever the mouse state changes.
 *
 * Read the mouse data and call the line discipline.
 */
bmintr(irq)
        int irq;
{
        struct bmouse bm;
        char bm_reg_1, bm_reg_4;
```

```
      /*
       * Freeze the counters so that we can read them
       */
      outb(BM_CTL, BM_REG_4);
      bm_reg_4 = inb(BM_DATA);
      outb(BM_DATA, bm_reg_4|BM_HOLD);

      outb(BM_CTL, BM_REG_1);
      bm_reg_1 = inb(BM_DATA);

      if (bm_reg_1 & (BM_MOUSE_MVD|BM_BTNS_MVD)) {

            bm.buttons = bm_reg_1 & BM_BUTTONS;

            outb(BM_CTL, BM_REG_2);
            bm.x = inb(BM_DATA);

            outb(BM_CTL, BM_REG_3);
            bm.y = inb(BM_DATA);

            (*linesw[BMLINE].l_input)(&bm);
      }
      /*
       * Release the counters
       */
      outb(BM_CTL, BM_REG_4);
      bm_reg_4 = inb(BM_DATA);
      outb(BM_DATA, bm_reg_4 & ~BM_HOLD);
}
/*
 * Call the line discipline l_read to pass an
 * event structure to the user.
 */
bmread(dev)
      dev_t dev;
{
      (*linesw[BMLINE].l_read)(dev);
}
```

Chapter 6 – A STREAMS driver

This is the final evolution of the Microsoft InPort Bus Mouse, modified to be a Stream driver. The clone driver in the SCO UNIX kernel is major device number 40:

```
/*
 * src/bmst.c
 *
 * Copyright (c) Peter Kettle and Steve Statler, 1992.
 *
 * Stream driver for Microsoft InPort Bus Mouse.
 */
```

```
#include ⟨sys/errno.h⟩
#include ⟨sys/types.h⟩
#include ⟨sys/stream.h⟩
#include ⟨sys/stropts.h⟩
#include ⟨sys/dir.h⟩
#include ⟨sys/param.h⟩
#include ⟨sys/sysmacros.h⟩
#include ⟨sys/user.h⟩
#include ⟨sys/cmn_err.h⟩
#include "bm.h"
#define    BM_BA        0x23c        /* Base Address for mouse
                                        registers */
#define    BM_CTL       (0+BM_BA)    /* Control Register */
#define    BM_DATA      (1+BM_BA)    /* Window to other mouse
                                        registers */
/*
 * Values written to BM_CTL
 */
#define    BM_REG_1     0            /* Select Internal Reg. 1:
                                        Buttons and Status */
#define    BM_REG_2     1            /* Select Internal Reg. 2:
                                        X Coordinate */
#define    BM_REG_3     2            /* Select Internal Reg. 3:
                                        Y Coordinate */
#define    BM_REG_4     7            /* Select Internal Reg. 4:
                                        Mode of operation */
#define    BM_RESET     0x80         /* Reset the mouse
                                        controller */
/*
 * Mask values used to read BM_DATA, when BM_REG_1
 * is selected
 */
#define    BM_BUTTONS   7            /* State of buttons
                                        1=Right Down,
                                        4=Left Down */
#define    BM_MOUSE_MVD 0x40         /* Set if the mouse is
                                        moved on the
                                        X/Y axis */
#define    BM_BTNS_MVD  0x38         /* Set if the buttons are
                                        pressed or released */
/*
 * Values written to BM_DATA when BM_REG_4 is selected
 */
#define    BM_HOLD      0x20         /* Freeze counters so they
                                        can be read */
#define    BM_INTR_ON   0x08         /* Enable interrupts */
#define    BM_INTR_30HZ 0x01         /* Interrupt at 30Hz */
#define    BM_QUADMODE  0            /* Set mode for data to
                                        be read */
/*
 * Module info for each QUEUE. Values need to be tuned.
 */
```

```
static struct module_info bmstm_info = {
    72,                    /* module ID number */
    "bmst",                /* module name */
    0,                     /* min packet */
    INFPSZ,                /* max packet */
    32,                    /* high water mark */
    16,                    /* low water mark */
};
int bmstopen(), bmstclose(), bmstsrv();
/*
 * QUEUE for read module
 */
static struct qinit bmstrinit = {
    NULL,                  /* XXput routine */
    bmstsrv,               /* XXservice routine */
    bmstopen,              /* XXopen routine */
    bmstclose,             /* XXclose routine */
    NULL,                  /* reserved */
    &bmstm_info,
    NULL
};
/*
 * Define the Stream driver
 */
struct streamtab bmstinfo = {
    &bmstrinit,            /* read QUEUE */
    NULL,                  /* write QUEUE not required */
    NULL,
    NULL
};
/*
 * bmstopen() copies the read queue here
 * for use by bmstintr()
 */
queue_t *bmstqueue;
/*
 * bmstinit()
 *
 * Initialize the mouse hardware and print a configuration
 * message on the console.
 */
bmstinit()
{
    outb(BM_CTL, BM_RESET);
    outb(BM_CTL, BM_REG_4);
    outb(BM_DATA, BM_QUADMODE);

    printcfg("bmst", BM_BA, 3, 5, -1,
             "InPort Mouse (Stream)");
}
```

```
/*
 * bmstopen()
 *
 * Called by the Stream head when the user process makes
 * an open(S) call.
 *
 * Clone open is here for completeness, even though we only
 * have one minor device available (minor = 0).
 *
 * Turn on interrupts
 * Return the minor device number if successful, else
 * OPENFAIL
 */
bmstopen(q, dev, flag, sflag)
     queue_t *q;
     dev_t dev;
     int flag, sflag;
{

     dev = minor(dev);

     if (sflag == CLONEOPEN) {

          dev = 0;
     }
     bmstqueue = q;        /* Use this in bmstintr */
     outb(BM_CTL, BM_REG_4);
     outb(BM_DATA, BM_INTR_ON|BM_INTR_30HZ|BM_QUADMODE);

     return(dev);
}
/*
 * bmstclose()
 *
 * Called by the Stream head when the user process makes the
 * last close(S) call.
 *
 * There is no STREAMS work for us to do, this is all being
 * taken care of by the Stream head
 *
 * Turn off interrupts
 */
bmstclose(q)
     queue_t *q;
{
     outb(BM_CTL, BM_REG_4);
     outb(BM_DATA, BM_QUADMODE & ~BM_INTR_ON);
}
/*
 * bmstintr(irq)
 *
 * Called whenever the mouse state changes.
 *
```

```
 * Call allocb() to get a buffer for the mouse data.
 * Copy the mouse data into the buffer, and adjust
 * bp->b_wptr
 * Call putq() to add buffer to read queue, then return.
 *
 * bmstsrv() will be called later at task time to move the
 * data to the Stream head, and it will then be available
 * for the user to read(S).
 */
bmstintr(irq)
     int irq;
{
     char bm_reg_1, bm_reg_4;
     struct bmouse bm;
     mblk_t *bp;
     /*
      * Freeze the counters so that we can read them
      */
     outb(BM_CTL, BM_REG_4);
     bm_reg_4 = inb(BM_DATA);
     outb(BM_DATA, bm_reg_4|BM_HOLD);

     outb(BM_CTL, BM_REG_1);
     bm_reg_1 = inb(BM_DATA);

     if (bm_reg_1 & (BM_MOUSE_MVD|BM_BTNS_MVD)) {
          bm.buttons = bm_reg_1 & BM_BUTTONS;

          outb(BM_CTL, BM_REG_2);
          bm.x = inb(BM_DATA);

          outb(BM_CTL, BM_REG_3);
          bm.y = inb(BM_DATA);
     }
     /*
      * Release the counters
      */
     outb(BM_CTL, BM_REG_4);
     bm_reg_4 = inb(BM_DATA);
     outb(BM_DATA, bm_reg_4 & ~BM_HOLD);

     /*
      * Now allocb() a buffer, copy bm into it,
      * and putq() it onto the read QUEUE.
      *
      * Note that allocb() sets db_type to M_DATA
      * by default.
      */
     if ((bp=allocb(sizeof(struct bmouse), BPRI_MED)) ==
         NULL) {
          cmn_err(CE_WARN, "bmstintr() couldn't allocb()");
          return;
     }
```

```
            bcopy(&bm, bp->b_rptr, sizeof(struct bmouse));
            bp->b_wptr += sizeof(struct bmouse);
            putq(bmstqueue, bp);
}

/*
 * bmstsrv()
 *
 * - called by the STREAMS scheduler
 * - Take messages off the read QUEUE and putnext()
 *   them to the Stream head.
 */

bmstsrv(q)
    queue_t *q;
{
    mblk_t *mp;

    while ((mp = getq(q)) != NULL) {

        /*
         * Check for room at the Stream head - but always
         * putnext() any priority messages
         */

        if ((mp->b_datap->db_type <= QPCTL)
            && !canput(RD(q)->q_next)) {

            /*
             * There is no room at the Stream head, so
             * return this message to read QUEUE.
             */

            putbq(q, mp);
            return;
        }

        switch (mp->b_datap->db_type) {

            case M_DATA:
                    putnext(q, mp);
                    break;

            case M_FLUSH:
                    if (*mp->b_rptr & FLUSHW) {

                        flushq(q, FLUSHALL);
                        *mp->b_rptr &= ~FLUSHW;
                    }

                    if (*mp->b_rptr & FLUSHR) {

                        qreply(q, mp);
                    } else {

                        freemsg(mp);
                    }
                    break;
```

```
            default:
                    cmn_err(CE_WARN,
                            "Unexpected message
                            type in bmstsrv(): %d",
                            mp->b_datap->db_type);
                    freemsg(mp);
                    break;
            }
        }
    }
```

Chapter 7 – Using the extended RAM disk driver

Use mknod(ADM) to create the following block and raw devices for the RAM disk, which we shall call ramd. The examples here assume that major device number 72 is available:

```
# mknod /dev/ramd b 72 0
# mknod /dev/rramd c 72 0
```

You will now be able to run

```
# fdisk -f /dev/rramd
```

to set up a partition table. Next, create the following device to access the entire partition:

```
# mknod /dev/rramda c 72 47
```

You will now be able to run badtrk(ADM) to set up a bad track table on the partition, and to add some bad tracks:

```
# badtrk -e -f /dev/rramda
```

Next, run divvy(ADM) to create a filesystem:

```
# divvy -m /dev/rramd
```

After running divvy(ADM), you should have four new device entries set up in /dev corresponding to the block and raw division table entries that you have just created.

Check that everything is working properly by mounting the filesystem on division 0, and copying some files into the RAM disk.

Chapter 8 – A raw device driver

Add these routines to the extended RAM disk driver from Chapter 7:

```
void
ramdbreakup(bp)
    struct buf *bp;
{
    dma_breakup(ramdstrategy, bp);
}
ramdread(dev)
    dev_t dev;
{
    if (physck(dksecsize(ramddip, dev), B_READ)) {
        physio(ramdbreakup, (struct buf *)0, dev, B_READ);
    }
}
ramdwrite(dev)
    dev_t dev;
{
    if (physck(dksecsize(ramddip, dev), B_WRITE)) {
        physio(ramdbreakup, (struct buf *)0, dev, B_WRITE);
    }
}
```

Raw transfers occur between user space and the device, which means that the paddr(bp) macro will now yield a user virtual address, rather than a kernel virtual address. To convert this to a physical address, you must replace the call to ktop(K) with a call to vtop(K) inside ramdio. Replace the line:

```
if (copyio(ktop(paddr(bp)), base, ramdreq.tsectors <<
    DKSSHIFT, flag) == -1) {
```

with the line:

```
if (copyio(vtop(paddr(bp), bp->b_proc), base,
    ramdreq.tsectors << DKSSHIFT, flag) == -1) {
```

APPENDIX A

Adding a new device driver to the kernel

A.1 Overview

This appendix describes how to use the SCO UNIX System V Link Kit to compile your driver source, to configure and link a new UNIX kernel, and how to boot the new kernel so that you can test your device driver.

Only a subset of the Link Kit utilities and their options will be described. When you have read and understood this appendix, you should feel comfortable with the concepts of configuring, linking and booting a UNIX kernel so that you can attempt all of the practical sessions included in this book.

A.2 The SCO UNIX Link Kit

The focal point for all of the configuration and linking activity for building new UNIX kernels is the set of directories beneath /etc/conf, as shown in Figure A.1.

Device driver writers should focus on the cf.d, pack.d and sdevice.d directories.

The contents of the directories are as follows.

A.2.1 bin

Contains the Installable Driver (ID) utilities which provide for building, configuring and tuning UNIX kernels. Some of these utilities are used internally by the configure(ADM) and link_unix utilities.

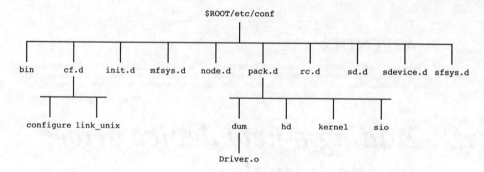

Figure A.1   The SCO UNIX Link Kit.

A.2.2   cf.d

Contains the configuration files describing the set of devices to be installed in the UNIX kernel, the values of the kernel resources (such as the size of the process table), a base version of /etc/inittab called init.base, and the two utilities configure(ADM) and link_unix.

A.2.3   init.d

Contains text files which are appended to cf.d/init.base to build the /etc/inittab file, which controls the actions of the /etc/init process (the first user process to run after the UNIX kernel has booted).

A.2.4   mfsys.d

Contains master configuration information for each of the filesystem types supported by the SCO UNIX kernel. Each supported filesystem type has its own configuration file, containing the filesystem name, some flags and a bitstring used to generate the entry points into the filesystem switch structure. This directory is not relevant for device drivers.

For further information, refer to the mfsys(F) manual page.

A.2.5   node.d

Contains configuration information for special device files that should be created in /dev by the idmknod(ADM) utility at the next kernel relink. For further information, refer to the idmknod(ADM) manual page.

A.2.6   pack.d

Contains a subdirectory called `kernel` and many device driver subdirectories. The kernel subdirectory contains the kernel object modules, and the device driver subdirectories contain the individual device driver object modules. The device driver subdirectory's name is the same as the device name, and the device driver object module within the subdirectory is called `Driver.o`. For example, `$ROOT/etc/conf/pack.d/hd/Driver.o` is the object module for the hard disk device driver.

The object modules in these directories are linked together to build the UNIX kernel.

A.2.7   rc.d

Contains device-dependent system initialization shell scripts that need to be executed as the system goes into multi-user mode (run level 2). The `idmkenv`(ADM) utility links the contents of this directory into /etc/idrc.d.[1]

For further information, refer to the `rc2`(ADM) manual page.

A.2.8   sd.d

Contains device-dependent system shutdown shell scripts that need to be executed as the system shuts down (run level 0). The `idmkenv`(ADM) utility links the contents of this directory in /etc/idsd.d.[2]

For further information, refer to the `rc0`(ADM) manual page.

A.2.9   sdevice.d

Contains files which describe the device-specific characteristics (including the device name, the interrupt level and the I/O space addresses of the controller registers) for each of the devices specified in the master device file, `mdevice`. The files in `sdevice.d` are maintained by `configure`(ADM).

A.2.10   sfsys.d

Contains configuration information used to determine which filesystem types from `mfsys.d` (see above) are to be included in the next kernel relink. This directory is not relevant to device drivers.

For further information, refer to the `sfsys`(F) manual page.

A.3   Building a new kernel

There are eight major steps to be followed whenever you want to add a new device driver to the kernel:

(1) Make your own copy of the UNIX Link Kit directory tree, so that you have a safe area to work in, away from the actual files and directories used to maintain your machine's own copy of UNIX. Set up an environment variable ROOT to point to the top of your Link Kit tree.

(2) Write the device driver in C, and provide a Makefile to compile it and to copy the object file into the correct part of the Link Kit directory tree.

(3) Determine the device-specific information, including the major device number, the interrupt vector and the priority level to be used (when applicable). This information is used by the kernel when it wants to call your device driver routines to handle I/O requests, to deal with interrupts, and so on.

(4) Use the configure(ADM) utility to add the details of your device driver to the system configuration files.

(5) Compile your device driver and copy the object module into your Link Kit hierarchy.

(6) Link a new UNIX kernel and copy the new kernel into a directory in /tmp.

(7) Shut down the system and reboot the new kernel from /tmp.

(8) Use the mknod(C) utility to create one or more special device files in /dev so that you can access your device driver.

These steps are described in more detail in the following subsections.

A.3.1   Make a copy of the UNIX Link Kit directory

Choose a directory where you want the top of your own UNIX Link Kit directory tree to be, for example, your home directory. Then use the copy(C) utility to make a copy of the directory /etc/conf. You will have to be the superuser to read some of the files and directories:

```
# copy -rv /etc/conf ⟨destination directory⟩
```

When the copy(C) has finished, use the chown(C), chgrp(C) and chmod(C) utilities to ensure that you have appropriate ownership and permissions to access all of the files in your new, private Link Kit directory.

Finally, set up an environment variable ROOT in either your .profile or .login file to point to the top of your Link Kit tree. Make sure that you export ROOT.

When you have finished, you should end up with the directory structure shown in Figure A.1.

A.3.2   Write the device driver

This book contains many practical sessions and model answers for real, working device drivers. We shall use the model answer for the exercise set at the end of Chapter 2 (the answer is given in 'Answers to Exercises') to illustrate the points covered in this appendix. Recall that this dummy driver does nothing other than announcing its presence when any of its routines are called. This device driver has the three-letter prefix *dum*.

We recommend that you set up an src directory somewhere beneath your $HOME directory, which will contain your device driver source files and a Makefile. Use your favourite text editor to type in the source for dummy.c (if you want to, you can simply type in the model answer for Chapter 2, given in 'Answers to Exercises').

Next, type in a Makefile to compile your device driver source to an object module, and then to copy the object module into your Link Kit hierarchy. An example Makefile is given in 'Answers to Exercises'. You can easily extend this to contain rules for your other device drivers from the exercises in this book.

To compile your device driver source, type

```
$ make dummy.o
```

To copy the resultant object module into pack.d, first ensure that you have appropriate write privileges on your $ROOT/pack.d directory, and then type

```
$ make cp
```

A.3.3   Determine the device-specific information

The major device number, and whether your device driver is for a block or character device, uniquely identify it to the UNIX kernel, so that user processes which make open(S), close(S), read(S), write(S) and ioctl(S) system calls can access the device via your device driver routines.

If your device generates interrupts, you must also provide an XXintr routine, and specify which interrupt vector your device is attached to, and at what interrupt priority your device's interrupts should be serviced at. Note that our dummy device driver does not have any interrupts.

Finally, you must specify whether your device is a character device or a block device. All of these pieces of device-specific information are described in Chapter 2.

For our dummy device driver, we need to determine the following pieces of information:

- The major device number. Our example will use major device 17.

- The names of the XXopen, XXclose, XXread, XXwrite and XXioctl routines. Our routines are called dumopen, dumclose, dumread, dumwrite and dumioctl.

- A character or block device driver. Our example is a character device driver.

When the kernel wants to access your dummy device driver, it will use the major device number from the inode of the special device file in /dev to index cdevsw[], which you will configure to contain the names of your device driver routines. This mechanism is described in more detail in Chapter 2.

A.3.4 Use the configure(ADM) utility

Important note: Before using configure(ADM) for the first time, we advise you to make copies of the following files and directories in $ROOT/etc/conf:

- Copy the file cf.d/mdevice to cf.d/mdevice.orig.
- Copy the directory sdevice.d to sdevice.d.orig.

Use the configure(ADM) utility to modify the system configuration files in cf.d and sdevice.d to contain information about your dummy device driver. Make sure that you are in the cf.d directory before starting, and that you have appropriate values prepared for all of the items described in step 3 above.

If you do not know which major device number to use, you can use configure(ADM) to tell you what the next available one is. The -j NEXTMAJOR option to configure(ADM) prints out the next available major device number:

```
$ ./configure -j NEXTMAJOR
```

Note that there is a ./ before the configure command, as you are working in the directory $ROOT/etc/conf/cf.d and this may not be on your PATH.

It is extremely important that you use a unique major device number for your device, otherwise you may disable other critical devices and prevent the kernel from booting. Unfortunately, configure(ADM) is not smart enough to spot many of the potential mistakes that novices can make (and experts too, sometimes!), so you must be very careful. For this example, we have assumed that major device number 17 is available, but you must check your own system and use a different major device number if 17 is already in use.

Type the following command to add the details of your dummy device driver to the system configuration files:

```
$ ./configure -a dumopen dumclose dumread dumwrite dumioctl -c -m 17
```

The command you have just used instructs configure to add (-a) the routines dumopen, dumclose, dumread, dumwrite and dumioctl for a character device (-c) with major device number 17 (-m 17). Note that not all of the routines are required for every device. For example, the XXioctl routine is only required if you want your device to respond to ioctl(S) system calls. Similarly, it is not necessary to configure an XXread routine for a printer driver! In general, all devices require XXopen, XXclose and at least one of XXread, XXwrite or XXstrategy. All the other routines are optional.

Configure(ADM) flags and options

The configure(ADM) utility has many flags and options, and some more are described later on in this appendix. However, the only other flags that you will need to use to complete the exercises in this book are as follows.

–b

This is similar to the -c flag that you have just used, but specifies a block device rather than a character device. Raw device drivers that have character and block device driver routines should be configured with both -b and -c in the same command.

–d

This is the opposite to the -a flag that you have just used. It is used to delete device driver routines and configuration options from the system configuration files.

–v IRQ

This flag is used to specify the interrupt request line, or interrupt vector, that the device is attached to on the i8259A PICs.

–l level

This flag is used to specify which particular priority level the interrupt should be serviced at. The lowest priority interrupts are at priority level 1, and the highest are at priority level 7. Note that there is no direct relationship between a device's interrupt vector and its interrupt priority level.

–T scheme

If your device is using interrupts, you *must* specify -T 1 to indicate that your device will use its own interrupt line, unless the driver's XXinit routine auto-configures entries in the interrupt tables for the device.

Failure to specify -T 1 will mean that configure(ADM) will not generate entries for your device driver's XXintr routine, and your device driver will not be able to receive interrupts from the device.

–s

This flag indicates that you are configuring a Stream driver.

For further information about configure(ADM) and its many flags and options, please refer to the manual pages in the *SCO UNIX System Administrator's Guide*.

The master device file, mdevice

If you compare the cf.d/mdevice file with the original cf.d/mdevice.orig, you will see that configure(ADM) has added a line to the end of mdevice describing the characteristics of your dummy device driver. The mdevice file contains a one-line description of each device driver to be included in the next relink of the UNIX kernel. The entry for your dummy device driver should be:

```
dum    ocrwi    irHc    dum    0    17    0    1    -1
```

The first field is the device name. This field may be up to eight characters long, and defaults to be the same as your device driver's prefix, unless you use the -h flag of configure(ADM) when you initially add the details of your device to the system configuration files.

The second field is the function list, and specifies which routines are present in your device driver. The contents of this field are used to generate entries for bdevsw[] and cdevsw[]. Your dummy device driver should have open, close, read, write and ioctl routines.

The third field identifies the device driver characteristics. Your dummy device driver is installable, it is required to be in every UNIX kernel, it controls Hardware, and it is a character device. The r and H flags are set by default whenever you add a device driver with configure(ADM), although since your dummy device driver is neither required nor does it control any hardware, you should reset them using the following command:

```
$ ./configure -d -R -H -c -m 17
```

The fourth field is the handler prefix, common to all of your device driver routines which you have added using configure(ADM).

The fifth and sixth fields are the block and character major device numbers respectively.

The seventh and eighth fields specify the minimum and maximum numbers of devices that can be supported by the controller (see Chapter 1 for a more detailed explanation of the differences between controllers and devices). These numbers can be changed by using the -M flag to configure(ADM).

Finally, the ninth field specifies the DMA channel to be used by this device. A -1 indicates that your device does not use any DMA. If your device does use DMA, you must specify the DMA channel with the -c flag to configure(ADM).

For further information about the mdevice file, please refer to the mdevice(F) manual page.

The system device file, sdevice

Configure(ADM) writes further information about your device driver to a file in sdevice.d. The name of that file is the same as the device name field in the mdevice file. In our example, the file will be called sdevice.d/dum. The file in sdevice.d is an extension of the corresponding entry in the mdevice file.

The entry for your dummy device driver should be:

```
dum    Y    1    0    0    0    0    0    0    0
```

The first field is the device name, and matches the corresponding entry in the mdevice file.

The second field is the configure field, which contains either a Y or an N. A Y indicates that the corresponding device driver object module from pack.d/XX should be installed into the UNIX kernel when the kernel is next relinked, an N indicates that the device driver should not be installed in the next relink, and that the pack.d/XX/stubs.c file should be used instead. This field can be changed by specifying the -Y flag to configure(ADM).

The third field is the unit number, and is used to specify how many devices are attached to the controller. Its value must be within the minimum and maximum values specified in fields 7 and 8 of the mdevice entry. This field can be changed by using the -U flag to configure(ADM).

The fourth field is the interrupt priority level, and is set using the -1 flag to configure(ADM), as described earlier in this section.

The fifth field is the interrupt type, and indicates the type of interrupt scheme required by the device (whether the device requires an interrupt, and if so whether it is shared with other devices).

The sixth field is the interrupt vector, and is set by using the -v flag to configure(ADM), as described earlier in this section.

The seventh and eighth fields are the start and end I/O addresses respectively, and contain the start and end I/O addresses in the I/O space through which the device communicates, if the device is I/O mapped (see Chapter 1). These fields are set with the -I flag to configure(ADM).

Finally, the ninth and tenth fields are the start and end controller memory addresses respectively, and should be used if the controller has on-board memory (some devices use buffers in the memory between 640K and 1Mb). These fields are set with the -J flag to configure(ADM).

Since your device driver is reasonably simple and doesn't control any real hardware, all but the first three fields of sdevice.d/dum are set to 0.

However, if you were writing a device driver for a complex piece of hardware, you would see that the corresponding entries in mdevice and sdevice.d have many more fields filled out. You may like to look at some of the other files in this sdevice.d directory.

A.3.5 Compile your device driver

If you haven't already done this, now is the time to compile your device driver to an object module and to copy it into pack.d/XX, using the command

```
$ make cp
```

as described above. Note that you will not produce an executable file as a result of this compilation. You must link and install a new UNIX kernel before you can test your device driver. There should be no errors from the compiler at this stage. If there are any errors, you must go back and correct the source before trying to link a new UNIX kernel.

A.3.6   Link and install a new UNIX kernel

Move into your $ROOT/cf.d directory, and relink a new kernel by typing:

```
$ ./link_unix
```

Depending on the speed of your machine, building a new kernel can take up to several minutes. Please be patient!

There should be no errors or warnings from the link_unix utility. If there are any, you almost certainly made a mistake when you used configure(ADM). Carefully note down all of the errors, make sure that you understand why they are caused, and go back and fix them. If you think that you made an error with configure(ADM), it is often useful to remove the original configuration information completely, and then to start over again. Use the following command to remove all the configuration information about your dummy device driver:

```
$ ./configure -d -c -m 17
```

Remember to substitute your own major device number if you are not using major 17.

When you have fixed all the errors, try relinking the UNIX kernel again. You will not be able to boot your new kernel unless you resolve all of the errors reported by link_unix.

When the new kernel has been relinked successfully, copy it into your test directory in /tmp.

A.3.7   Shut down the system and reboot the new kernel

Now you are ready to reboot the new UNIX kernel that you have just built with link_unix. Use the shutdown(ADM) command to bring the system down cleanly – don't get too excited and be tempted to simply power the machine off and back on again!

```
# /etc/shutdown -y -g 0
```

Remember that you have to be the superuser to be able to shut down the system.

To boot your new kernel, type its full pathname at the boot prompt:

```
SCO UNIX System V 386
Boot
: /tmp/peterk/unix
```

Important note: If your new UNIX kernel doesn't boot, power the machine off, restart the boot sequence and reboot either /unix or /unix.orig.

A.3.8   Use the mknod(C) command

Before any utilities will be able to access your device driver, you must create a character special device file in /dev with the correct major device number. The major device number is the only way that the kernel has of accessing your device driver. This has two important implications:

- It is essential that you specify the correct major device number.
- The actual name of the special device file can be anything that you want, providing that it doesn't clash with any existing entries in /dev.

The following command will create a special device file for your dummy device driver:

```
# /etc/mknod /dev/dummy c 17 0
```

You will have to be the superuser in order to run this command.

The command you have just used instructs mknod(C) to create a special device file called /dev/dummy, which is a character device (c), with major and minor device numbers 17 and 0 respectively.

A.4   Testing the device driver

Test your driver with the cat(C) utility:

```
$ cat /etc/motd > /dev/dummy
$ cat /dev/dummy
```

If all is well, you should see your device driver routines being called by the UNIX kernel as the cat(C) utility makes open(S), read(S), write(S) and close(S) system calls.

You can test your XXioctl routine with the stty(C) utility:

```
$ stty < /dev/dummy
```

At this stage, you need not concern yourself with any errors from cat(C), stty(C), or any other utility that you are using to test your device driver – these errors are being reported because your device driver routines are only stubs.

NOTES

1.   The current release of SCO UNIX ignores this directory.
2.   The current release of SCO UNIX ignores this directory.

APPENDIX B

Debugging device drivers

B.1   Overview

Unless you are extremely lucky or extraordinarily clever, sooner or later you will write a device driver that doesn't behave exactly as it should when you test it for the first time. The malfunction might be reasonably trivial, such as mouse coordinates changing in a positive direction only, or more serious, such as a hanging process, or even a kernel panic.

This appendix provides some advice about how to debug device drivers, starting at the moment that you first put pen to paper (or fingers to the keyboard). It is divided into three sections:

(1) Defensive programming.

(2) Debugging device drivers.

(3) Dealing with hanging processes and kernel panics.

The information gathered in this appendix comes from a variety of sources, including the authors' own experience of debugging the device drivers in this book, and watching students on SCO's *Writing Device Drivers for SCO UNIX* training course, on which this book is based.

B.2   Defensive programming

The easiest way to get device drivers to work properly is to write them correctly in the first place. Although this does sound like a rather condescending statement, it is nevertheless true. It is surprising how often programmers make trivial mistakes such as forgetting to pass the correct number of arguments to functions, dividing by zero, using variables before they are initialized (particularly pointers), and so on.

In a user program, such errors can only cause problems for the particular process when it runs, as the kernel protects all processes from each other and themselves. At worst, the process will receive a SIGSEGV or a SIGBUS signal, drop a core file into the filesystem, and terminate before any damage can be caused.

However, a device driver is part of the kernel, and therefore has access to the entire address space of the machine, including all the processes and all parts of the kernel. Therefore, trivial mistakes such as using uninitialized pointers can corrupt any process that is running, and any kernel data structure, such as the process table, the buffer cache contents, and so on. Depending on the exact nature of the problem, the kernel may continue to run apparently normally for a period after the corruption, before it eventually panics. The first notification that you will receive of any problems will be when the kernel panics, perhaps a long time after the original damage has been done by your device driver.

Here is a list of things to check before testing your device driver for the very first time:

- Check that you are passing the correct number of arguments, in the correct order, to every routine that your device driver uses. For example, use outb(addr, byte) rather than outb(byte, addr), or even outb(addr).

- Check that all variables, particularly pointers, are initialized before you use them.

- Check that you are using user or kernel addresses as appropriate. Check whether you should be using physical or virtual addresses, particularly when calling kernel support routines such as copyio(K).

- Check that your variables are signed or unsigned, as appropriate. This is particularly important when making calls to inb(K), which returns an 8-bit quantity. If the top bit is set, and you assign the result to a signed integer, you may get problems caused by sign extension.

- Don't be tempted to go all-out for glory at the first test. If the device uses interrupts, consider testing it with an XXpoll routine before testing it with interrupts. Get the basic mechanisms working first, to give you confidence in yourself, your device driver and the hardware.

  For example, during development of the mouse driver at the end of Chapter 3, consider getting changes in the X coordinate reported properly first. Afterwards, try for the Y coordinate, and then the buttons.

- Check that your driver will communicate correctly with the device, according to the manufacturer's hardware specification.

- Make a copy of /unix, called something other than /unix.old (for example, /unix.orig), before you build a new kernel for the first time. You will be able to boot this kernel with confidence if you get into difficulties later on.

- Create an emergency floppy set, with mkdev fd, which will allow you to reboot the machine even if you corrupt the primary and secondary bootstraps on the UNIX partition.

- Check that your device driver is properly configured into the kernel. Remember to recompile your device driver, copy the new object module into pack.d, *and relink the kernel*, before each new test.

Reconfiguring should not be necessary unless you are adding new routines or deleting old ones.

- If your device is using interrupts, remember to specify an IRQ line (-v), an interrupt priority level (-l), and an interrupt scheme (normally -T 1).

- Make sure that the hardware configuration matches the information which you have given to configure(ADM). For example, if you have specified -v 4 for the IRQ line, check that any jumpers on the device are set accordingly.

- Check that the specified IRQ line is not already in use by another device (examine the kernel startup messages in /usr/lib/adm/messages, or run hwconfig(ADM)).

- Check that the task-time and interrupt-time parts of your device driver are properly interlocked with spl(K).

  Initially, it pays to be over-cautious and to interlock for longer than might finally prove to be necessary.

- If your device driver calls sleep(K), use printf(K) to display the wait channel and priority parameters, which can be compared with the output from ps(C) if the process appears to hang (see Section B.4 below).

- Make sure that you boot the correct kernel, with the latest version of your device driver in it.

- Make sure that you have created a special device file of the correct type in /dev, with a major device number which matches that which you have specified with configure(ADM).

  If your test programs receive ENOENT (No such file or directory) from their open(S) system calls, you have forgotten to create a special device file in /dev.

  If your test programs receive ENODEV (No such device) from their open(S) system calls, you probably have your device driver configured with a different major device number from that which you specified to mknod(C).

  If your test programs receive ENXIO (No such device or address) from their open(S) system calls, your device driver is probably not configured into the kernel.

  Verify that your device driver is there (or not) by using nm(CP) to examine the kernel object file, and look for your device driver routine names.

- Assume initially that the kernel and the hardware will function correctly, and that any bugs that manifest themselves are being caused by your device driver.

Remember that Rome wasn't built in a day!

B.3   Debugging device drivers

Once your device driver starts to show signs of life, you can be confident that many of the teething troubles outlined above have been overcome. The next step is to test each of the functional components of your device driver.

B.3.1   Testing the device driver

Think carefully about the design or choice of test programs that you intend to use. For example, to test a block device driver, read from it before you try to write to it, thus ensuring that the basic mechanisms are operating correctly before you risk writing over the top of the process table!

Begin testing by using cat(C), od(C), hd(C), and then move on to dd(C), before trying to use tar(C). Put cmn_err(K) or printf(K) statements into your device driver's routines so that you can see when they are invoked by the kernel. Although these tests will not return any useful or sensible data, they will enable you to verify that your device driver is properly configured into the kernel, and is responding correctly to open(S) and read(S) system calls.

To test the write mechanisms, use the same commands again. For example, cat(C) a small file, such as /etc/motd, to the device, and then cat(C) it back again onto stdout. Repeat the same sequence with progressively larger files. Verify that your device driver behaves correctly at the end of the device, for example, reading or writing the last block of a filesystem. As your confidence builds, try more complex commands, such as mkfs(ADM), fsck(ADM) and mount(ADM). Copy some files into the filesystem, unmount the device, mount it again, and check that the files are still all there and that they have not been corrupted. Try writing a file to the block device and reading it from the raw device, and vice versa.

Testing a character device driver, such as the mouse driver, is a little more difficult and may require a small test program to be written. Write the least complex test program possible, and present the data in an easily-understood format. A good example of a simple test program is mouse.c, given in 'Answers to Exercises'. If your program displays hexadecimal numbers with the %x formatting string, prefix the numbers with 0x, and so on.

As a general principle, you will maintain a faster rate of progress if you think and then test, rather than testing and then thinking.

B.3.2   Using debugging diagnostics

If you suspect that your device driver is not functioning correctly, insert some debugging diagnostics which printf(K) variables, results of decision statements, arguments to functions, and so on. It is good practice to enclose all debugging diagnostics inside a #ifdef DEBUG preprocessor directive, so that you can leave them in the device driver during testing, and choose whether to use them or not by specifying -DDEBUG in the Makefile. You can also associate the diagnostics with a debugging level, which determines how much output will be produced. One advantage of this is that it is possible to use adb(CP) to change the debugging level without having to recompile the device driver and relink the kernel, which saves time.

For example, consider the following code extract from the mouse device driver:

```
...
...
#ifdef DEBUG
int bmlevel = 1;
#endif
...
...
/*
 * bmopen()
 *
 * Turn on interrupts
 */
bmopen(dev, flag, id)
     dev_t dev;
     int flag, id;
{
#ifdef DEBUG
switch (bmlevel) {

     case 1:
          printf("DEBUG: bmopen()\n");
          break;

     case 2:
          printf("DEBUG: bmopen(dev=%d,%d, flag=%d, id=%d)\n",
                  major(dev), minor(dev), flag, id);
          getchar();
          break;

     default:
          break;
}
#endif
     outb(BM_CTL, BM_REG_4);
     outb(BM_DATA, BM_INTR_ON|BM_INTR_30HZ|BM_QUADMODE);
}
```

The device driver declares a debugging level, bmlevel, and switches on its value to determine how much debugging information is required. The initial value is 1, which produces the least amount of debugging information.

B.3.3   Patching kernel data with adb(CP)

To change the value of bmlevel to 2, which will produce more debugging information, use adb(CP) as follows:

```
# adb -w /tmp/peterk/unix
* bmlevel/x
bmlevel:       0x1
* /w 2
bmlevel:       0x2
* Ctl-d
# reboot
```

The command /w 2 patches the value of bmlevel in the data segment of /tmp/peterk/unix in the filesystem, so that when the kernel is rebooted, the driver will produce more debugging information. Although this technique may appear a little daunting at first, it is easily mastered and can save a lot of unnecessary edit–recompile–relink cycles.

Note that with bmlevel at 2, the device driver calls getchar(K). This will stop the kernel running until you press a key on the console, and will give you an opportunity to examine the debugging information before allowing the device driver to continue.[1]

Using the getchar(K) kernel support routine is the first step to writing your own kernel debugger, which might print out data structures from the device driver, dump the process table, change variables (including debugging levels) in the running kernel, and so on.

B.3.4   Patching kernel text with adb(CP)

It is also possible to use adb(CP) to patch instructions in the kernel's text segment! This is much more difficult than patching data, as you are only able to give numeric values to adb(CP), not instruction mnemonics. However, with a reasonable amount of patience, and access to a CPU reference manual, most things are possible.

Consider the following example from a disk interrupt routine, which tests an error count against a threshold value. The author suspected that a hard disk was causing an abnormally high number of soft errors (errors that were being reported to the disk driver's interrupt routine, but which could be eventually corrected by retries). To find out how many retries were being required, without recompiling the driver and relinking a new kernel, the instruction that was testing against the threshold was modified.

The actual C statement was:

```
if (++XXtab[ctlr].b_errcnt <= MAXRETRY) {
```

Adb(CP) was used to find, and then disassemble, the instruction:

```
# adb /tmp/peterk/unix
* XXintr+0x127?i
XXintr+0x127:  cmp  Byte Ptr [edi-0x2fef05e5],0x4
* ?x
XXintr+0x127:  0xbf80
* (Return)
XXintr+0x129:  0xfa1b
* (Return)
XXintr+0x12b:  0xd010
* (Return)
XXintr+0x12d:  0x7f04
* Ctl-d
#
```

The description of the CMP instruction from the *80386 Programmer's Reference Manual* was used to determine that the 04 of the 0x7f04 was the value of the threshold being tested against. It was now straightforward to patch a new value for the threshold:

```
# adb -w /tmp/peterk/unix
* XXintr+0x12d?x
XXintr+0x12d:   0x7f04
* ?w 0x7f00
XXintr+0x12d:   0x7f04=   0x7f00
* XXintr+0x127?i
XXintr+0x127:   cmp  Byte Ptr [edi-0x2fef05e5],0x0
* Ctl-d
# reboot
```

Even after this modification, the disk heads could still be heard seeking over and over again, but no diagnostics were being reported on the console, indicating that the disk controller was not reporting soft errors. Soon afterwards, the disk controller was replaced, and the problem was cured.

B.3.5   Timing problems

When your debugging diagnostics indicate that your device driver is working properly, it is time to remove the -DDEBUG flag from the Makefile, and recompile your driver. At this stage, *do not* remove any of the #ifdef DEBUG clauses from the device driver.

If your device driver really is working properly, it should behave exactly as before. However, turning off the debugging diagnostics makes subtle changes to the timing of the device driver, and you may discover that the driver has now stopped working altogether! The reverse is also true – adding debugging diagnostics to a device driver that does work can make it stop working properly!

This is particularly relevant for devices that interrupt. The only advice that we can offer is to be patient. Step by step, turn the debugging diagnostics back on (or change the debugging level), until you reach a threshold beyond which the device driver's behaviour changes. You should at least have some clues about where to start looking in your device driver for the problem.

B.4   Dealing with hanging processes and kernel panics

In this section, we shall describe how to use the crash(ADM) command to display system stacks from the running kernel or from panic dumps in the swap device.

B.4.1   Hanging processes

In Chapter 4, we explained how processes can sleep at a priority less than PZERO, and that they will stay locked in the system if they are not woken up by a wakeup(K) issued from an XXintr routine. If you suspect that your process is hanging (for example, tar(C) starts writing to your device but never returns to the shell, and doesn't respond to signals), it is likely that there is a bug in your device driver.

Almost certainly, there is a problem in the interrupt routine. Either your device driver is not receiving interrupts at all, or it is not issuing the wakeup(K) call correctly.

There are two things that you can do to help determine the cause of the problem. The first is to switch to another console multi-screen, run ps -el, and look for the hanging process. Here is an extract from a ps -el command:

```
PID PPID  C PRI NI    WCHAN TTY      TIME CMD
  0    0  0   0 20  d014a919 ?        0:00 sched
  1    0  0  39 20  e0000000 ?        0:01 init
  2    0  0   0 20  d00a63ec ?        0:00 vhand
  3    0  0  20 20  d00a018c ?        0:00 bdflush
275    1  0  30 20  d00e0c18 01       0:02 sh
276    1  0  30 20  d00e0d70 02       0:02 sh
277    1  0  28 20  d00c680c 03       0:00 getty
308  275  0  20 20  d100bea0 01       0:00 tar
242    1  0  26 20  d0137a08 ?        0:00 lpsched
339  276 49  84 20           02       0:02 ps
```

The tar(C) command is asleep at priority 20 (PRIBIO), waiting for block I/O. Because it is asleep at a priority less than PZERO, it is impossible to interrupt it by sending it a signal.

To find out exactly why it is asleep, we can use crash(ADM) to examine the system stack.[2] The p option displays the process table, and allows us to identify which process table slot is being occupied by the tar(C) process (our process was in slot 9). We can then specify t slotno, to print a kernel stack trace for the process. For simplicity and formatting purposes, we have replaced the possible arguments and some of the register values with w, x, y and z. These are not important to our discussion:

```
# crash -d /dev/mem -n /tmp/peterk/unix
dumpfile = /dev/mem, namelist = /tmp/peterk/unix, outfile = stdout
> t 9
STACK TRACE FOR PROCESS 9:
STKADDR    FRAMEPTR   FUNCTION  POSSIBLE ARGUMENTS
e0000cb8   e0000cdc   swtch     (x,y,z)
e0000ce4   e0000cf0   iowait    (w,x,y,z)
e0000cf8   e0000d08   bread     (w,x,y,z)
e0000d10   e0000d54   breadm    (w,x,y,z)
e0000d5c   e0000db4   s5writei  (w,x,y,z)
e0000dbc   e0000dec   rdwr      (x)
e0000df4   e0000df8   write     (w,x,y,z)
e0000e00   e0000e2c   systrap   (x)
           e0000e38   sys_call from a00037a4
  ax:   4 cx:   0 dx:   4 bx:7fff8000 fl:  216 ds:  1f fs:  0
  sp:   x bp:   y si:   z di:7fffff3f err:  14 es:  1f gs:  0
> quit
#
```

We can see that the tar(C) process is asleep inside iowait(K), the last routine that was called before the context switch inside swtch. This strongly suggests that iodone(K) is never being called from the device driver's interrupt routine, or if it is, it is being called with incorrect arguments.

Examination of the offending device driver revealed that the call to iodone(K) from XXintr was not being passed any arguments. This was easy to fix.

B.4.2   Kernel panics

If the kernel panics and dumps a copy of physical memory to the swap device, the same t option can be used to analyse system stacks of processes that were running at the time of the panic.

It is not necessary to save the panic dump, as crash(ADM) can analyse it directly from /dev/swap. Once again, the suspicious process can be determined with the p option. Look for processes that have a p (running on a processor) or an r (on the run queue) in the ST column. Here is a sample crash(ADM) output from a kernel panic resulting from a kernel page fault, reported on the console as follows:

```
PANIC: Kernel mode trap. Type 0x0000000E
```

The trap type can be compared against the list of Exception IDs in the Intel *80386 Programmer's Reference Manual*. A trap type 0xE is a page fault. Under normal conditions, the kernel is not supposed to cause page faults, and this immediately makes us suspicious that our device driver is doing something strange with pointers. We can use crash(ADM) to investigate further. As before, we have replaced the possible arguments and some of the register values with w, x, y and z:

```
# crash -d /dev/swap -n /tmp/peterk/unix
dumpfile = /dev/swap, namelist = /tmp/peterk/unix, outfile = stdout
> t 16
STACK TRACE FOR PROCESS 16:
STKADDR   FRAMEPTR  FUNCTION  POSSIBLE ARGUMENTS
e0000b60  e0000b78  prf_task  (w,x,y,z)
e0000b80  e0000ba4  cmn_err   (w,x,y,z)
e0000bac  e0000bd0  k_trap    (x)
Trap e    e0000bdc  cmntrap   from d0010fe4 in bcopy
   ax:  x cx:  10 dx:   bx:  0 fl:     10246 ds:  160 fs:  0
   sp:  x bp:   y si:  z di:  x err:  e0000002 es:  160 gs:  0
e0000be4  e0000c2c  bcopy     (w,x,y,z)
e0000c34  e0000c44  copyio    (w,x,y,z)
e0000c4c  e0000c64  ramdio    (w,x,y,z)
e0000c6c  e0000c88  ramdxfer  (x,y,z)
e0000c90  e0000c9c  ramdstar  (y,z)
e0000ca4  e0000cac  ramdstra  (x,y,z)
e0000cb4  e0000cc0  dkrdmb    (w,x,y,z)
e0000cc8  e0000cfc  dkgetmb   (x,y,z)
e0000d04  e0000d10  dksetdri  (w,x,y,z)
e0000d18  e0000d3c  dksetup   (w,x,y,z)
```

```
e0000d44  e0000d64  ramdopen  (w,x,y,z)
e0000d6c  e0000d88  s5openi   (w,x,y,z)
e0000d90  e0000dac  copenl    (w,x,y,z)
e0000db4  e0000de0  copen     (w,x,y,z)
e0000de8  e0000df8  open      (w,x,y,z)
e0000e00  e0000e2c  systrap   (x)
          e0000e38  sys_call from a00036dc
   ax:   5 cx:  x dx:  d bx:  403700 fl:  202 ds:  1f fs:  0
   sp:   x bp:  y si:  z di:  403848 err:    5 es:  1f gs:  0
> quit
#
```

We can see that the last two stack frames before the kernel trap are from bcopy(K) and copyio(K), and that copyio(K) was called from our device driver's ramdio routine. The problem would appear to be related to the arguments passed to copyio(K).

Inspection of the source code revealed that we had forgotten to convert paddr(bp) to a physical address with vtop(K), before calling copyio(K). Again, this was easy to fix.

B.5 Summary

This appendix has provided a selection of useful hints and tips about how to go about testing and debugging device drivers on an SCO UNIX machine. Section B.4 demonstrated that even if the kernel panics, all is not lost.

NOTES

1. Calls to getchar(K) should be avoided at interrupt-time.
2. A detailed description of the crash(ADM) command is beyond the scope of this book. However, it is relatively straightforward to use it to examine system stacks.

Index